HARUN IBRAHIM
SHARING
JESUS
SHAKING ISLAM

HARUN IBRAHIM
SHARING
JESUS
SHAKING ISLAM

ONE ARAB'S JOURNEY FROM JERUSALEM
INTO PIONEERING MEDIA MISSIONS TO MUSLIMS

Edited by Heikki Salmela

Published by Al Hayat Ministries in 2025.

Harun Ibrahim, edited by Heikki Salmela

SHARING JESUS, SHAKING ISLAM:
One Arab's Journey from Jerusalem
into Pioneering Media Missions to Muslims

Bible references are from the New King James Version by Thomas Nelson Publishers.
Qur'an references are from the Hilali-Khan translation (The Noble Qur'an) by King Fahd Complex for the Printing of the Holy Quran.
Unless otherwise noted, all photos are from the archives of Harun and Sari Ibrahim, Keymedia (Avainmedia), and Al Hayat Ministries.

Cover picture by Eero Antturi
Book layout by Zarief Mina
Cover design by Bob Makdisi

ISBN: 979-8-89463-019-9

Table of Contents

Foreword

History knows few successful attempts to take the gospel to Muslims. The crusades of the Middle Ages were a travesty of the missionary command of Jesus. Even then, however, there were other voices. Francis of Assisi (c. 1181–1226), for example, thought that Muslims must be overcome by love. But the distorted image of Christianity created by the Crusades has acted as a stumbling block and a wall between the Christian church and Muslims to this day.

At the end of the last century, an international prayer movement for the Muslim world arose. Millions of Christians prayed, and breakthroughs began to come. One of these wall-breakers was Harun Ibrahim.

I was working as the Executive Director of Fida International (named the Finnish Free Foreign Mission at the time) when Harun and his wife Sari headed to Sweden in 1988 to study Christian media ministry and reach out to the country's large Muslim refugee population. I later visited Harun and his colleagues in person to learn more about their work. Although I had had some exposure to practical mission work in other countries, reaching Muslims with the gospel was new to me. Harun's and his colleagues' bold approach caught my attention.

In the 2000s, I deepened my cooperation with Harun as chairman of the World Pentecostal Fellowship (PWF)

Mission Commission and later as chairman of the Pentecostal Commission on Religious Liberty (PCRL). In 2014, I asked Harun to join the PWF Mission Commission to bring expertise in reaching the Islamic world. About five years later, I also invited him to join the newly formed PCRL. In the latter body, he represents former-Muslim converts to Christianity, an area in which we continue to work together.

Today, Christians with Muslim backgrounds are also represented in the World Evangelical Alliance, where their membership is expressed especially through the Communio Messianica, a denomination of former Muslims. Harun chairs its board of council and, interestingly, the community has close links with Messianic Jews. Harun is valued and listened to in Communio Messianica—something I have found out by participating in the MBB Global Prayer Days, the community's worldwide virtual prayer meetings.

In the Middle East, emotions run high. I admire Harun's balanced way of dealing with people from different backgrounds and opinions.

I have also had the opportunity to visit Harun's home region of Kirjath Jearim in Israel, mentioned in the Bible. This autobiography also opens up the story of his family—the roots from which he grew into his ministry. The reader learns how God's guidance and plan have been woven into the various stages of Harun's life and the choices he has made. The characters, attitudes, and values of his parents, Said and Fatima, shaped the character and worldview of the son growing up with ten siblings in ways that God has taken as instruments for the fulfillment of his plan.

Raymond Lull (1232–1315) was one of the pioneers of the Christian Muslim mission. Working in Tunisia, he boldly pointed out the contradictions he saw in Islam but was also filled with love. After him, however, the Islamic world was a virtually untouched region from a missionary perspective for centuries.

To our delight, we are now living in a new era where Harun, Keymedia, Al Hayat, and a host of other Christian ministers and organizations are creating change.

Arto Hämäläinen
Doctor of Theology (DMin)
Executive Director Emeritus of Fida International
Chairman of the Pentecostal Commission on Religious Liberty
Chairman of the Africa Pentecostal Mission Network
First Chairman of the World Missions Commission of the Pentecostal World Fellowship 2005–2022

For the Reader

When I decided to start writing this book, I didn't want to just write about the story of my life. The book's concept came to me after meeting many Muslim-background believers (MBBs) who suggested that if I ever wrote a book about my story, it should include some of the challenges I have faced as an MBB and even mistakes I have made and learned from. I thought this was a good suggestion, and I have tried to follow it.

In addition to my personal experiences, I will, for example, talk about the persecution faced by former Muslims and the difficulties we face in searching for our place in traditional Christian ministries and communities. It is my hope that an open examination of these challenges could help resolve them; after all, many of them are still quite common among MBBs.

For Muslim-background believers, I want my book to encourage them to nurture relationships with their Muslim family members. Sometimes, some MBBs get advice from other Christians or even other ex-Muslims to keep away from their Muslim family to avoid persecution. I do not think this advice is biblical or constructive. I firmly believe it is possible that also you who come from a Muslim background can have a good relationship with your family even though you are a follower of Christ and they are not.

For the Western reader, I want to emphasize two things. First, I want to underline that as Muslim-background believers, we come from a strong community culture where the Muslim community—*ummah* in Arabic—is the basis for one's identity, belonging, and purpose. When we come to Jesus, we lose that Muslim community—we know that we must lose it to the extent that we cannot confess both Islam and Jesus—but at the same time, we are yearning for a new Christian "ummah" in which to belong. This is a need of every Muslim-background believer.

Secondly, I hope a Western reader will take this as a story of how we, MBBs, have been searching for our place in fulfilling the Great Commission. We are a part of the body of Christ, and also we are responsible for spreading the gospel. We want to fulfill this responsibility together with other Christians.

When I started to write this book, I didn't expect the project to bring up so many emotions inside me. I wrote through tears, laughter, sadness, gladness, and thankfulness. I remembered people I met in my childhood; I remembered stories that I had almost forgotten. After all the reminiscing, I realized how blessed I was to have the childhood family I had. I love my mom, my brothers and sisters, and their families. It was not easy for them to accept me when I abandoned the religion of the fathers—there were times when I was on the outside of my closest "ummah," my childhood family—but still, they eventually accepted me. We have had good relationships for years now, which I'm so grateful for.

For me, my family members are my heroes, especially my mom.

I want to use this opportunity to also thank my wife, Sari, and my children, Ali and Sami, and their families for the great support they have shown me during this project. Sari has been my most significant supporter in all my life and ministry.

I want to thank my friends, especially David Meyer from the Joyce Meyer Ministries—you have always been a faithful partner and friend; I loved every time we traveled together. Gary Preston—thank you for being a true friend who has stood by me, given valuable advice, and loved and prayed for me. I want to thank Samuel Arra, Heikki Salmela, and Susanne

Ihatsu-Seppälä, who greatly helped me to put my memories and experiences into a book. I want to thank all of you who have worked or are still working with me, such as Leslie and Peter Strong, David Denmark, Niilo Närhi, Abu David, Dr. Yassir Eric, Abu Yehia, and Latif El Qochairi.

If I mentioned all the names, it would be a very long list, but everyone who has been a part of this ministry—I want you all to know that you are special to me.

Thank you so much for being a part of my life.

Harun Ibrahim

The book has been voted as the "Christian Book of the Year 2024" in Finland based on public votes.

Prologue

The afternoon sun was still high over the Algerian Houari Boumediene airport in February 1992. Inside, people were queuing for immigration control. Dozens of bearded customs officers in blue uniforms were going through the suitcases of the arrivals. Every bag was searched, and it seemed that every pair of socks was rummaged. Not a single one of the officers smiled.

I had entered the country with my Finnish evangelist colleague Niilo at the invitation of a local pastor, Mahmood. He had invited us to visit Algeria and asked if we had any Bibles that we could bring with us. When I spoke with him on the phone and heard the word "Bibles," I thought maybe he wanted a suitcase full of Bibles. So, we decided to take as many as possible with us, even at the risk of not being allowed through customs.

While waiting in line at the station building for passport control, the thoroughness of the customs officers brought beads of sweat to our foreheads. This was not our first time in Algeria, but it was the first time we had a suitcase full of Arabic Bibles with us. We knew that the regime restricted things they interpreted as spreading Christianity among the people. So, if the officer discovered the Bibles, there was a high risk that we would lose the Bibles, and we would probably also be expelled from the country.

We were very nervous and prayed in Finnish, "God, you have created eyes for this man. We pray he will not see what we have because we are bringing your Word into the country."

When it was our turn, the officer asked us to place the suitcases before him. He started to inspect them one after another. Then he came to the suitcase with the Bibles. The Bibles were covered with a simple towel. He removed the towel — and didn't react in any way! Other things captured his attention, like blank cassette tapes we had with us (Pastor Mahmood had asked us to bring them, too). The officer told us cassettes were included on the list of prohibited imports, so he confiscated them and let us go.

For us, it was a miracle and an answer to our prayers. The Bibles looked like Bibles, so there was no chance he could have mistaken them for other books.

Pastor Mahmood was also astonished. It turned out that he had meant for us to bring only a few Bibles; he had not believed that any more would pass through. He wondered how we could get so many Bibles into the country. Later, he delivered them to the members of the church.

In August 1992, six months later, Niilo and I were back at Houari Boumediene airport. We were coming to the country again to participate in a Christian pastors' conference. At the airport, we stood in the queue for immigration control just like the time before. This time, we didn't have Bible freight with us—we wanted to get into the conference, and we didn't want to take any risks.

Usually, when I travel to an Arab country with a Westerner, I like to be the first to go through passport control in case of any trouble. But Niilo doesn't like to wait in lines, so he quickly decided to go through first. An officer checked his luggage and stamped his passport, and he got through.

When it came to my turn, the officer said unexpectedly that I would not be allowed in because I didn't have permission from the PLO—the Palestine Liberation Organization—to enter the country. That was strange. Yes, I was an Israeli Arab, and Algeria had strongly supported PLO since the 1970s, and the organization influenced the country's internal politics. Still, my visa was in order, and Niilo had gotten through without any "PLO permission." I argued with the officer until he got upset with my questions. Without warning, two other officers grabbed me by my arms, hauled me away, and locked me in a cell.

The cell was a small, around 4 x 4 meters (12 x 12 feet), and packed with thirteen other people. Everyone looked worried. In the corner, there was a hole in the floor. This was not a golf green; the hole was the toilet. I had the urge but no desire to make a hole-in-one with so many people around. There was a small window with bars high up the wall, and a cat sat up there, watching us.

I was there for hours, sitting on the floor. I was afraid of what would happen to me and what would happen to the new Algerian converts who had listened to our Christian radio programs. In my luggage, I had a list of more than seventy Algerians who had written to us and told us that they had become Christians or wanted to know more about Christianity. We had intended to give the list to local pastors at the conference. Would the officers find the paper? What would happen to the people mentioned? I berated myself for our carelessness.

Was this the end of my vision? How long would they keep me in this jail? Then something happened that was even more scary, something I had never experienced before. It was like the devil spoke directly into my mind: *Are you sure that God did not allow you to enter Algeria because you have done something terrible?*

My trust in God was shaking, and I began to consider all the bad things I had ever done. Could there be something in them that might explain why I was being punished like this?

As I was anxiously pondering them, I suddenly felt the Holy Spirit reminding me of a prayer and Bible study with my wife Sari a few days before. Sari had said to me, "Wow, look at this beautiful verse, here in Psalms 103:9, 10: 'He [the LORD] will not always strive with us, nor will He keep His anger forever. He has not dealt with us according to our sins, nor punished us according to our iniquities.'"

This Bible verse came to me in a dirty cell at the airport, just like a drop of fresh water to dry land. Peace returned to me, and I said, "Thank you, Jesus." It was a great confirmation from the Lord that His mercy is above all our understanding.

Then, at some point, an officer came in and told me, "You have two options: You can stay here four more days, or you can go back home, through Paris, three hours from now."

The choice was easy for me. I left Algeria, stayed overnight in Paris, and got home safely. Niilo stayed in the country and participated in the conference. I was disappointed, but God had His good reasons, as it turned out later. The list of more than seventy Algerians had also survived, safely hidden, and was later delivered to the local congregations.

1

A Village on a Hill

I was born on November 18, 1959, into a Muslim family living in Israel in an Arab village called Abu Gosh.

The village is located on a mountain slope some 700 to 760 meters (2,300–2,500 feet) above sea level, about eleven kilometers (seven miles) west of Jerusalem, towards Tel Aviv. Because of its mountainous location, the area is known as Little Switzerland. The hillsides are covered with forest, and I dare say that our village is one of the most beautiful in Israel.

Historically, many believe that Abu Gosh is Kirjath Jearim ("a village of forest"), mentioned in the Bible. The book of Jeremiah states that God's prophet Uriah came from this village (Jer. 26:20). In the first book of Samuel, Kirjath Jearim is said to have been the temporary resting place of the Ark of the Covenant before King David had it brought to Jerusalem:

> *Then the men of Kirjath Jearim came and took the ark of the LORD, and brought it into the house of Abinadab on the hill, and consecrated Eleazar his son to keep the ark of the LORD. So it was that the ark remained in Kirjath Jearim a long time; it was there twenty years.* (1 Samuel 7:1, 2)

Today, at the top of the mountain, there is an old Catholic nunnery called Our Lady of the Ark of the Covenant. The place is famous for the scenery, loved by both Arabs and Jews alike. Walking about a hundred meters west of the monastery church, you can see Tel Aviv and the sun setting into the sea in the evening. Walking east from the church, you get a broad panoramic view of Jerusalem.

As a child, I played around the monastery buildings with my siblings and friends. As an adult, I have been encouraged by how the place has withstood several fires and attacks during its long history. The beautiful church is built on the ruins of a fifth-century Byzantine church, and it still stands as the highest building on the Mount of Abu Gosh, towering over the whole village.

On the hillsides are hundreds of white stone houses, shops, another monastery, and more than thirty Middle Eastern restaurants. The village has a reputation for having the best hummus in the country. When you add that the village is also known for friendly relations with the Jewish community, you shouldn't be surprised that thousands of Jewish people come to Abu Gosh every Shabbat to eat and spend time with their family and friends. Countless foreign tourists have also discovered the place.

A famous Messianic Jewish community, Yad Hashmona, established by two Finnish friends of Israel, is located just outside the village.

When I left Abu Gosh in 1980, its population was about 4,500. Now, more than forty years later, the number is almost 8,000. Virtually all the inhabitants are Muslims, aside from some Christians who are a part of the monasteries.

My Father, a Generous Man

One of those white stone houses dotting the Abu Gosh hillsides is the one where my family lived when I was a child. Like most houses, it had a flat roof where my siblings and I could play or hang out. And we certainly needed room to play, as my family consisted of seven boys and four girls in addition to our parents—thirteen people in total. I am right in the middle (number six) among us siblings.

The forests surrounding the village also offered plenty of places for us to play or have adventures, to hide, climb, and run. Our uncles, aunts, and cousins lived in the village also. For example, my aunt's home was right across from us, on the opposite side of the street.

My father's name was Said. He was a nominal Muslim, but he did not practice much religion. Instead, he was known for his generosity and being a man of his word. Our whole community held him in the highest regard. In my childhood, he owned a grocery truck and drove it for a living. The army green truck had a big hood and made a big noise. As I recall, the truck's brand was Autocar. I remember how he would often drive through the village to stop and give out fresh fruit for free to those in need. He was never too busy to help.

An artist's drawing of my father Said. He was a living example of how Arabs and Jews can live together in harmony.

My father had two close friends: a Jew named Harun (Aaron), after whom I was named, and Hussein, after whom my brother was named. My father had good relationships with both Jews and Arabs alike. I don't remember ever hearing any negative words come from his lips about Jews or anyone else. He was an example of how Arabs and Jews can live together in harmony, and I believe I've inherited this gift from him.

Managing a family with eleven children and having a job, the time my father could individually devote to each of us kids was limited. Still, I remember him as a kind and loving person at home. Sometimes, I wished I could have received more attention from him and my mother, but now, as a father and a grandfather myself, and as busy as I am, I appreciate the remarkable job he did in caring for each of us despite his limitations.

In the spring of 1968, at thirty-five, my father fell sick with lung cancer—he was a heavy smoker. Only about six months later, he passed away after living his whole life in Abu Gosh. I became fatherless at the age of eight, burdened with grief and uncertainty about the future. On the funeral day, hundreds of people watched as my father's coffin was carried out of the house all the way to the cemetery. I remember the tears in my older brothers' and sisters' eyes, but for some reason, I did not cry. Maybe as a distraught and bewildered boy, I thought my father was only on a trip and would soon return. After about a month, I realized I would be without a father for the rest of my life. It was painful to understand that whenever we had a party at home or any special occasion at school, I would never again have a father with me like my friends had.

My Mother, My Hero

My mother, Fatima, is a strong and smart woman. She is just a tiny little thing, but she has never hesitated to fight for her children under any circumstances. She usually deals with problems by being quiet at first and taking time to think rather than acting too quickly. It sometimes takes her an hour or two to even address an issue, which is unique in the Arab culture. She is kind, generous, and loving.

My mother was born in Israel, in the port city of Jaffa, on the Mediterranean Sea. Her father was from Abu Gosh, and her mother had a Turkish background. Later, the family moved back to Abu Gosh, and both my grandfather and his brother worked as imams at the local mosque. My mother has also been a religious person her whole life.

In 1952, she met a handsome young man, Said, my father, and they married. At the time, it was customary in Israeli Arab culture for the groom's parents—and often a number of other relatives—to visit the maiden's home and ask her parents for their consent to the marriage. (The arrangement was often already agreed upon when the girl and boy were young, but a formal visit from the groom's parents was still part of the process.) For the couple, the result was often a marriage of convenience, where feelings of love matured only over time.

The beginning of my mother and father's common life followed such cultural traditions. Yet, it differed from many other marriages in that—according to my mom—it was a union of love from the start.

When my father died, my mother became a thirty-four-year-old widow with eleven children aged from two months to fourteen years. She wanted to do her best and to be a good example for her children. As we grappled with our father's death, she was amazingly supportive of me and my siblings. Many women at this age get remarried, but who would marry a woman with eleven children? In the absence of a father, my mother did her best to meet our needs while playing the dual role of father and mother at the same time. We all love her and still highly esteem her for watching over us with her limited resources. I believe my mother is a hero. At least she is my hero.

Some of us kids were quiet, and some were active day and night. I was one of those active ones. I always felt that I had the energy to do many things simultaneously. I loved to make friends and be a part of a group. I also remember defending my brothers—even my older brothers—when they had fights with other children. You could say that I functioned as the Minister of Defense in our family. I didn't want to be a troublemaker, and I don't think I ever started a fight, but I usually was the one to finish it.

I remember going home after such conflicts and seeing the other kids' mothers complaining to my mom. Even though these other children were in the wrong and often came home with bloody noses, my sisters and brothers were not always happy with me at those moments. My mother was even more disappointed because she never wanted to hear anything negative about her children. Once, she said to me, "Why do you disappoint me like this? Your brothers and sisters are more peaceful. I sometimes wonder if I came home from the hospital with the wrong baby."

As a child, I took these words seriously and was deeply hurt by them. I wanted to go far from home and find a place to cry. I remember thinking, in my young mind, that I should take my own life, and then she would realize that she had lost the best of her children. But praise God, I never did that. Later, I told her what she said was wrong, and she was very sorry.

My mother, Fatima. Even the trials of life
haven't hardened her loving heart.

As a family, we had a lot of different personalities, but collectively, we had a strength of character and a will to thrive despite the hardships we encountered. Thanks to our parents' wisdom and good heart, our home became a miniature model of a diverse community where each of the eleven siblings lived respectfully of the others. One of my mother's educational goals was to teach us to embrace others and love everyone—no matter how different they were from us—which was reflected, for example, in the fact that it was forbidden to tell racist jokes in our home. I think this is how I learned to accept many kinds of personalities and viewpoints. Anyone who constantly hears eleven distinct opinions will learn to get along with others.

Tolerance of difference also applied to gender. Thanks to our parents, the boys in the family learned to treat our sisters as equals, which resulted in deep love and friendships that have bound us together since childhood. My father seemed to show no preferences in how he cared for the boys and the girls. After his death, my mom never allowed us boys to think that we were any better than our sisters or that women were less superior in their intellect and spirituality. When I got older and started to understand Islam a little more, I rejected the inherited Islamic culture, which sanctioned gender inequality and disrespect towards women. I am sure all this has helped me in my Christian ministry later.

Even though I was fully aware of my mother's love, I always missed my father. As I was growing up, I wished I could jump into his truck, join him on his work trips, and give him a chance to be proud of me.

School Years: In the Shadows of Two Wars

In my childhood, our family lived through two terrible wars. The first of them was called the Six-Day War, and it was fought in 1967. Israel had received news that some of the neighboring Arab countries were planning an attack. So, in the early morning of June 5, Israel staged a sudden, preemptive air strike that destroyed more than 90 percent of Egypt's air force on the tarmac. A similar air assault incapacitated the Syrian air force. Without cover from the air, the Syrian and Egyptian armies were left vulnerable to Israel's military operation.

Within three days, the Israelis had achieved an overwhelming victory on the ground, capturing the Gaza Strip and the Sinai Peninsula from Egypt and reaching the east bank of the Suez Canal. An eastern front was also opened on June 5 when Jordanian forces began shelling West Jerusalem—disregarding Israel's warning to King Hussein to keep Jordan out of the fight. The shelling resulted in a crushing Israeli counterattack. By June 10, Israel's army drove Jordanian forces out of East Jerusalem and the entire West Bank. Both sides of Jerusalem were now controlled by Israel, including the holiest place for the global Jewish community—the Western Wall in the Old City of Jerusalem. Israel also took a big part of the Golan Heights from Syria.

The West Bank border runs less than two kilometers (one mile) from Abu Gosh, and in 1967, one of the battles between Israeli and Jordanian armies was fought on the Har Adar ("Radar Hill") next to the village. Fortunately, Abu Gosh remained safe; I don't remember a single shell hitting the town. Long after the war, there were destroyed tanks on the slopes of the Har Adar, and as children, we played on and even in them.

Israel gained victory because, as they claimed, God was on their side. All that happened in only six days. I remember my mother used to say, "Goodness me. Who on earth are these Jews? Sometimes, they make you feel as if God is Jewish."

In October 1973, another conflict between Israel, Egypt, and Syria erupted, known as the Yom Kippur War. The war started when Egyptian forces crossed the Suez Canal while Syrian troops simultaneously launched an offensive against Israeli positions in the Golan Heights. After heavy losses on both sides, a cease-fire negotiated by the United Nations, the US, and the Soviet Union went into effect.

For me, these wars created a great deal of confusion and even affected my spiritual journey. The Muslim Arabs were sure that Allah had given them the land and that, politically, it was their right to take the land back from Israel. On the other hand, Israel claimed that God had enabled them to regain their power in the area. I was a schoolboy then and could no longer figure out who God was and whose side He was on.

As I mentioned, Abu Gosh is located near Jerusalem, and during peaceful times, it was a nice spot to live. In the village, there was only one primary school. After finishing it at the age of thirteen, I had to decide where to continue my schooling. It was 1973, and the Yom Kippur War hadn't broken out yet. I had several options: to go to Jerusalem or some Arabic-majority city, such as Nazareth or Haifa, to attend an Arabic secondary school, or to go to a Jewish school.

I chose a Jewish school in southeastern Jerusalem, in an area called Talpiot, which was on the way to Bethlehem. The school was named the Ort Kennedy Elementary and Secondary School (based on the name of President John F. Kennedy) and was about 16 kilometers (ten miles) from my home. I had to take two buses to get there, but it didn't bother me: I wanted to attend a Jewish school because they were considered high quality, and all the other secondary schools were also far from our home.

Me *(back)*, my cousin Musa *(right)*, and my little brothers Hussein and Ibrahim.

The secondary school system in Israel is good because it combines studies and hands-on learning. We worked three days a week and studied for three days. In my case, it meant I got a professional education in engine mechanics during that time. In addition, I came to know Jews, Christians, and Muslims and mingled with many Jewish immigrants from various parts of the world.

Still, as an Arab child, studying in a Hebrew school was not always easy. In the first year, I had to catch up with everybody and learn Hebrew more fluently. Besides that, my Jewish classmates gave me a hard time. There were only three other Arab kids in the school, and whenever I was in an altercation, I was called "*Arabi Melukhlakh*"—"a dirty Arab." The days when the PLO carried out explosive attacks were even worse. One such day, I was beaten up quite badly.

It is extremely difficult to live in the middle of such a political conflict without being part of the problem. I wonder, if my personality wasn't as it is, what could have happened? I may have turned into a terrorist or reverted to revenge, which could have been disastrous. Or, I could have become someone who fights theologically and politically with the Jewish people and the State of Israel. But I thank God for my mother and father and the good example I had in my home. At times, I did feel bitter and wanted to react in a destructive manner, but I didn't. I made a rule for myself that when any conflict arose I would instead stay out of school for two or three days. I escaped to the Old City of Jerusalem, where cinemas showed two movies in a row from 10 a.m. to 2 p.m.

"Harun Is Our Friend"

After my first year in secondary school, I had reached my limit with the treatment they gave me—I couldn't take any more bullying. So, I made a plan to end it. I chose the tallest guy from my class, Zion, and followed him for two days, discovering he took bus number 24 to go home from school. Then, one day after school, I hurried ahead of him towards the bus stop and hid behind a tree, clutching a big stone in my hand.

When he approached, I jumped out and said, "Zion, I chose you because you are the biggest kid in the class. You came with your gang to beat me up, and that's not fair. Now that you are alone, I've decided to split open your head. Though I'm smaller than you, I've chosen you to take my revenge on. But I'm giving you a choice; either we make peace, and you make the others stop persecuting me, or your head will meet my rock."

Suddenly, this giant, Zion, began to cry and apologized for what they had done to me. I said, "It's OK, but stop treating me like this in class." We were only 14 years old then, but Zion and I made peace there on the spot. The following day, he stood up in the class and said, "Harun is our friend. It's not his fault he was born an Arab, and I will not allow anyone to harm him from now on."

Another guy, Gabby Johari, stood up and agreed with Zion. Gabby looked at me and said, "Harun, I will ask my mom to invite you over next Shabbat to our home, and I will stand by you in school." His mom agreed, and I spent Shabbat with a Jewish family for the first time in my life.

Gabby's parents were from Kurdistan, Iraq. His mom was so sweet, and his father also hugged me. The family even influenced the development of my musical taste. Gabby's brother, Meir, loved the music of Greek-Egyptian folk-pop singer Demis Roussos. His songs caught on with me and became my favorites, too. I started to like the Western style of music in addition to the classical Arabic music that I was used to.

There was another friend from the Jewish school named Eli Elphasi. His parents were Jews from a Moroccan background, and he also invited me to his home. Gabby and Eli became my best friends. Around this time, my mom said, "Please invite all your friends to our home to stay for a night." Gabby and Eli came. Zion couldn't come because his mom didn't want him to be away on Shabbat. This was the first time these Jewish boys stayed overnight with an Arab family. I loved them very much. I visited them, and they visited me. I still keep in contact with them from time to time. Gabby lives in New York, and Eli is in Israel.

So, I was not mistreated anymore in school. I had my friends; my Hebrew had become more than acceptable and was about on par with the rest of my classmates. There were still some negative attitudes towards me in school, particularly on the part of one of the teachers who taught mathematics. Once, he assigned us some homework, and when I brought it back, he asked me to go to the board and write my answer.

When I had finished, he said, "It is wrong."

I knew I had answered correctly, so I stood my ground and said, "My answer is correct."

We argued back and forth until the teacher suddenly realized I was right. He looked at me and said, "Your answer is correct, but your stubbornness to prove you are correct bothers me. I will let it go this time, but next time, you can go to your Arab schools and study there."

It was too much for my friends. They stood up and screamed at him, "We do not want a racist teacher!" and went to the headmaster. Soon after, the headmaster gave us a new teacher.

I finished secondary school in 1976. After that, I took some additional courses to upgrade my professional skills. As I had done before, I worked and studied at the same time and during summer vacation as well. In 1977, I decided to take an accounting course, which qualified me to work as an account manager. Classes were taught in Hebrew and English.

Looking back, I can praise God that all these experiences—including the most negative ones—have turned out to be for the best. I believe that even the hardships, with the support from my family and friends, strengthened my character, set me free from fanaticism and narrow-mindedness, and endowed me with resilience in dealing with crises. As far as the Arab/Jewish conflict is concerned, I believe that we need our eyes opened to see that there are victims on both sides. That's why, for me, it's been more helpful to pray for the situation rather than take one side against the other.

2

Questions and Sweet Dreams

My study in the Hebrew school with Jewish people did not significantly change my political or religious views. Most of my friends and their families were secular Jews, so their Jewishness was not a big problem for me. But I did find myself uncomfortable when I met Jews who were more religious—the orthodox and ultra-orthodox types—so I didn't go out of my way to include them in my friendship circles.

My most profound religious breakthrough happened a couple of years before starting secondary school. As I mentioned, the Six-Day War in 1967 confused me spiritually. I had believed that God existed, but after the war, I had begun to doubt who He was and whose side He was on. So, around twelve years old, I decided to search for answers by making the Islamic prayers more a part of my life.

During my childhood, the Muslim people in Abu Gosh were not very religious. Going to the mosque for Friday prayers was not popular. The few times I went there with my uncle and cousin, there were only around ten people—mostly elderly. For a child, there seemed to be nothing interesting there for me. Only on some special holidays did more people attend the mosque. So, when I decided to pray like a true Muslim, I did it at home.

I remember how I prayed—or at least tried to pray—but after only three days, I felt bored. The biggest reason was that I had so many unanswered questions about religion: Does God really hear me when I pray? Was I supposed to pray the Muslim way without addressing my personal issues? Why couldn't I have a personal relationship with God? Why did I have to pray at certain times?

When I tried to pray, all these questions stirred in my mind. Finally, I stopped trying and gave up.

The religion of Islam rests on five pillars, and despite my young age, I had critical objections to all of them:

- *The Shahada, the profession of faith, which says, "There is no god but Allah, and Muhammad is his prophet."* To be a Muslim, one must recite the *Shahada*. According to Islam, you can't say only the first part, "There is no god but Allah," but you must include Muhammad, or otherwise it is incomplete. I started to wonder why Muhammad was included here. Why was he a part of witnessing God's existence?

- *The prayer, Salat.* In Islam, one needs to pray five times a day and, every time, perform four to seventeen different series of prescribed motions and prayer phrases. In addition, every Muslim must perform a ritual washing called *wudu* before praying. All the required prayers must be recited in Arabic—even if the one praying doesn't understand it. Already at a young age, I began asking myself, what happens if I miss my prayer? Would I be punished? Why did I need to repeat the same expressions and motions without really knowing why I was doing them? Why was there a need for *wudu*—what if I had just taken a bath or a shower and washed?

  Apart from these questions, I think I rejected the Muslim prayer concept mostly because I felt it didn't help me to know God or have a real relationship with Him. I felt like I was literally "just going through the motions." Already as a child, deep in my heart, I wanted to have a personal relationship with God, even though I didn't know this term then. Later, I understood that the repetitive rituals of certain verses associated with corresponding motions lock people into a routine void of life and impact. As a child, I wasn't getting anything out of it (and I don't think God was either).

- *Sawm, fasting during the holy month of Ramadan, which means that an adult Muslim must not eat or drink from sunrise to sunset.* In my childhood, I was taught that the Ramadan fast was so that the rich could empathize more with the poor. I wondered, then, why the poor had to fast. I was also told that if I traveled more than 25 kilometers (15 miles), I wouldn't need to fast, and if I didn't fast, I could feed sixty people to make up for it. Again, it made me think of the poor: if they didn't fast and didn't have the money to feed sixty other people, what would happen to them? I even had questions about why Muslims follow the lunar calendar. In it, a year is eleven days shorter than in the solar calendar, and Ramadan can sometimes come in the summer and at other times in the winter.

  When I brought up these questions with my mom, she never knew how to answer them. As a result, truth be known, I don't think I fasted more than three days in my entire time as a Muslim.

- *Zakat, giving alms. Zakat* is similar to the Christian tithe. According to Islam, Muslims are supposed to give 2.5 percent of their income to the poor. In addition, they are encouraged to give money to spread Islam all over the world. These were not a big issue for me because I had learned to give at home. Yet I felt that the system was unfair to those struggling to make ends meet in their own lives.

- *Hajj, the pilgrimage to Mecca a Muslim must make once in their life.* Once again, the poor are not able to fulfill this pillar either. It seemed strange to me that obeying God was made so difficult for poor people.

So, there I was, a teenage boy full of questions and objections. I enjoyed the things boys of that age enjoy, such as soccer and other sports, but inside, I was empty. I began to doubt everything about Islam, religion, and even God's existence. After that, I lived years without believing in anything. A profound unbelief formed deep in my heart and was revealed in my words and behavior. Despite my young age, I committed all sorts of sins and transgressions, both big and small.

Sari – An Amazing Young Lady from Finland

Though I had no sense of direction, I wanted to get on with my life. After secondary school, I continued my studies, but at the same time, I wanted to work and make some money. In 1976, I applied for a job at a kibbutz called Kiryat Anavim, close to my village. A kibbutz is an agrarian, communal settlement unique to Israel, in which all the wealth is held in common, and profits are reinvested in the community. At Kiryat Anavim, one of the things that contributed to the common treasury was the hotel, and that's where I worked. My responsibility was to coordinate the cleaners' work and ensure the rooms were ready to accept new customers.

A beauty and an adventurer in 1978. A photo of Sari as a recent high school graduate. At the same time, I continued my studies and worked on the kibbutz.

In the summer of 1978, I met there a young Finnish woman named Sari. During this time, many young Western people came to Israel and worked on kibbutzes as volunteers. It was a cheap and easy way to spend time living and traveling in the Holy Land. In a kibbutz, they received a place to stay, and their meals were included. The settlement asked them to work four days a week for six hours a day; the rest of the week was free.

In the kibbutz hotel, I worked with many Finnish people, but only a few of them spoke English. Sari did. She was very nice to me, and we quickly became friends. Whenever I saw her, I volunteered to carry bed sheets or whatever she needed to the area or floor where she worked. She called me a gentleman, which made me proud of myself.

The hotel was on a hill, and my home village could be seen from the top balcony. Some other Finnish people volunteered to take Sari to show her the town, but others from the kibbutz warned her not to go there because the inhabitants were Arabs. They told her, "You see that village? It's called Abu Gosh. You should avoid going there, and you should not even have friends from that place, though we have some of them working here on this kibbutz." But, praise God, Sari did not listen to them.

One day, I gained the courage to invite Sari to the movies. At the film's end, I got a little bolder and asked her to consider dating me. That was September 6, 1978, and Sari's answer was positive. After that, we openly walked around together, and several Finnish people warned her about dating an Arab. I understand that they were only trying to look out for her. Again, lucky me, Sari didn't listen to their advice.

During the period Sari was in Israel, she visited my home many times, and my family came to love her and Sari to love them. She told me many times how she thought my family was friendly and that she felt my sisters' love for her. In fact, my whole family—my mother and brothers included—were drawn very quickly to her.

At the same time, Sari learned to love my culture. She loved it when there was an Arab wedding in the village. Usually, it would be a three-day party—from Thursday evening to Saturday—but the actual wedding day was special. On that day, there might be as many as one or two thousand guests, and food would be served to all starting around 2 p.m. One never knew who was invited and who was not; that never mattered. All were welcome. Sari and her Finnish friends had the opportunity to attend some of these weddings, and, usually, they were treated like VIP guests. This is part of Arab culture; outsiders are treated well, and it's essential to show generosity.

One of the peculiarities of the wedding feast was that the bride could wear as many as twelve different dresses during the party. She would begin with a white dress but then change from one dress to another, and after each change, she would dance with friends and family. Though this was something new and strange for Sari and the Finnish girls, they were all impressed and thought it added some additional "flare" to the wedding celebration and called special attention to the bride. I was so proud that Sari saw this side of our culture and embraced it.

In the summer of 1979, Sari's year in Israel came to an end, so I decided to visit her in Finland. I told my mom about my plans, but she was not enthused. Still, she blessed me and didn't protest too hard about my leaving.

Because of the flight arrangements, I arrived in Finland the day before Sari. I stayed at a friend of Sari's, and in the morning, I met Sari's father, Erkki, for the first time when he came to pick me up. He didn't speak English (or Hebrew or Arabic!), and I didn't speak practically a word of Finnish. We had to drive together to the airport to bring Sari home. It was July, and summer in Finland is beautiful. Still, the journey felt long! I tried speaking English slowly, thinking he would understand, and he spoke Finnish loudly and slowly, thinking that I would understand. But neither of us had a clue what the other was saying.

My visit to Finland shaped the next phase of my relationship with Sari. We realized it was more than friendship or light dating; it was love.

Having an Israeli passport, I was allowed to stay in Finland for three months. I met many of Sari's family members, including her aunts and uncles, two grandmothers, and her grandfather. I loved Finland, and I loved her family. I was introduced to the Finnish culture and food, but the most amazing thing above everything else I discovered in the country was the Finnish sauna. For sure, this is the best thing in all of Finnish culture. The sauna is a small building or room designed for heat sessions. The high heat and steam make the bathers perspire. I am so much in love with the sauna that now I have four of them—two at home (electric and steam saunas) and two at our summer cottage (electric and wood-fired).

The three months in Finland passed quickly, and it was time for me to return home. Sari and I were uncertain about our future, but we knew we loved each other.

After arriving back in Israel, I decided to go and work in Eilat, a southern Israeli port and resort town on the Red Sea near Jordan. The town is well known for its snorkeling and diving. The Coral Beach Nature Reserve attracts many tourists, so I had many opportunities to find work. I found work in a nice hotel and worked there for five months.

At the time, making a phone call to Finland from Israel was very expensive. To call an international number, you had to buy the minutes in advance. If I remember correctly, I had to work four hours to cover the costs of a five-minute call! Consequently, I used to call Sari only once a week. Between calls, I wrote letters. Well, to be honest, I didn't write the letters myself—I needed help.

While working in Eilat, I met an Argentinian man named Miguel, whose English was excellent. He approached me tentatively after seeing me writing to Sari and said, "Your handwriting is terrible and full of mistakes. Let me write your letters." He was right; my handwriting was and still is terrible. Sometimes, even I myself am not able to read what I have written before.

So, I dictated to him, and he wrote the letters. But things changed one day. Miguel let me know he was a homosexual and had feelings for me. I said to myself, "Oh my God, what a situation I am in!" I realized we had a profound conflict of interest. I told him I didn't want him to write any more of my letters, and from that day onward, I never saw him again. Instead,

I decided to subject Sari to more of my miserable handwriting and use more money to speak with her directly by phone.

During one of our calls, Sari informed me that I would be a father. This made me miss her so much more. I decided to go back to Finland for a visit. I was young but wanted to take responsibility for my actions. I called my mother, older brothers, and a few others and told them the news.

When these people heard about the new situation, many of them wanted to give me advice. Yet, most of those recommendations were different from what I had expected. One person said, "So what? You are not the first or last to whom this has happened. Western girls can take care of themselves." Another's advice was even worse, "It would be easy for her to get an abortion." The third said, "It's up to her. She can have an abortion or give it up for adoption." The fourth piece of advice came from my mother. She was proud that I was thinking about taking responsibility, and she said to me, "Call her and tell her to come back to Israel. We will build you a house, and if she declares faith in Islam, everything will be fantastic."

At least my mother's advice came from a loving, motherly heart. Yet, because I was no longer truly Muslim in my heart, I was confused but thought I should try to make her happy. I called Sari and shared what my mother had told me.

I knew Sari was a Christian, but now she had something more to tell.

"Look, Harun," she started. "Just a short while ago, I went to a church and renewed my relationship with Jesus, and I will never give Him up. Never! I can raise my baby with you or without you, but never without Jesus."

I thought, "Who is this Jesus competing with my love?" However, I respected Sari's willingness to give anything up for her faith. Her decision helped me make my choice. I wanted to be a man and take responsibility, not run away from it. I decided I did not want my child to be without a father. I had lost my own father at an early age, and I knew how painful it was to grow up fatherless. That was the last thing I wanted my child to feel. So I had no other choice—I knew I would break my mother's heart, but I would have to leave and go be with Sari.

I credit my mom for teaching and instilling a sense of responsibility in me. Moving to Finland was the right thing to do.

I didn't have much money but saved up enough to buy a flight ticket from Tel Aviv to Helsinki on April 14, 1980. When I arrived in Sari's hometown of Kuopio, she was at the train station waiting for me. It was great to see her again, face-to-face. It was an emotional meeting. All the pent-up longing came out in one big, long hug.

At the time, Sari was studying to become a marketing secretary and lived with two other girls in an apartment, so staying there was not convenient for me. I looked for a cheap guest house but ended up staying in a hostel, which was an old one-story wooden house light-years away from being a five-star hotel. I slept in a big room with six beds. Everything I owned at the time fit into one bag. I didn't know the language, and later, I found out that I was one of only six foreigners in the city at that time.

One day, I woke up and felt someone touching my hair. I thought Sari might have come and wanted to wake me up. But instead, I saw an alcoholic lady with a very weird look. She was wearing white lipstick. That was the first time I had ever seen such a thing! I jumped off the bed and screamed at her. She just casually and calmly walked away, briefly stopping at the dresser and taking my cigarettes. I could not even go after her because all I had on was my underwear.

During my first days at this lousy hostel, Sari and I decided to do something significant towards building our future: we got engaged. We bought the cheapest gold rings in town that we could find. Sari also had an application pending to move into student housing, and luckily, we got the apartment just before I ran out of money.

We got married on June 6, 1980. Our wedding was not even close to what I was used to in Abu Gosh. But it was *our* party. We had only two guests: the witnesses from the court. Following the brief ceremony, we found a nice cafeteria and ordered coffee and cake.

Soon after getting married, we applied for a more extensive student apartment in married student housing and were accepted. We were very limited with our financial resources. I was looking for a job and soon found one at an engine machine shop. The people working there were very kind. Only two of them spoke fragments of English, but they were nice to me. Sometimes I misunderstood their jokes, but we resolved the misunderstandings quickly. At that workplace, I learned Finnish a lot and picked up some local slang, too. I also learned a lot about Finnish culture.

Sometimes after work, I went to a bar for a few beers with my colleagues. The more beer I had, the better my Finnish became! That was my first introduction to real, Finnish secular life. At the same time, while hanging out with these new friends, I began to become aware of the immorality in Western cultures. So, I was keen to tell them that my wife was a practicing Christian and not worldly like other women. But this only made me realize the double standard I was living by; I was not as moral of a person myself nor committed to godly principles as she was.

So, this is how my life with Sari started. I couldn't have imagined how much her spirituality and character would influence me. Later, I learned to know her as a true woman of God. Sari is honest, humble, trustworthy, an excellent mother, an excellent grandmother—all our four grandchildren love her dearly—and a loving wife. When asked a question, she will always give a truthful answer. She's also a prayer warrior, and her Bible knowledge is remarkable.

God has been very gracious to me. He has put in my life two women who have tremendously affected how my life has turned out. One is my mother—a real model of a virtuous woman— and the other is my lovely wife, Sari.

Becoming a Father

On July 12, 1980, my life changed forever when I became a father. I was only 20, but I was so proud to have a son. I wanted to name him Ali, which is a typical Arab name, and it was okay for Sari. However, she also wanted him to have a Christian name. So, we also gave him the name Marko, a Finnish form of Mark, one of the four evangelists in the New Testament.

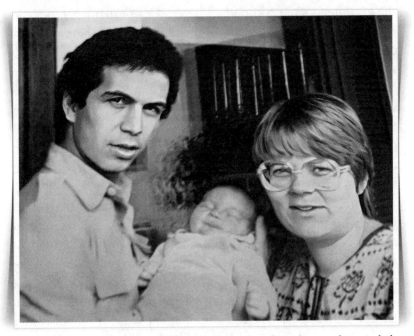

Ali's and Sami's *(in the picture)* birth revolutionized our lives and reminded me of the father's importance to a child.

Ali has an extraordinary personality. One of his unique features is that he is always thankful. This means that it has always been easy to make food for him; he eats almost everything he is served and eats it thankfully. One time, when he was a child, Sari had food on the stove, and she just forgot about it. Later, she remembered it when she smelled something burning in the house. Ali had just come home and asked for something to eat. Sari told him she would have to cook something else because she burned the food. But Ali ate it anyway, thanking her and telling her what an excellent meal it was.

When Ali was born, I had just started working in the engine machine shop that I mentioned. That work lasted less than a year, and then I had to look for another job. After months of looking, I finally found a job in paper waste management for the local newspaper company. There were not many people who were interested in this type of work. Much of the work was done outside, and in winter there were many days when the temperature was −20 degrees Celsius (−4 Fahrenheit) or even colder. The pay was less than what I would have received as unemployment compensation. That wasn't fun, but I decided to take the job anyway because I didn't want the government to support me. I still think that when you move to another country, you shouldn't be too picky about your work before you learn the language and how society works.

On one of my after-work bar trips, I met an Israeli man named Isaac, who was a tourist in the city. He had a Spanish friend named Pedro with him. Pedro was married to a Finnish woman and had just arrived in Finland. Isaac told me Pedro was looking for work, and I told him that my company was looking to hire somebody. He got the job, but we had a terrible communication barrier between us. He did not speak a word of English and only a few words in Finnish. My Finnish was far from perfect, but I tried to teach him. I would point at an object and tell him what it was in Finnish. In turn, he would say the object's name in Spanish. A year later, I was able to speak Spanish, but he still did not speak Finnish.

However, we became good friends. He and his wife visited us, and we visited them. Neither of us men were satisfied with our salary or job, so Pedro decided to quit. I also started looking for other options and came across a job advertisement for a pizza chef. I applied and got hired. The salary was huge compared to what I used to make. I learned how to cook and became a good chef.

At the pizzeria, my shift usually ended around 10 p.m., and I had to wait for a while to catch a bus that would take me home. So, I often went to a pub for a few beers, sometimes a little more. I made some new friends, and once, they offered me a joint with hash. After that, smoking hash became a regular habit for me, but I never told Sari what I was up to or doing. I always made up excuses about why I came home late. Graciously, she always forgave me and let it go. Whenever I think about this, I feel sorry for what I did to her.

Work was sometimes hectic at the pizzeria. The most spectacular tricks were practiced when there were fewer customers. Our children took their father's example and threw round doilies into the air at home.

In July 1984, we had our second child. We named him Sami, which is a common name both in Arabic and Finnish. In addition, we gave him the Christian name Mikael.

One day, when Sami was four years old, he came home looking nervous. He wasn't looking straight into our eyes. I asked him, "What's going on? What happened?"

He said, "Well, Dad, I went to the supermarket with my friend Kalevi, and he took a small piece of chocolate and then bit into it. He gave me some, and I ate it, but I feel terrible because I know I shouldn't have done that."

The way he said it, clearly embarrassed and with a guilty conscience, wringing his fingers, filled my heart with empathy. I tried not to smile but said to him, "OK, let's go back to the supermarket and fix it."

When we got to the supermarket, we asked to see the manager. Then I told Sami, "OK, go ahead and confess to the manager," and Sami did. The manager listened to him, smiled, and said, "Well, young man, this time you will only need to pay for it because you confessed, but next time, you will have to come here and work for me, and it will not be easy." Since then, I have never seen Sami take anything that is not his, and I think he learned his lesson.

I can't say I have been an exemplary father, but I loved my children and trusted Sari with raising them. I don't think there was much difference between how Sari raised our kids and how my mom raised my siblings and me, except that Sari would raise Ali and Sami to be Christians. Later, as adults, Ali and Sami became good friends, for which I am very happy.

3

A Restless Man Faces the Truth

Despite all those good things, life was—though I didn't want to confess it—off the rails for me. I smoked weed and drank but continued to work. Luckily, there were some things I didn't do. I never laid a hand on Sari or verbally abused her. I guess it was because my mother was strict about how we treated women. Still, sometimes, when I came home late and drunk, it was too much for Sari. I wondered how she was able to bear it.

One day, I came home late again. I had lost my key and couldn't get into the building. We lived on the top floor of a three-story building. I threw stones at the window until Sari woke up. I don't know how serious she was, but she said she would not open the door; she'd had enough. But I climbed up the fire escape, went up to the roof, and swung myself over the roof's edge onto the balcony. Sari was terrified and opened the balcony door and said, "How could you do that? You could have died." She was startled and angry with me, and who could blame her?

At that time, Sari and three other Christian women who lived in the neighborhood decided to start a prayer group. In addition to a shared faith, all the women had one other thing in common: they had husbands who were not Christians. The woman decided to pray for their husbands to get saved. They developed a prayer list and prayed every week together and every day on their own for the men on this list. Sari later told me that she thought that all the husbands would accept Christ, but not me. She felt it would be easier for a cow to learn to fly than for me to accept Christ into my life. Still, she challenged God with this. Lucky for me, God took this challenge seriously. Gradually, something started to happen in my life. Sari and I started talking more about Christianity, Islam, and Judaism.

Isn't it strange that when God is on the move, usually, the evil one comes up with distractions? Never before had Jehovah's Witnesses knocked on our door, but one day, two of them showed up at our house. I had started reading the Bible and even had several dialogues with Sari about biblical issues. Just as I was beginning to move in the right direction, the devil wanted to push me away from the path God had for me.

Many Jehovah's Witnesses are friendly people. They think that they are true Christians, but they deny the divinity of Jesus, believing Him to be one of the creatures made by God—a lesser god, but not "the God." This belief is enough to exclude them from Christianity. So, from a Christian perspective, you can compare them to Muslim preachers, Mormons, or Hare Krishnas, who may all be sincere but lead people in the wrong direction.

Of course, I didn't know this at the time. So, I opened the door for these two visitors and let them in. Sari knew better and was not delighted with what I did.

Who Are the 144,000?

These two witnesses started to talk to me about the translations of the Bible. They said the then-official Finnish translation was all wrong and that the Jehovah's Witnesses founder Charles Russell's translation was the best. They didn't know that I was from Israel and read Hebrew.

I asked them, "What is the original language of the Bible?" They said the Old Testament was written in Hebrew and the New Testament in Greek. I said, "Great! I was taught about the Old Testament in Hebrew in Israel. Let's compare the texts."

I had a Hebrew Bible, and we compared it to the official Finnish version. Every verse we compared was translated well. They disagreed, verse after verse, until they gave up and moved on to the New Testament.

Then they started attacking the deity of Jesus. It didn't matter to me, but I wanted to prove them wrong again. So, I took my chance with the New Testament. They asked questions, and every time, I snuck off to ask Sari about the issue and then returned to give them the answer.

We spoke about many things. One of the topics was the 144,000 people that will be in heaven, as mentioned in Revelation 7:4: *"And I heard the number of those who were sealed. One hundred and forty-four thousand of all the tribes of the children of Israel…"*

The Jehovah's Witnesses think this number refers to the humans who will be resurrected to heavenly life and that the crowd is comprised of their members. I went again to Sari and asked her about it, and she said they misunderstood the chapter because the verse does not speak about 144,000 Gentiles but about the tribes of Israel.

Sari's quick reply was fantastic. They didn't mind that I kept leaving the room because I let them think I was checking on the baby.

I returned and asked them, "Who are the 144,000?"

"Jehovah's Witnesses," they replied.

I said, "Well, that is not true. This passage has nothing to do with Gentiles. This is speaking about the tribes of Israel."

I had pushed them into a corner, although I was not even a Christian yet. They asked me how I could be so sure about my interpretation. I said, "Well, now that you ask directly, I want to be honest. Every time I went out of the room, I told your question to my wife because she speaks the truth, and I trust her."

Then one of them said, "Maybe your wife is one of those."

"One of what?" I asked.

"One of the 144,000."

I told them that she was not a Jew. Then they realized that she was a devout Christian who knew the Bible.

Next, they changed the subject to the gifts of the Holy Spirit. They said that people have misunderstood the gifts and that there are no such things. I went to Sari and asked her if she practices the gifts of the Spirit.

"Do you have them?" I asked.

"Yes," she replied.

I returned to them and said, "Guys, the gifts of the Holy Spirit are true, and you are wrong."

"Who told you this?" they wondered.

"My wife, Sari, of course."

Then they tried politely to say that Sari was not telling the truth. Finally, without any political correctness, I asked them, "Are you saying my wife is a liar?"

They froze. Then I said, "Get up and leave my house."

Sari and her prayer group continued to pray for their husbands, and Sari started to practice a brilliant way of sharing the gospel with me. She reminded me how clever I had been with the Jehovah's Witnesses and how I could convince them with my knowledge of Hebrew. She began to ask me about the Hebrew origin of certain verses in the Old Testament, like Psalm 22, Isaiah 53, Isaiah 7:14, and others that mention the Messiah. She would say, "Harun, could you please check if this is a good translation?" I did not know what she was up to, but I was proud to be able to help her.

On New Year's Eve 1984, I had a shift at the pizzeria. It closed at 10 p.m. As usual, I went to the bar for a while, and after that, I went to the taxi stand with my friend to wait for a cab. On New Year's Eve, the taxi line was long. Suddenly, a man came out of nowhere and started talking to us, asking if we would like to discuss spiritual issues. The man's name was Jouni.

"If you'd like," he said, "we could go to a small café nearby and have a cup of hot tea."

It was approximately –20 Celsius outside, so a warmer place with a hot cup of tea sounded great. After we sat at the café and began drinking our tea, he began sharing Christ with us. I listened to him for a while, until I said to him, "Listen, I am a Muslim. I studied in a Jewish school. My wife is a committed Christian. So I have everything in order with God." (My reaction was typical of a secular Muslim when challenged about his faith: I stressed my own religiousness, even though I wasn't religious at all.)

I did not expect what Jouni said next.

"I don't care if you are a Muslim, studied in a Jewish school, and your wife is a Christian; I see that you are drunk. The Bible is clear: If you do not have Jesus in your own heart, you will not go to heaven."

"You are rude!" I replied.

He shot back, "I'm not rude. That's what the Bible says. Do you want me to lie to you? Do you want me just to please you? The truth is what will set people free. Jesus said, 'No one will come to the Father, except through me.'"

I respected the guy because he was honest. When he laid the truth out, I said, "I like you, and I would like to invite you to dinner at my home." After that, Jouni offered to take me home so that he could find out where I lived. He also asked me if he could bring a friend with him, and I agreed it would be fine.

I went home and found Sari awake. Now I had a good excuse for why I was late. I said, "I'm late because I met a Christian like you. He gave me a tract with the church's address on it." I showed it to her. She could not believe her eyes. It was her church!

A Divine Encounter

I set up an appointment to meet with Jouni a week and a half later on Friday. I was sober this time and ready to discuss Christianity again with him. I had even prepared for it: I had just finished reading the Gospel of John seven times in a row from Sari's Bible!

Jouni brought along a friend named Niilo Närhi, who, unknown to me then, would later become my close colleague.

They both talked about God and how God loves me and all mankind. They also told me how God loves each person in a special way and how man's evil resulted in all the suffering on earth. They said that God wasn't pleased with all this wickedness and suffering that we see around us, but many of these troubles we bring upon ourselves—"we reap what we sow." In the midst of all this misery, God's nature is love, and He is the source of goodness, holiness, peace, and contentment. I was listening attentively to them, soaking in every word.

While we were talking, Niilo realized my knowledge of the Old Testament was more profound than the New Testament. Suddenly, he asked me, "If someone came today and claimed to be the Messiah, how would we know if he is true or false?"

I told him that that person would need to prove he was from the seed of David.

Niilo agreed. "That's correct, but how do we prove it?"

I told him there are some books regarding David's genealogy. Niilo listened to me, but it seemed that he was not as satisfied with this answer as my previous one. He had another question ready.

"Where are these books?"

"Somewhere…" I started, but I couldn't end the sentence. I didn't know.

Then Niilo said, "Let me tell you, in my opinion, these books have been burned. Let's read what it says in the Book of Daniel, chapter nine, verses 24–27."

So, we read together:

> *Seventy weeks are determined*
> *For your people and for your holy city,*
> *To finish the transgression,*
> *To make an end of sins,*
> *To make reconciliation for iniquity,*
> *To bring in everlasting righteousness,*
> *To seal up vision and prophecy,*
> *And to anoint the Most Holy.*

Know therefore and understand,
That from the going forth of the command
To restore and build Jerusalem Until Messiah the Prince,
There shall be seven weeks and sixty-two weeks;
The street shall be built again, and the wall,
Even in troublesome times.

And after the sixty-two weeks Messiah shall be cut off, but not for
Himself;
And the people of the prince who is to come
Shall destroy the city and the sanctuary.
The end of it shall be with a flood,
And till the end of the war desolations are determined.
Then he shall confirm a covenant with many for one week;
But in the middle of the week
He shall bring an end to sacrifice and offering.
And on the wing of abominations shall be one who makes desolate,
Even until the consummation, which is determined,
Is poured out on the desolate.

When we had finished reading the text, Niilo continued saying, "In the year 70 AD, Titus, the Roman emperor, burned the temple and destroyed it, which this prophecy speaks about. And this proves that the Messiah Daniel spoke about was born before 70 AD. Only someone born before that time could prove he is the Messiah."

I read it in Hebrew several times and tried to be as smart as possible so I wouldn't have to capitulate, but I had to be honest and say that Niilo was right. The text contained strange expressions about the number of weeks and was difficult to understand. Yet I saw it was a prophecy about the Messiah, and, historically, Titus did destroy and burn the temple, and Daniel had prophesied that the Messiah, Christ, would come before that. At least, that is what I understood from these verses.

I met Niilo and Jouni again several times, and during those meetings, I felt they were nice people. Their behavior and lifestyles were something I had never seen before, except in Sari, and this exemplified for me a model of how to be a

Christian in action. Also, since Sari and her close friends were all women, Niilo and Jouni were the first men I met who were real Christians. I realized that Christianity is not just a religion for women. After years of wasted time and doing nothing, my focus turned to religious discussion and research.

Sari did her best to help me discover that the anticipated Messiah in the Jewish Bible was Jesus. In a very clever way, she directed me to the root of revelation because she knew I had mastered the Hebrew language of the Torah. She introduced me to many of the prophecies about Jesus. She mentioned that over 300 prophecies about Jesus have been found in the Old Testament—about His miraculous birth, life, suffering, death, and resurrection.

I discovered that all these prophecies had been announced centuries before Jesus came to earth. This discovery shook me, and I was so astonished that the Jews did not believe in Jesus as the anticipated Messiah, though they read their holy Scriptures every day. I realized that both Jews and Muslims are still expecting a Messiah to come in the future—Jews for the first time; Muslims, like Christians, for the second time, but as the prophet of Islam, a just ruler and the judge of all. Christians, instead, recognize Jesus as the fulfillment of the Messiah prophesied in the Old Testament and anticipate him to come again as God and King.

I was now becoming convinced that Jesus of Nazareth of the New Testament was the Messiah and the one all these religions were searching for. Even Jesus' miracles were not the same as the other prophets' miracles. He was the only prophet absolutely compatible with God in His attributes, character, and behavior. The more I read about Jesus, the more I discovered and appreciated his extraordinary character. God was beginning to reveal His Son's uniqueness to me.

Finally, the conflict within me peaked. Even though I was not a practicing Muslim and had been an atheist for a long time, religion still ran through my veins and the marrow of my bones. Nothing is more difficult than letting go of the beliefs one has adopted. I understood that if doing good deeds would be the answer to canceling out my evil ones—as Islam teaches—I would need another lifetime to do that. Therefore, good deeds could not be the way to earn my salvation. Who, then, could save me and rescue me from all my sins and filth?

This period was one of the most challenging seasons of my life. Now that I know what was going on, I can describe it theologically: the Holy Spirit was convicting me of my sins, though I was still very confused. Here I was, a man born into a Muslim family, who studied in a Hebrew school, married a devoted Christian woman, and was a father of two boys. Though people could not see it on the outside, I knew my life was miserable. I had all these questions that kept circling in my brain. What is the religion of God? Is it Judaism? Is it Islam? Is it Christianity?

I had no peace and found myself thinking continuously about these things. I thought about the negative consequences of converting to Christianity. For sure, it would break my mother's heart, and that concerned me. On the other hand, I understood that it was my life. I had a family and kids to raise.

One day, I did something I haven't shared with many people. The act shows how desperate I was. I took a sheet of paper and wrote in Arabic: "Judaism, Christianity, Islam." I folded the paper, went to a forest, put that paper under a stone, and told God I wanted Him to somehow mark on the paper which one of the religions was true. I would return a week later to see how He had answered.

It was a long week as I waited expectantly for the answer. It was early spring, and the temperature was above zero, and I didn't remember that the ground underneath the stone would be wet. So, when I went there to pick up the paper, the ink had washed off, and I only saw blue smudges. I was disappointed. Later, the event has reminded me that, in essence, the way to God is not any religion itself; you need a personal relationship with Him.

During that time, the spiritual battles I was fighting made me a different person. I forgot things at work and burned pizzas. Even my boss noticed. It was a tough time. All the questions were running in my head all the time. Finally, I came to the point of having no choice but to make one of three decisions:

1. Accept Christ, knowing it would break my mother's heart.

2. Convert to Judaism. Yet I knew I couldn't really accept Judaism with all its rules and—after learning about what the Old Testament says about Christ—the way Judaism ignores all the clear Messianic prophecies in the Bible. So, I concluded soon that this wasn't the answer for me.

3. Become a practicing Muslim. But for this option, too, I immediately thought, no way! I couldn't even imagine that I would like an Islamic life, wishing and hoping that God would forgive me, and even after that, not being sure. According to Islam, even Muhammad was unsure about being accepted into heaven.

I knew I had to decide because I couldn't live that way anymore—wrestling with all these thoughts and ideas from morning until night. So, I decided that I would try Jesus. If He were the way to God, I would be the winner here. If believing in Him were a mistake, I would be in deep dung anyway.

So, I devised a plan. On March 31, 1985, just after work, I walked to the bus. It was 10:20 p.m. I was the only passenger, and as I rode along, I started talking to God.

I said to Him, "If you, Jesus Christ, are my God and Savior, change my life and turn my black heart into a clean heart... from a hateful heart into a loving heart... from a defiled heart into a pure heart, filled with holiness and self-control."

When I had finished my prayer, I didn't feel anything special. I am an emotional person, but it was a purely rational decision, and at first, it also stayed that way. Later, I started to realize that my heart was filling with love and the power of regeneration.

A New Tone in Family Life

When I arrived home, Sari was asleep. I woke her up and told her I had just prayed on the bus and accepted Jesus in my heart. She yawned and didn't act too excited right away. It took a while for her to see the change in my life. Finally, she rejoiced because she saw the harvest of her tears and prayers. None of the other men these women prayed for had accepted Christ yet—I was the first to do so. The others made their decisions later.

That spring, my life was radically changed. I had received Jesus as my Savior, and peace began to grow inside me. My life took a sharp turn toward happiness without drugs or alcohol. My old drinking buddies asked me to join them in the bar, but I didn't want to go there anymore. I was utterly fed up with that life. They said I had lost my mind, but I felt just the opposite: only now had I found it. I felt I had clear goals now and firm principles to follow. I knew it was God—the God of Christianity—who was my sufficiency and who made my life meaningful. I was prepared to sacrifice everything for Him.

Our home turned into a Christ-centered home. Following Jesus became the target I lived for, and I wanted nothing else as long as I lived. My life with Sari also became easier after I had accepted Christ. I tried my best to become a better father and husband. Sari and I were now a family with the same faith and desire—to keep Christ at the center of our lives.

I decided to call my mother and tell her about my decision. I told her, "Mom, I have decided to start following Jesus."

She didn't understand me at first and said, "So what? We all believe in Isa [Jesus], the son of Mariam."

I repeated, "No, Mom, I now believe that Jesus is my God and that the Bible is the only book of God."

She had my brother Zakaria close to her, and he told her, "Mom, he doesn't believe in Islam anymore—not in the Qur'an or Muhammad."

My mother was unhappy but said, "OK, son, it's your life."

My brothers and sisters, instead, were very upset with me, and it took them years to accept my decision. Later, I told my mother more about Christ.

Although my conversion had started from the prophecies of Jesus and falling in love with His character, the most noteworthy thing in my new faith was probably the concept of God as a father. God's fatherhood is the firm foundation I stand on for deliverance. Since I lost my earthly father, it was rewarding to call someone my father again. I had no idea, before I met Jesus, that God is a compassionate, loving father that anyone can run to, irrespective of their background. That was something I missed in Islam.

After growing deeper in my knowledge of God as a father, I began asking myself: What was my earthly father's destiny? Did he have the chance to hear about Christ as I did now? What is my mother's destiny as a Muslim woman with genuine faith? Have I told her about Christ in the right way so that she understands enough to lead her to salvation? What more could I do?

4

The Birth of a Ministry

Two months after accepting Jesus into my heart, I was baptized. The congregation to which Sari, Niilo, and Jouni belonged was part of the Finnish Pentecostal movement, and the baptism was administered in the traditional Baptist style by immersing the whole man in water.

I had changed jobs and worked at another restaurant, but my shift was still always in the afternoon. That made it possible for me to attend daily seniors' prayer meetings at the church, where I listened, learned, and studied the Bible with them. I was so active in my church that soon I was asked to oversee the prayer meetings in the area where we lived.

The owner of the restaurant was a short Italian man named Renzo. He worked all the time and was proud of his restaurant. At the same time, he was weird. He would sometimes come to the kitchen and make some noises behind the employees' backs, apparently either so that we would make mistakes or to scare us. Sometimes he shouted and swore at us. I, in particular, seemed to be the target of his tricks. Renzo knew that I had just become a committed Christian, so he really wanted to see if he could make me lose my temper.

I was really confused. By nature, I am a hot-blooded person, and the man drove me nuts. Sometimes I had to do my best to keep from cursing or punching him out. All I could do was just simmer inside, like the spaghetti I cooked as a chef.

At home, I complained about Renzo's behavior to Sari. She told me to try my best to be calm. I got the same advice from my pastor at the church, Martti Kallionpää. When I told him about my struggle at work, he used to laugh loudly and say, "Just be calm. God put this man in your life for a reason." And Pastor Martti was right. God put Renzo in my life to shape my temperament. It was not easy, but now, as I write this, I thank God for Renzo and how God used him to make me grow.

"Come Help Us"

I loved my congregation and wanted to do whatever I could with my gifts to serve. In addition to overseeing the prayer meetings, I was active in church outreach. I also tried out for the congregation's youth choir, Kulmakivi (The Cornerstone), which was pretty famous in Finland at the time, but I was unsuccessful. Unfortunately, I wasn't blessed with the voice of a nightingale, but closer to that of a crow.

Occasionally, I prepared meals for the church members to collect donations for the new church building. The Pentecostal movement in Finland holds an annual mid-summer conference with around 30,000 attendees at that time. So, I suggested to the organizing committee that I could run a pizzeria at the event. The idea was happily received. I gathered a team of volunteers, put up a tent the size of around 300 square meters (3,200 square feet), bought a pizza oven, and trained the volunteers to make pizza. We did this for several years. I wanted to be active because I felt that this was my new life, and every time I did something, it made me feel happy to serve God.

One day, my friend Niilo Närhi, a youth pastor in our congregation, told me about a mission conference he had attended. At the meeting, he had been leading a prayer session for Muslim ministry when one of the participants had seen a vision of an Arab man, wearing Arab clothing, stretching out his hands, and saying, "Come and help us." God had been calling Niilo to serve among Muslims before, but the vision and special atmosphere during the prayer session made his burden for the Muslim people even more intense. Niilo felt we should do something to spread the gospel among them. I agreed. He suggested that we start by gathering for a weekend twice a year to pray and fast with those who want to reach Muslims.

Around fifteen people came together for the first meeting. Every time, the group grew bigger. Although I am from a Muslim background, I was not an expert in Islamic studies, so in between the gatherings, I read and studied books in that field.

In 1987, my emerging passion for the Muslim ministry gained a new impetus. That year, the Lord opened the door for me to attend two important gatherings. The first was a Pentecostal mission conference held in March in Helsinki, the capital of Finland. Missionary work among Muslims was one of the topics there, and the main speaker was a Welsh missionary to Pakistan named Terry Lewis.

He was blond, over six feet (about 190 cm) tall, with a wooden leg and a powerful voice. He stood up to preach and said, "Nine hundred and fifty million Muslims are on their way to hell without Jesus, and you are still here doing nothing." Every time he pointed his finger, it was directed at me. I was both excited and sad at the same time. I felt God was talking directly to me through Terry Lewis and wanting me to move into full-time ministry.

When I told Sari about this, she was surprised. She told me that in her youth, she had felt God was calling her to be a missionary. Later, she had forgotten about it, but then someone prophesied that she would be doing missionary work among Muslims. She hadn't believed it, but now it seemed that the call and the prophecy were from God.

Later in the same spring, Niilo, Sari, and I attended another conference for those interested in reaching out to Muslims. That event was held with Swedish Pentecostal congregations in Mariehamn in Åland, Finland. There, I met a Swedish missionary named Sune Elofsson, who worked for the Swedish Christian organization IBRA Radio.

At the time, there were several radio-broadcasting Christian mission organizations around the world such as IBRA Radio,

Trans World Radio, and Far East Broadcasting Company. IBRA Radio was founded by the Swedish Pentecostal movement in 1948, and it had subsidiaries established in Finland, Denmark, and Norway. Sune told me that he was producing Arabic radio programs with the help of many Arabic-speaking people. Then he asked me if I was interested in starting a ministry to Arabic-speaking Muslims through media with their team.

Sune's words were like a kiss from God to me. Then he added, "Did you know that in a thirty-minute segment on air, you can reach a larger number of people than the Apostle Paul during his whole ministry?"

I went to my congregation's elders and shared what I had heard from those two men, Terry and Sune. My pastor at that time was Onni Haapala. He contacted an organization working in media within the Finnish Pentecostal denomination. The organization was called HSR-TV (now Keymedia) and was part of the Nordic IBRA family.

Visiting Abu Gosh, Antti the Lamb

In May 1987, Sari, the boys, and I visited my family in Abu Gosh. This was the first time we saw my Israeli family after I had permanently moved to Finland. We asked my parents-in-law, Erkki and Eila, to join us. It was a great visit. Ali and Sami met their Israeli grandmother, cousins, uncles, and aunts for the first time, and it was a big thing for them all. During the two weeks in Abu Gosh, no one asked me anything about my new faith. Most of the resentment my family members had felt about my conversion seemed to have subsided. My mom welcomed us all very generously and warmly. She was happy to meet my Finland family, and her happiness was very authentic.

Our visit happened during Ramadan, the holy month of fasting for Muslims. Even though it was the fasting time, my mom and sisters cooked for us. They had no problem with us eating while they fasted. The way my family treated us shows that there is a big difference between the teachings of Islam and the behavior of Muslims. We can see a lot of Muslims who are very friendly, kind, and generous to non-Muslims, but that is not what Islam, as an ideology, teaches them to do.

In Islam, there are two main holidays: Eid al-Fitr and Eid al-Adha. Eid al-Adha means the Feast of the Sacrifice (or the Holiday of Sacrifice), and it honors the willingness of Ibrahim (Abraham) to sacrifice his son as an act of obedience to Allah's command. (According to Islam, that son was Ishmael, not Isaac, as stated in the Bible.)

Another feast, Eid al-Fitr, means the Holiday of Breaking the Fast, and it is celebrated at the end of the fasting month in honor of the inspirations of the Qur'an. On these two holidays, Muslims worldwide sacrifice animals—mainly lambs. So, when we were in Israel, in preparation for ending the Ramadan fast, my brother bought a lamb they planned to kill and eat. The lamb was brought to my mother's house, and Ali, Sami, and their cousins had lots of fun feeding and playing with it. It became their friend, and they named the lamb Antti, a Finnish man's name.

On the morning of the feast, my brothers woke up early. First, they went to the mosque to pray, and then came the time to sacrifice the lamb. Sari, the boys, Sari's parents, and I had left to visit Jerusalem and then returned for dinner. Once we had gathered around the table, Ali and Sami asked, "Where is Antti?" They hadn't seen him in the yard.

I said, "Mmmmm, well, it is here right in front of you." Immediately, they realized that I was speaking about what was on their plates. That was a big shock for the boys. Then Ali said, "I am not going to eat this; no one eats his friend." Luckily, my mom had some grilled chicken that she fixed for them.

"I Will Become a Missionary"

In Finland, our future began to take shape rapidly. In the following months, we met the committee of Keymedia and visited IBRA Radio's headquarters in Stockholm.

Keymedia's chairman, Pastor Kai Antturi, told me they had been praying to start an Arabic department but didn't know anyone who could head the initiative. Now, they felt our meeting was particularly ordained by the Lord. The board decided to send Sari and me to Sweden to minister to the Muslim world with the IBRA Radio team.

In Stockholm, the reception was equally warm. Sari and I also visited their recording studio in Cyprus twice. There, I was introduced to sound engineering and program production with the help of Swedish young men who worked in the studio: Matthias, Lars, and others.

When the time came for us to move to Sweden, Sari quit her job as a sales secretary, and we gave up our apartment. I called my boss at the restaurant where I worked at that time. I told him I was quitting to become a missionary.

He said, "You must be mad. Are they going to pay you more than I do? You are a good chef, but if you want to go, I can't stop you. Remember, my door is always open if you want to return."

In the summer of 1987, we visited IBRA Radio's Cyprus studio. The boys were with us, and to their delight, we also made it to the beach during the trip.

This photo is from Jerusalem, which we visited in July 1988.

In July 1988, we made another visit to Israel, and on August 14, 1988, we were ordained by our church as missionaries. Surprisingly, however, we didn't immediately find a flat in the Stockholm area. We were already wondering if we had made a mistake—maybe it wasn't God's will to move? However, after a short stay in one believer's apartment in our home town Kuopio, we got a rental apartment in Tumba, a Stockholm suburb.

At the beginning of September, we moved to Sweden and started in the media ministry with IBRA Radio.

5

In Sweden and Beyond: Impact of Christian Media

In Stockholm, I started ministering with Reverend Sune Elofsson and an Egyptian man named Hussein, who shared the same office as me. He had started there a few months earlier.

At that time, IBRA Radio broadcast several Arabic program series on short waves from Lisbon, Portugal. I joined the team to produce the programs and help others in sound engineering. In addition, I did follow-up, which meant taking care of the listeners' responses, answering their questions, praying for the prayer requests, compiling statistics, and having a correspondence registry. When I discovered there were a lot of Muslims in Sweden, I also wanted to begin street evangelism among them.

As a family, we started to attend a Finnish-speaking Pentecostal church, Finska Filadelfia (The Finnish Philadelphia Church), in Stockholm. In addition, I started attending a small Pentecostal congregation in Tumba, which included a handful of Arabic-speaking Christians. There were four Muslim-background believers (MBBs, as we usually put it) there, and five or six women from a Christian background. The group organized Arabic meetings, and sometimes, the women's husbands also attended.

In that group, I made a shocking discovery: I realized that my Arabic was not so good anymore. This became particularly clear when it was my turn to lead a meeting for the first time. I started, and according to the other participants, I translated my Finnish spiritual language to poor Arabic, which they all found very amusing.

Later, I understood what caused my stumble. Firstly, I hadn't thought about Arabic grammar since I was in primary school. (I had completed my studies at the Jewish secondary school in Hebrew.) Secondly, my spiritual language was Finnish. By then, I had read the Bible and prayed almost only in Finnish, which caused me to feel it very difficult to pray and express my thoughts to God in Arabic. In fact, I was so alienated from Arabic that in my dreams, sometimes even my mother would speak to me in Finnish.

When I was leading the church meeting, one of the women present, Sonia, hit me in the head with all this. She interrupted me and said, "Listen, my son, you are not speaking Arabic. You just said 'song' in Arabic, not 'hymn.' We are not going to accept it. I have also listened to the radio program that you made and have to say your Arabic is awful. You have more grammatical mistakes than proper sentences."

I must admit that her feedback made me angry, but God was in control. Today, I thank God for Sonia. She is one of those people who told me the truth, straight to my face, without being politically correct. She's now a good friend of Sari and me.

In response to Sonia's candid criticism, I called my sister Izdihar, who was a teacher in Abu Gosh. I asked her to send me Arabic textbooks, from first-grade level to as far advanced as she had. She sent me the books, and I started to learn Arabic properly. I noticed that Sonia was right. My Hebrew was much better than my Arabic. At the same time, I had to learn Arabic Christian vocabulary instead of translating Finnish religious sayings into Arabic in my mind. In many cases, you can't just translate spiritual phrases (or any other phrases) from one language to another—it doesn't work that way.

I had to change and learn, and so I did. Later, I also became fluent in different dialects of Arabic.

Sune Elofsson coordinated the Arabic ministry in the Swedish IBRA Radio in the 1980s. He was one of those who believed in me in my early days in ministry.

Six Hours in the Army

My ministry in Stockholm was just taking off when I was unexpectedly summoned to return to Finland to serve in the army.

In Finland, all male citizens under 30 must serve the country by going to the military or civil service. At the time, one had to serve a minimum of eight months in the Finnish Defense Forces or sixteen months in civil service. I had applied for Finnish citizenship just before we moved to Sweden, and thought I was so close to turning thirty that they would not summon me. But I was wrong. We had been in Sweden for around ten months when I received the summons. The letter was delayed, and when I did receive it, I had less than two days' notice to be at a military base in Northern Finland, or I would be detained.

That was one of the worst days ever, and as a family, we were all very sad. I couldn't think about leaving Sari and the boys for eight months. We were all so confused and very emotional. Ali was almost nine years old then, and Sami was nearly five. When it was time to say goodbye, Ali asked me with tears in his eyes, "Are you coming back?" This broke my heart, but I did not want him to see my tears.

I tried to book a ferry from Stockholm to Finland, but it was full, so the only other way to get to Finland was to drive far north to Lapland, cross the border, and make my way to a city called Kajaani where the military base was located. The distance between Stockholm and Kajaani is around 1,350 kilometers (more than 800 miles).

I called the army base and told them I couldn't make it there by midnight but would arrive by approximately 5 a.m. I started driving, and that trip became the longest prayer meeting I have ever had. It was summer, and the Nordic night was bright. I prayed the whole way.

I arrived at the base at about five o'clock, as I had estimated. They showed me to my bed, but at 5:30, the wake-up call came. After washing up, I joined all the other recruits, and we marched to breakfast.

After eating, I went to get my army uniform, but since I was the last one there, they couldn't find a uniform in my size. The trousers were too big, the jacket was too small, and the boots were at least two sizes too big. From there, I went to the doctor's office for my physical. Then, a man by the name of Captain Mäkinen gave us a welcome speech in an auditorium.

I was almost thirty, and everyone around me was eighteen or nineteen. Captain Mäkinen was probably about twenty-five. As he started to speak, I quickly noticed that every third or fourth word he used was profanity. It bothered me a lot, so I stood up and said, "Captain Mäkinen, my name is Private Ibrahim. I left my two sons and wife in Stockholm, where we were called to be missionaries. You have welcomed us with curse words. I am sick and tired of this, so would you please behave? I am almost thirty years old and don't need this kind of foul language."

Captain Mäkinen was shocked that someone like me, a private, would dare to stop him in the middle of his speech and say something like this. During the rest of his speech, every time he said something, he looked at me and said, "Am I behaving, Private Ibrahim?"

I nodded as a sign of approval with a smile on my face.

When I had time to think about the situation, my thoughts were a mixture of sadness and worries. I wondered how my family would manage in Stockholm while I was in the army. What was the future of the ministry going to look like now? Why was God allowing us to go through this? Did it mean it was too early to move to Sweden, or was it an attack to discourage us and cause us to give up? All this time, I couldn't get Ali's tears out of my mind.

When I had the opportunity, I called the Keymedia CEO to give him an update on my situation. He gave me the phone number of a man who was working in the army as an officer. I called him, and after telling him my situation, he said, "I am not recommending that you do so, but if a private says he will not bear arms, he will be sent home. It will take approximately half a year before they reach out to discuss the matter, and if that person happens to be over thirty by that time, he will not have to serve."

So, I took his advice and was sent home. Thank God, my Finnish army service lasted for only six hours! When I write this, I am telling myself: Lucky me, I have an army story to tell my friends and grandchildren.

To the Streets, Squares, and even a Mosque

In 1990, Timo Närhi (Niilo's brother) moved with his family to Sweden. He is fearless and one of the best evangelists I have ever met. Together, we started to invite young Finnish Christians to Sweden for short-term mission trips that lasted around six months at a time. Some of them ministered with us for a whole year, and a few for even longer. We walked around streets and squares telling young Muslims about Christ. We also visited refugee centers to invite Arabic-speaking refugees from Iraq, Lebanon, Syria, and other countries to the church, where hot meals were served for dinner.

During the meal preparation and dinner, people watched the *Jesus* film and other Christian films, like *Christian Pilgrim* or *Sadhu Sundar Singh*. We also saw testimonies from Muslim-background believers like Abu Youssef Al Maghrabi. Abu Youssef was a Moroccan man who had accepted Christ into his life and turned his testimony into a thirty-minute documentary film.

After watching the film, we encouraged people to ask questions and engage in discussion. We usually got thirty or forty questions that we had to respond to on the spot without preparation. It forced me to read the Bible more and dig deeper into biblical studies. We also dedicated Wednesdays as a day of prayer and fasting for God's blessing over the ministry.

Later, I discovered that while Muslims' questions arise out of genuine personal interest, many questions are repeated by person after person, such as: How could God have a Son? If Jesus and the Holy Spirit are also God, how can there be one God? How can Christians prove that the Bible is the true Word of God? Why don't Christians believe in the prophet Muhammad? Why was a sacrifice needed—Couldn't God have just forgiven the sins? How could God become a man and feel hunger and pain?

We still hear the same questions today.

Once, the imam in the local mosque heard about us and sent a man to invite me to the mosque on a Friday after prayers. I took on the challenge and went, together with Timo. The imam was Lebanese, and his name was Ziad. He started the meeting by accusing me of directing good Muslims into the path of perdition by preaching the false teachings of Christianity. I asked him if he would give me twenty minutes to share why I was doing this. I also asked him to promise that neither he nor the ten others there would interrupt me during this time. He agreed. So, I preached and told my testimony. But they felt my speech was so interesting that after twenty minutes had passed, the others—not the imam—asked me to continue talking. In the end, I spoke for two-and-a-half hours!

Before I left, Imam Ziad told me he wished I would burn in hell. I told him I wished to see him on his knees before Jesus, of his own will, declaring, "Jesus is Lord."

I offered him a Bible, but he said he already had one and didn't need it. We left, and I don't know what discussions went on behind closed doors between the imam and the other Muslims present. But word did get out about our evangelistic team, and many Muslims sought me out and wanted to meet with me and talk.

We preached the gospel also to Muslims elsewhere in Sweden and prayed for many people during these years. Looking back, we estimated that about 250 to 300 Muslims came to Christ in Sweden between 1988 and 1993 within the ministry we and the Finnish and Swedish Christians with us were doing.

At one baptism service, something funny happened. At that time, there were twelve MBBs who wanted to follow Christ's teaching and be baptized. We decided to baptize them at Finska Filadelfia, the Finnish Pentecostal church in Stockholm. It was winter, and one of the elders oversaw filling the baptismal pool. He did this often and had a system.

First, he started by filling the pool with hot water, and then he added cold water. In the end, it would be at a suitable temperature. That day he started as usual with the hot water but forgot to add the cold water until it was too late. He told me to please not baptize anyone at the beginning of the service because he had forgotten to add cold water. Instead, we should wait until the end of the service so the water would cool down.

We tried waiting as long as possible. Finally, we thought it must have cooled down somewhat. I was the one designated to baptize these MBBs. I put my feet in the water, and it was very warm. Not boiling, but it was hot enough that it got me sweating. Yet, I had no choice but to go through with it.

I told my MBB friends that the water was hot. They said it was okay because they would go in one at a time. But I was in the pool for a *long* time. So they came in quickly and got baptized. After baptizing the twelve, I was in pain. From my waist down, I was red. I looked like I had red pants for many days after that and became a major consumer of cooling creams.

Our family fit in quite well in Sweden and were getting adjusted to life there. Sari was mostly at home caring for the children and making my ministry possible. Our sons Ali and Sami started to speak Swedish, made more friends, and life was easy for them.

Part of the radio evangelist's work was to answer the listeners' letters, pray for their prayer requests, and update a correspondence registry.

Adel and His Jacket

The outreach work in Sweden had many sides to it. There were times of rejoicing and sadness, victories and defeats. Together with Timo, we visited many refugee centers. The refugees that were living there had many problems, and we tried to help them the best we could. Some became Christians when they saw Christian love in action. Some others tried to exploit the Christians financially or otherwise, which led to some disappointments among the outreach workers. Some refugees, who we thought were genuinely interested in Christianity, turned out to be cheats. Nevertheless, a seed of the gospel was planted even in their hearts. And who knows, maybe it will bear fruit one day.

During this period, Timo and I witnessed many miracles. One happened to a young Moroccan man named Adel, who attended some meetings. Adel came to us complaining that he had no work, money, or shelter. It was early spring, and the nights were still cold. We called Mauri, an elder in the Finnish congregation, and explained the situation to him. Mauri had a house he was in the process of renovating. "There is enough space upstairs for the boy to come and live there for now," Mauri promised.

We gave Adel a lift to Mauri's place. Adel continued to come to the meetings. In May, our family had a short holiday and traveled to Finland. As soon as we returned about two weeks later, the phone rang, and it was Mauri, wondering, "Do you know what happened to that Moroccan fellow? I haven't seen him for quite a while now."

"I have no idea," I replied. "Maybe he returned to Morocco."

"It's just that he left an old worn-out jacket here," Mauri said. "What should I do with it?"

"Throw it in the garbage can, I guess," was my reply.

A few days later, the phone rang. Someone on the other end was trying to explain something in Swedish. Since I didn't understand much of what was said, I gave the phone to Sari. After hearing that the call was from the police station, she changed the conversation to English and gave the phone back to me.

"We have a Moroccan man here named Adel," the policeman explained. "On May Day, a wallet was stolen from a Norwegian man, and when we arrived at the scene, a group of North Africans ran off. Only this one was caught. He claims he is innocent but has no ID papers or his passport. He told us you would know where his passport is."

"Yes, I do know Adel, but I don't know where his passport is," I said. "I'll come by tomorrow to visit him if it's OK."

The next day, I went with my colleague to the police station. Adel had been locked up for several weeks already. Since he said he was Moroccan, police officers had taken him to the Moroccan Embassy. There they had been told that no one could know if he was a Tunisian, an Algerian, or someone who wanted to get into Morocco. They would need official proof from Morocco, which would take some time.

When Adel saw us arriving, he cried and clung to my neck, asking, "Please help me! You must help me. Go get my jacket. It's at Mauri's place, and my passport is in the pocket!"

I felt cold inside. I remembered my last conversation with Mauri. I hoped Mauri hadn't thrown the jacket away yet. Adel had to stay back and wait for our return. When I left him, I called Mauri.

"Yes, I did throw that jacket away," Mauri said. "It should be at the garbage dump already."

We were wondering if it would be worth looking for the jacket.

"No way," was Mauri's opinion, "It's such a big area; there is no hope of finding it among all the garbage."

The next day, we went to see Adel again and explained the unfortunate situation. Adel cried and asked, "Now I don't know what to do. Please call my father in Morocco and ask him to send my birth certificate."

I tried to call Morocco but couldn't get ahold of Adel's father. Still, we felt that we needed to help our friend in some way. We decided to try our best and go to the garbage dump. Maybe we could find the passport.

Timo and I drove to Mauri's place and asked if he had any shovels.

"We are going to the dump to look for Adel's jacket! Would you come along as a guide?"

Mauri must have thought we were crazy, but he threw the shovels in the car, and we went to the dump. Adel's jacket was a light beige cloth jacket, so we knew what we were searching for. But the area was huge. The more we dug around, the more we started to sweat. Finding a needle in a haystack would have been easier than finding Adel's jacket in that dump. We walked around digging here and there for about an hour or an hour and a half. But nothing. There was no sight of a light beige jacket anywhere. If Adel's proof of nationality depended on finding this jacket, he was in deep trouble.

There was an unmanned Caterpillar tractor nearby, so we stopped to rest on its treads. At the same time, we prayed, "Dear God, can't you help us a bit since we're trying to help Adel? Please, Lord, show Adel that you are almighty. Amen."

We opened our eyes and started for the car. Despite the prayer, we felt it was useless to look any further. We hoped that God would help Adel in some other way. However, after we had walked for only five meters (around twenty feet) or so, I saw a small piece of familiar-looking material peeking from under all the garbage! I bent over and pulled it up. We couldn't believe our eyes. I held Adel's jacket with the passport in its pocket in my hands! With thankful hearts, we praised God for helping us.

It was evening, and the next morning we went back to the police station. Finding the jacket and the passport was a great witness to Adel about God's ability to answer prayers. Adel was rejoicing. After the trial, he was released, and I prayed with him as he started his new life with Jesus. Adel confessed to me, "Listen, I never heard much of what you were saying about Jesus. I was not even interested. But now that you guys showed me the love of your God in action, I accepted him as my Lord."

Afterward, Adel returned to Morocco and continued his studies at the university. Later, he moved to the Ivory Coast.

Spaghetti and the Bread of Life

As the number of converted Muslims grew, we wanted to start a special discipleship program for those who showed potential for being leaders. So, we selected five of these new converts to attend a once-a-month meeting on Saturdays to go deeper into the word of God with us. We informed these young men that we wanted to keep these meetings small and stressed that it was just for them and that they shouldn't let anyone else know about what we were doing.

Before leaving home for the first of these meetings, Timo called me and said, "Hey, my wife Roosa just made a batch of spaghetti sauce. Do you have any pasta at home so we could serve food at the Bible study?" I thought it was a good idea, so I grabbed a packet of spaghetti that would feed about ten people and brought it with me.

When we got to the church, Timo and I were shocked. The five men we invited hadn't been able to keep quiet about the Bible study. Instead of five, thirty-five turned up!

"What are we going to do now?" Timo and I were thinking. The shops were already closed, and we didn't have any money with us. Two girls from the outreach team were helping in the kitchen, and they were wondering what to do. Finally, we advised them, "Just cook the spaghetti."

Our meeting room was a small cafeteria room upstairs that could hold up to forty people. I started my speech and asked everyone to stand. Then I took my Bible and read the story of Jesus feeding 5,000 men and many women and children with five loaves of bread and two fish. One of the guys asked, "Are we going to eat fish today?" I smiled and said, "No, but we have a similar situation here."

I explained to the listeners more about the story. Then I said, "Let's bless this food so there would be enough for all of us."

We blessed the food, and the girls served it. The spaghetti didn't increase in the pot, but it didn't visibly decrease either until everyone had gotten their serving. The group ate in respectful silence. The blessed spaghetti went down well, and so did the Bread of Life, which was shared after the meal.

All the other new MBBs needed Bible teaching as well. Timo and I served together for a year until God called Niilo, my pastor from Kuopio, to join us in Stockholm. Timo and I were evangelists, but we needed a teacher on our team, and Niilo was one of the best Bible teachers we knew. I learned a lot from him.

Evangelists in Morocco. Markku Tuppurainen *(left)*, Timo Närhi *(right)*, and me with two of our local friends.

An Iraqi believer named Nadir Allawardi also began working with us, so we decided to split up. Timo and Nadir formed a team, and Niilo and I worked together as another team. On Tuesdays, one group would lead the evangelistic meeting while the other group visited the refugee centers. On Thursday, we switched roles so each team could participate in both ministries.

6

Sharing the Gospel with Muslims — A Risky Business

Looking at the history of church missions, we can see that the Muslim world has been almost completely ignored. When Sari and I started ministry in the 1980s, I heard an interesting statistic: for every $100 given for foreign missions, only $1 was targeted to the Muslim world. Yet the Great Commission is very clear. In Matthew 28:19, Jesus says, "Go therefore and make disciples of all the nations." All nations mean the whole world, and since we were not going there, it seemed God was sending the nations to us—through migration.

Muslims have been moving to Europe for decades, and the issue has its upsides and its downsides. The former includes the new opportunities migration has provided for reaching them with the gospel. Since then, many churches and Christian ministries have fruitfully reached Muslims in the West. Numerous new MBB brothers and sisters have enriched local churches. Many of the converts have also become very effective in evangelism.

All this starkly contrasts with the fact that Muslim immigration has also had a remarkable negative impact on some communities. The biggest reason is that in most Western countries where Muslims have become sizeable minorities, a significant number of them choose not to integrate into the society where they've settled.

Locally, this is reflected in the emergence of Muslim "ghettos" in several European countries, such as in France, the Netherlands, Belgium, and Germany. Those Muslim-majority neighborhoods have become "no-go" zones even for the police—it is too dangerous to go there.

When looking at society as a whole, Muslims' reluctance to assimilate has affected other people's religious freedom and has caused restrictions on people's free speech. For instance, Muslim violence (or the threat of it) occurring when someone has commented negatively about the prophet Muhammad or the Qur'an has silenced many rational and dispassionate critics of Islam. Some Muslims have gone so far as to petition their Western governments for the implementation of Sharia law in the country alongside the country's formal legislation and judiciary.

"I Won't Guarantee Your Life"

I received my first death threat in 1991 at a public debate I attended. The debate was initiated by a well-known Muslim professor, Ahmed Deedat, who had dedicated his life to fighting against the Bible and against those who believe in it. He was Pakistan-born but lived in South Africa, and from there, he traveled worldwide, challenging Christians to public debates about Christianity and Islam.

In Sweden, the challenge set by Deedat was taken up by a Pentecostal minister, Pastor Stanley Sjöberg. He and Deedat agreed on a two-part debate for the last weekend of October 1991. The first night, the theme would be, "Is the Bible the word of God?" The second night it was, "Is Jesus God?".

Sometime before the event was to take place, Stanley called me asking for literature on Islam and any other material that might prove helpful. Upon hearing of the issue, Niilo, Timo, and I went straight to Stanley's office. We spoke with him for a few hours and gave him some helpful hints for the coming contest. Debates aren't usually beneficial, but since the Muslims issued the challenge, it had to be accepted.

The stage for the event was the Folkets Hus (People's House) of Stockholm, the big congress center. As the first part of the debate was about to start, the place was packed to the rafters. Around 4,000 people jammed inside the hall, and many were left outside. Deedat marched in proudly with his Muslim entourage. The atmosphere was tense from the start.

During the weekend, Deedat did his best to ridicule Christians' faith in the Bible and Jesus as the Son of God. But still, he seemed to be losing. The real winners were our outreach workers, who distributed over 4,000 booklets to people standing outside and, after the debate, to those who came out of the hall.

A press conference was held the next day. Niilo, who knew my character well, warned me not to get involved. So, I tried my best to keep my mouth shut.

Deedat arrived again with his large group of followers. His supporters were shouting, "Allahu Akbar! Allahu Akbar!" which means, "God is greater," or "God is the greatest." Deedat sat next to Stanley. Someone from the Swedish Christian newspaper *Dagen* asked the Muslim professor, "What is your opinion about the debate last night?"

"Well, it could have gone better, but my schedule was too tight. I didn't have as much time as I would have liked to prepare. Plus, Stanley had the advantage over me because I spoke first," Deedat complained.

"So, you admit you lost the debate?"

"I didn't say that," Deedat replied.

Then *Dagen*'s journalist asked, "You claimed the Bible isn't God's word. Later, you said that *parts* of the Bible are God's word. What do you mean?"

At that point, I couldn't keep quiet any longer and raised my hand to ask a question. As a former Muslim, I knew what Deedat would say next. Given the go-ahead, I turned to him and said, "You claimed the Bible is partly God's word and partly isn't. I'm a former Muslim. My sins have been forgiven through my faith in Jesus of the Bible. This same Jesus that you made fun of has changed my life. Now, my Muslim family accepts me and has no problem with me believing in this Jesus, who is the only Savior of the world. I want to ask you how do you know which part of the Bible is God's word and which isn't? Have you received a revelation from God concerning this?"

That question is a hard one for a Muslim to answer. I knew the Qur'an didn't promise another godly revelation after Muhammad. If Deedat responded that he had a revelation about the issue, he would contradict the Qur'an. And if he answered that he hadn't received a revelation, his argument would be treading on thin ice. Deedat was quiet for a couple of minutes thinking. Then he gave me a stern look and hissed, "Next question, please."

The discussion moved on. I noted a Muslim cameraman filming me at length with a camcorder. I approached the man and asked, "Why are you filming me all the time?"

"I want to document you on the tape," he replied.

"I don't want myself on your tape," I told him.

Deedat's Pakistani bodyguard came close to me and warned me, "So, you're a former Muslim. Something might happen to you, and I won't guarantee your life."

I explained the situation to Niilo, who advised me, "Let's be careful now. We don't need any corpses. When we leave, you walk between me and Timo."

Stanley had invited us to lunch after the press conference. Deedat and his party were also going to be there. With my "bodyguards" Timo and Niilo by my side, I sat down to lunch with the forty other guests. The menu consisted of a nice plate of lamb with rice.

"May we continue the discussion here?" Stanley asked Deedat politely.

"Yes, we may," Deedat answered. "You can ask me anything you like."

My hand was up immediately before anyone else. I couldn't miss this opportunity. When Deedat saw me raise my hand, he growled, "Oh no, not this man again."

I repeated that I was from a Muslim background. Then I said, "I've become a Christian. If I go back to my home village to visit my family, there is a chance that I could be killed. I know people from there who would do it. Islam doesn't accept my work, and according to the Qur'an, it is acceptable to murder an apostate. It happens all the time in the Islamic world." I said this even though our family's trip to Abu Gosh in 1987 had gone well. However, there had been a risk of persecution present during the journey.

I gave Deedat a challenging look and continued, "One thing I don't understand is that you came to preach Islam as a religion of love and peace, and yet your bodyguard warned me that I could be persecuted for turning to Christ and that he couldn't guarantee my safety. Is this the sort of Islam of 'love' you were telling us about? Maybe this is real Islam? You are here preaching about your religion and at the same time threatening me in a free country."

Immediately, Deedat stiffened in his chair. Then he jumped up, crushing the white napkin in his hands, throwing it on his plate, and yelled, "I hate you! I'm leaving now."

The refined Swedes were embarrassed as Deedat marched out with his party in the middle of the lunch. I felt it wouldn't be right to leave all that fine lamb on my plate, so I just continued to eat.

Rachid and the Two Muhammads from Morocco

In addition to evangelizing Muslims and teaching the converts in Sweden, we encouraged local Christian-born believers from Arabic-speaking backgrounds to minister to Muslims. At the same time, I had a lot on my hands with radio program production and follow-up, which I also loved.

In those days, our team at IBRA Radio received twenty to forty letters weekly, and part of my radio ministry was to travel to different countries and meet listeners who had accepted Christ. Letters came in from many countries, but most were from Morocco. I think it was because the programs were broadcast from Lisbon, and the coverage was particularly good in North Africa. The Moroccans also seemed to be very keen listeners of shortwave broadcasts.

One letter in particular caught my attention. It was very genuine, kind, and full of questions. The person who wrote it was a sixteen-year-old Moroccan who called himself Rachid. I decided to go to see him. The year was 1989.

In Morocco, I went to the address Rachid had given. It was his uncle's house, and Rachid's cousin opened the door. He told me that his father had found out that Rachid was a Christian and kicked him out, and Rachid had moved to his aunt's house. The cousin offered to show me the place, but when we arrived, we discovered the aunt had also kicked him out. I decided to drive the cousin back home, but while driving, we saw Rachid walking on the street. It was such a moment of joy to finally meet him.

With my friend Rachid in his hometown.
On the right, another Moroccan believer, Abdul.

I found Rachid to be a brave young man. Each time I visited Morocco and met him, we did crazy things together.

We bravely preached the gospel in the streets and handed out Bibles in the marketplace. This was a big "no-no" and very dangerous in a country like Morocco, which was almost totally Muslim at that time. But we did it anyway. Once, we had several copies of the New Testament with us, and while we were delivering them, a man in the market shouted, "Call the police! These infidels are evangelizing!" Rachid was brave enough to say a few more words to the man, and then we decided to return to the car.

Rachid and I continued to be friends and saw each other in Morocco several times until he moved to the USA.

Back in Stockholm, one of the new believers was a Moroccan man named Muhammad Bakkali. He was a good and honest man, but the Swedish government rejected his asylum application and sent him back to Morocco. He wrote a letter to us about his situation, how he had no job and was lonely because all the people around him were Muslims. It was a very sad letter. We decided to visit him and bring a love offering—a small sum of money—to help support him.

Muhammad lived in Fez, an inland city south of Gibraltar. The population of the city was over 600,000 already at that time, making it the second-largest urban center in the country. We landed in Morocco in Casablanca, so the rest of the way we had to go by car. Taking a local believer with us, we drove to Fez to look for Muhammad. Upon arriving there, we went to find him at the address he had given us but found no building with that address in the area. We were thinking, "Did he write it down wrong? Or did he do this on purpose? Or was this divine intervention?"

We stopped the car and, after prayer, felt urged to knock on the door of a particular house. A little boy answered the door, and we asked, "Does Muhammad Bakkali live here?" He replied, "Yes, I will go and get him." When he returned, he had a short, stooped older man with him.

I asked, "Does Muhammad Bakkali live here?"

"Yes, that is me," he replied.

I was confused because the Muhammad we sought was not so old and was in good shape.

"I'm sorry, the Muhammad I am looking for is a younger man," I said.

"I know who you are talking about," he replied. "I sometimes receive his mail. We have the same name. Let me take you to him."

He got in our car, and we went to the younger Muhammad's home. On the way, this older man said a few things that got my attention. He began to speak as if to himself: "I am the door," "I am the way," and "I am the truth." I then asked him, "Where have you heard these things?" He told us he had become a believer in Jesus Christ many years ago. Because he did not own a Bible, he listened to Christian radio programs and wrote down every Bible verse he heard. He also told us that his dream was to take part in Holy Communion, the Eucharist.

When we found the younger Muhammad Bakkali, we all spent the day together. Then we agreed to meet again at the older Muhammad's home the next day and celebrate Communion together. So we did, and Niilo blessed the bread and juice as the wine, and, for the first time, the older Muhammad took part in Communion. We also gave him a Bible. He was overjoyed.

After Niilo and I left, the Muhammads continued to meet for a while. Then the older Muhammad sadly passed away, and the younger one left Morocco. He is now in the Ivory Coast.

Further Study

During my five years in Sweden, I carved out time also for theological studies. I enrolled at ICI Institute (now Global University), which is a Bible college offering correspondence courses with homework assignments. I undertook these studies not only to enrich my own spiritual life but also to help me answer questions posed by fellow MBBs and correspond more effectively with our listeners.

Courses covered topics such as the Christian life, faith, sin, the Holy Spirit, and the Apostle Paul's letters. In addition, I read dozens of theological books, such as books on Christian doctrine, church history, miracles of Jesus, missiology, apologetics, comparisons of religions, and the Old Testament. I even read the Qur'an, the Hadith (traditions containing sayings and actions of Muhammad), and biographies of Muhammad—and Christian and critical literature about them. I understood that to speak with Muslims effectively, I had to demonstrate that I was familiar also with their religion and belief system.

Between the years 1988 and 1993, Timo Närhi, Nadir Allawardi, Niilo Närhi, and I, along with others on our team, distributed more than 25,000 New Testaments and whole Bibles, as well as tens of thousands of tracts and other books produced by the Call of Hope in Stuttgart, Germany. During this time, I was also invited by a Finnish Bible college called Iso Kirja to give lectures on Islam and Muslim ministry. All the time, I continued to produce radio programs that were transmitted through shortwave radio to the Arabic-speaking world. During those five years, our team at IBRA Radio recorded over 3,500 episodes of numerous program series.

My trips to North Africa also continued. During my visits, I met many people who wrote to us. I discovered that many had come to believe through ministers who had already been discipled through correspondence and had become our ministry partners. We were strongly bonded together as an MBB community there.

In addition to preaching the gospel, I was concerned about how we could look after the psychological and physical needs of converts. The decision to abandon Islam and follow Jesus, particularly in the Arab world, has serious consequences. Muslims who do so can be killed, imprisoned, tortured, disowned by their families, and rejected by their society and friends. Consequently, they struggle to find an alternate community in a local church or with another body of believers that can be a new "family" for them.

In the winter of 1990–1991, I was introduced to an MBB group from Egypt whom I had heard of through the media—the news of three MBB men who spent eleven months imprisoned for apostasy spread everywhere. As a result of international pressure from human rights organizations, the men were eventually released. I was burdened to meet them, so I booked a flight to Egypt to be by those brothers' side to encourage them after their agonizing ordeal.

When I arrived in Cairo, the weather was cold. I can assure you that winter weather can be uncomfortably chilly even in the sunny Middle East. The cold and humidity seem to sink deep into the bones. And if you try to go indoors to get warm, it's useless because it feels even colder inside the houses than outside. You need many blankets for sleeping.

All I knew about the men were their first names. I had no addresses or other information to guide me to find them—just my heart and faith and a strong conviction that I should meet them. For lack of a better idea, I decided to start my search by going to a church meeting. There I met a sister who was interested in ministering to Muslims. She asked me if I was a Christian, and I told her I was an MBB. She said that she knew other believers like me. When she mentioned their names, I realized they were the ones I sought. So, with her help, I found them.

The series of events was yet another example of how much God loves Muslims and Muslim-background believers. After meeting with the men and getting to know them, we soon learned that my trip wasn't just about encouraging them, but it was the beginning of an amazing ministry in Egypt. We set up an informal organization (it is impossible to create formal MBB organizations in Muslim countries), which is still in operation. We named it *Awlad Ismaeel*—"the Children of Ishmael."

My new Egyptian friends wanted desperately to start something for the MBBs in the country.

7

Big Dreams
and Special Guidance

My new MBB friends and I started dreaming about a ministry that would radically change the Muslim world. We were confident to press forward even though some of our dreams seemed like they would be impossible to achieve.

We dreamed about:
- A publishing ministry
- A 24/7 Arabic Christian satellite TV channel
- A 24/7 Arabic Christian radio channel
- Bible schools for MBBs
- A training program to educate churches on Muslim ministry
- A denomination or movement that would unite MBBs all over the world

We had already worked on some of these sectors in Sweden, Morocco, Algeria, and elsewhere. Regarding the publishing ministry, we took the first steps with the Children of Ishmael organization we had established in Egypt.

Our first product was a magazine named *Awraq-leltanweer* ("Pages of Enlightenment"). It was the first Christian magazine in Egypt edited by Muslim-background believers, and it contained non-denominational articles on various topics ranging from the person of Jesus to enhancing the missionary work of the churches. One of the articles has especially stuck in my mind.

It was written sarcastically, and it criticized the unjust treatment the religious minorities had to face in Egypt.

The magazine was published from 1991 to 1995. Later on, we also started publishing books.

Unexpected Twists and Turns

As IBRA Radio's Arabic programs received more and more listener feedback, Niilo and I traveled to more countries to see firsthand what was happening on the field. During these trips, we witnessed several extraordinary situations which we took as miracles of God. Those included the two cases in Algeria in 1992 that I told in the prologue.

The passage of the Bible shipment through airport immigration control was a miracle for us but also for our local pastor friend Mahmood, who was amazed at how we were able to bring so many Bibles into the country.

On another trip, my unexpected experience of going to the airport cell and returning home early also led to an unexpected advancement of the Kingdom of God. After getting back to Stockholm, I visited a refugee family who was to be deported back to Lebanon. I shared the gospel with them, we prayed, and they all accepted Jesus Christ that day. Later, they joined a Baptist congregation in Lebanon and started to hold a Sunday school for children. This visit to the family would not have happened if my trip to Algeria had gone as Niilo and I had planned. This way, God used these circumstances to win this lovely family to the Lord.

Later that year, one of my best friends, a godly and precious brother named Victor Hashweh, informed us about the needs of the Kurds in Northern Iraq. He told us about the atrocities Saddam Hussein's forces had committed against the Iraqi Kurds and how thousands of them were killed. The Kurds didn't have much food and lacked just about everything. Victor was going to visit the area and asked us to join him.

I had met Victor three years earlier when I was invited to Finland to participate in a conference intended for refugees who had come to the country. Many of them were Muslims, and one of the conference's organizers was sister Marketta Kakriainen. She had also invited Victor and his wife, Maha, there. Victor is a Jordanian who lived in England at the time. We spent a week together, and I came to know him as a gentleman and a true man of God. I used to say, "Victor lives as he teaches: he preaches with words but also through his life." He has significantly impacted my life, and I love him and his family dearly.

Jesus Film into Kurdistan

So, after Victor had told us about the needs of the Kurds and the aid mission he was planning, we shared the situation with the Finnish congregations and received a sizeable donation to take with us. Niilo and I decided to go together. We met up with Victor and Maha in Istanbul. The next morning, we took the flight to Diyarbakir in southeastern Turkey, and from there, we hired a taxi to take us south into Iraqi Kurdistan. We had to travel this way because, at that time, it was impossible to reach the area from Baghdad because Saddam Hussein had blocked off the routes.

Kurdistan is a geographical and cultural territory in northern Iraq where the Kurds represent a majority of the population. There are also significant Kurdish populations in southeastern Turkey, northwestern Iran, and parts of northern Syria, and sometimes the name Kurdistan is also used for the whole of this area. In all these regions, the people have dreamed about a sovereign Kurdish state or, at least, an autonomous position within the existing countries. Unfortunately, even autonomy has only been officially implemented in Iraq. The region is rich in minerals and oil, making the governments in Ankara, Baghdad, Tehran, and Damascus even more reluctant to allow the Kurds to establish their own independent state.

The area is said to be one of the most mountainous regions in the world, but when we left Diyarbakir, the landscape didn't look like that. All around us, vast plains opened up. The distance from Diyarbakir to the border was around 300 kilometers (190 miles). The road was mostly highway, but the trip took about five hours, although the driver tried to drive as fast as possible. The reason for the slow progress was at least twenty security checkpoints along the way. The Kurdistan Workers' Party (PKK) and Turkish armies often fought battles in the region, and the road from Diyarbakir to Iraqi Kurdistan went through one of the most dangerous areas in the world. The terrified taxi driver didn't want to get caught on the roads at night.

Welcome to Kurdistan. Niilo and I near the Turkish–Iraqi border.

The mountains grew more prominent as we approached the border. At the border checkpoint, I showed the Kurdish officer my Finnish passport. When he saw it and noticed my birthplace was Jerusalem, he asked if I had an Israeli passport and, if so, if I had it with me. I answered yes to both of his questions, so he asked me to show my Israeli passport. I have both Israeli and Finnish passports, and sometimes I take both documents with me when I travel.

When the officer took my Israeli passport, he did something I didn't expect—he kissed it.

"I love Israel," he said. "When Saddam Hussein's army started to surround our country, and we were short of food and supplies, Israel was the first country to send us help. So, it is an honor to welcome you into Kurdistan as an Israeli."

Hearing his words made me even more excited to get into the country.

We had a significant amount of money with us, and I carried it under my shirt in a money belt. The following day, we bought a lot of food, oil, and tea and filled several trucks full of goods. We even got some Peshmerga fighters—military forces of the autonomous Kurdistan region of Iraq—who came with machine guns to protect us.

We delivered the relief supplies around the city of Dahuk. We especially wanted to assist widows and orphans, but we also distributed aid to others regardless of people's religion. Most Kurds are Muslims, but there are also Yazidis, Christians, and adherents of other faiths. It was an emotional experience for us to see these people with next to nothing to live on.

One day while we were there, I asked someone if there was a local TV station nearby. I was told there was, so I asked the man to take me there. When I got to the station, I told them I worked in media. The station manager was proud to show me their equipment and facilities. I asked if they had any programming for Christians. He replied, "No."

For some reason, while packing my suitcase for the trip at home, I had felt like I should take one VHS copy of the *Jesus* film dubbed into Arabic. At the film's end, there were a few Christian songs, and the audience was invited to become followers of Christ. (The funny thing was that, in the film, the voice role of Jesus was played by my fellow traveler and friend Victor.) So now I said to the station manager, "I have something for Christians with me. I know you have problems getting electricity, and fuel for generators is very expensive."

Then I proposed that if he showed the *Jesus* film on his channel, I would buy them fuel. I thought that if I could help them out, they might agree to broadcast the film. The value of the Iraqi dinar had plummeted against the dollar, so even buying a large amount of gasoline was not a problem for us.

The station manager agreed, and I was so happy that I happened to take the film with me on the trip. I didn't know what would come of it, but ten years later, I met a Kurdish man who told me that he had accepted Christ when he watched the *Jesus* film broadcast on that channel. It made me cry. I'm sure that there were others also. What an investment this turned out to be!

During the trip, we visited many cities and villages. One town was called Sersink. In that little town, Saddam Hussein had built a palace for himself, which had since been badly demolished. When we went there, it turned out that there were Kurdish families living in the ruins. At one entrance, there was a brick on the wall that read in Arabic: "This palace was built for His Excellency Saddam Hussein, President of Iraq."

I asked one of the Kurds if I could have the brick, and one of the men knocked it off the wall with a hammer and gave it to me. On the way home, the X-ray machine at the Turkish airport discovered my souvenir. The officer didn't speak English, and I do not speak Turkish, but he motioned by crossing his wrists and said to me in English, "You, prison!"

We were all nervous and did not know what to do. Victor said to me, "Why did you have to do this?" Meanwhile, the officers brought an archeologist to the airport to look at the brick, which meant we might miss our flight. He came an hour and a half later, and luckily, the result was good news. The archeologist said that the brick had no historical significance. We were relieved when we were allowed to continue our journey home.

Meanwhile, back home, Sari and the team had worked on recruiting prayer warriors to pray for the Arab world. We had developed a specific tool for this purpose: prayer frames. They were posters, each containing general information about one Middle Eastern or North African country and the spiritual needs of the inhabitants. There are 22 Arab countries, so we divided 240 Finnish Pentecostal congregations into twenty-two groups so that around ten congregations would pray for each country. Then we planned to visit the congregations, give them one prayer frame each, and ask them to put it on the wall near the entrance of the church to inspire people to pray for the Arab world.

It turned out to be a great idea. Sari and her team did the hard work by collecting the information from *Operation World*—a famous Christian fact book—and other sources, and made the material available for the prayer warriors.

As a family, we continued to live in Sweden. Ali and Sami had integrated into their school nicely. Both spoke Swedish so well that they even communicated with each other in that language. Keymedia had planned for us to spend a year there, but because the work had been fruitful, our return to Finland had been delayed. Now, time had flown by so fast that we had been there for five years. During that time, Swedish congregations had started to take more responsibility for the Muslim ministry, and some Arab Christian couples from the Middle East had joined the work. One of them was Pastor Merzek, a wonderful man of God originally from Egypt, and his Lebanese wife, Lena.

So, in the spring of 1993, Sari and I felt the Lord say it was a suitable time for us to return to Finland. Of course, it would take a lot of work to move again from one country to another. It would also mean that our children had to leave their school, friends, and routines, and it is seldom easy to uproot one's kids to a new place. Still, the idea of moving grew stronger in our hearts.

We shared our thoughts with Keymedia's board, and after discussions they agreed, and we headed back to Finland in the summer of 1993. The idea was that we would start doing Arabic radio ministry and follow-up in their headquarters in Kerava, in southern Finland. It sounded great to us, but deep down in our hearts, there was also maturing a new dream: to start a TV ministry.

8

Starting Television Ministry

When our white Mercedes moving truck made the journey from Stockholm to Kerava, it also meant that our ways with Niilo parted again. Niilo and his family also moved back to Finland at the same time, but they moved to the city of Kuopio, where our friendship had first started. There Niilo became the secretary for short-term mission trips with another Finnish mission organization called Fida International. We still made some trips together but mainly worked separately from then on.

Although Sari and I believed it was the right time to move, settling into a new place wasn't easy. First, we had to fill out all the official papers again and apply for the kids to start school. Next, we began attending a new church and tried to make friends. But, for months, we still felt like outsiders in a strange land. Thankfully, Ali and Sami adjusted quite well to the move. They made new friends quickly in their new school close to our home.

There were also humorous incidents. In Kerava, we got a home in a neighborhood called "The Arabic Village." It was ironic because, before me, no Arabs lived in the area. It had gotten its unusual name because the houses in the neighborhood were made of white brick and had flat roofs, as in the Middle East. So, I became the first Arab in that "village."

Another humorous episode started when we were unloading the moving truck in Kerava, and a white paint can fell from the load onto the asphalt, causing the paint to splash everywhere.

The splatter was unsightly, and I couldn't get the color off the asphalt. So, I took a paintbrush and filled in the edges of the splash to make it square. It looked neater that way.

Matti, the man living next door, saw the white square in front of our house and wondered what it meant. At some point, he found out that we were Pentecostals, and one day he ventured to ask about the pattern.

"Is it related to your religion?" he asked. The question was strange, and the prankster in me couldn't resist the temptation. I said to him with an earnest look on my face, "Yes. It's for the day of Jesus's second coming. By the sign, the angels know where to come and pick us up."

Matti listened to my answer, and it seemed to satisfy his curiosity. At home, Sari and I had a good laugh. Later, I thought I must reveal the truth about the pattern to him. He listened to me, laughed, let a curse word out of his mouth, and said, "Oh, I so believed what you said!"

We had excellent neighborly relations as long we lived there.

An Unexpected Call from Sudan

In Finland, Sari became more involved in the ministry than in Sweden. She officially became the assistant of the Arabic team I led and, later, also the executive assistant at Keymedia. We shared everything about the ministry.

One month after the move, I received a phone call from a Sudanese Orthodox priest seeking our support to begin Christian programming on Sudanese TV. I was amazed at this rare opportunity and praised God for the open door.

Of course, I wondered how on earth such contact could come from a fanatic country like Sudan, where Christians were being massacred in its southern regions. The land was ruled by fundamentalist Islamic extremists. Didn't they know about our evangelistic radio programs? Or was there an assassination plan behind the invitation?

I soon decided not to let fear determine my decision. I wanted to go, and I enlisted two friends to accompany me to Sudan: Niilo and a Finnish Canadian named Steven Antturi, who knew much about TV production. Sari came with us too, but only to Egypt, where we stopped to film material for some Arabic Christian music videos (we had just decided to start TV productions and a set of music videos were our first programs). After that, Steven and I would fly to Sudan, and Niilo would join us after taking care of some appointments in Finland a couple of days later. Sari would stay in Cairo and meet with us on our way back.

One of the filming sessions in Egypt took place next to the pyramids in Giza near Cairo. In one of the music videos, we wanted the vocalist to perform some parts of the song while riding on a camel, so we rented one. When the music started, the owner of the camel suddenly jumped in front of the camera and started to dance. He obviously thought it was an ordinary love song and that we wanted to film a dancing Arab, too. Politely, we asked him to step aside, and the filming continued. But then the camel got nervous and threw the singer onto the ground. He hurt his leg a bit, but thank God, it was not broken. Finally, we got enough footage. The accident was unfortunate, but overall, the session had been so absurd that it was like a scene out of a comedy movie.

After three days in Cairo, it was time for Steven and me to fly to Sudan. We had stayed in our friend's apartment in the suburb of Heliopolis, around ten kilometers (six miles) northeast of downtown Cairo. We were just leaving the house when the phone rang. It was from the airport, and the caller informed us that our Kenyan Air flight would be delayed for two hours. It was noon and sweltering outside, so we took our time and sat down to eat lunch in the apartment. Only ten minutes later, about 200 meters (700 feet) from us, a car full of explosives blew up precisely on the corner where we were supposed to meet our taxi. The explosion was so intense that some plaster from the roof dropped onto our food.

The event is still well-remembered in Egypt because this was an assassination attempt to kill Egypt's then-Prime Minister, Atef Sedki. The attack was made by the terrorist organization Islamic Jihad, and it happened adjacent to a girls' school, resulting in the death of a twelve-year-old girl named Shayma Abdel-Halim.

Twenty-one people were injured. But Prime Minister Sedki, who was riding in an armored car, was not harmed.

It was horrible. We felt, and still feel, sorry for the victims, especially for Shayma and her family. Yet, at the same time, we felt thankful that God had protected us. If our flight hadn't been delayed, we would probably have died or been badly injured. Even now, the writing of this makes me emotional. I don't have the answer to why some are protected and others are not. Only God knows.

The flight from Cairo to Khartoum is not long, but at that time, it seemed to take ages. So many people had warned me and tried to scare me, saying I would be killed there for being an MBB. I wanted to think about something else, so I picked up a *Reader's Digest*. To my surprise, the issue had an article about Sudan in it. The article was about a man named Hassan Al-Turabi, one of the most-wanted terrorist leaders in the world at that time. The text also said that many Muslim terrorist organizations got their training in Sudan and were killing and torturing Christians and other non-Muslims. The Islamic Jihad, the organization behind the Cairo attack, also had its exile base in Sudan. The article did not put my mind at ease.

We landed in Khartoum, and to my surprise, a smiling Orthodox priest was waiting for us. It turned out he was the same priest who had called me earlier. His name was Father Philetos. His all-black outfit, light grey beard, and white teeth flashing from his smiling mouth made for an unforgettable contrast. His whole appearance emanated joy, friendliness, and genuine warmth.

Father Philetos took our passports, and we got into a black Mercedes. It was amazing. They treated us like royalty from the start. Our bags were carried on our behalf, and no one questioned us at the immigration control. We hadn't been informed beforehand that we would participate in several official events. We had assumed that we had only come to the country to train TV programmers.

Khartoum, the capital of Sudan, is a beautiful African city. It is located at the confluence of the White Nile and the Blue Nile, so the rivers divide the city into three parts. From there, the Nile continues north towards Egypt. At the time, it seemed that only the main roads were asphalted, and there were only a few tall buildings in the whole city. The streets were full of dark-skinned people from the south of the country.

While in the car, Father Philetos told us that we were going straight to a big celebration of the Coptic church and would be meeting some bishops, priests, and church members. I asked the driver to stop at a shop because I had no suitable shirt or tie with me. So, we stopped at a small clothing store with shirts in the window. I went in and bought a green striped shirt with a matching tie.

People at the meeting were very kind and welcoming. Afterward, the driver took us to a nice hotel on the bank of the Nile. We were told we were guests of the government and all we needed to do was to sign for whatever we needed. We also had permission to call home for free. The minute Steven and I went to our rooms, we looked at each other and laughed. It was not out of humor but a feeling of great relief. Niilo arrived a couple of days later.

During the visit, we saw the president of the parliament and many government members, such as the Minister for Media and the Minister for Interior Affairs. We also visited both national TV stations. We were told that the Christian programs were given one hour of weekly broadcasting time. Still, Christians were only allowed to use the studio for thirty minutes per week. To solve the problem, we promised to cover the remaining thirty minutes by filming suitable content in Finland. We also pledged to help the church leaders produce their programs, although we didn't yet know how.

Every member of the government we met told us how fantastic the religion Islam was, giving freedom to everyone. I wondered if they really believed what they said. The weather was hot in Sudan, and in some cases, I struggled to keep awake while these important people spoke for so long about their great political system.

The visit to Sudan included many surprises. One was a dinner with terrorist leader Hassan Al-Turabi (top, third from the right). To his left is our always-smiling host, Father Philetos.

One day, we were invited to have dinner at the largest university in Khartoum, the International University of Africa, and guess what? Dr. Hassan Al-Turabi—the terrorist leader I read about in *Reader's Digest*—would host the event. He was a terrorist but also a prominent Sudanese politician. In the 1990s, he was a central ideological leader behind President Omar Al-Bashir's regime, which was responsible for numerous human rights abuses, including summary executions, torture, arbitrary detentions, and denial of freedoms of speech, assembly, and religion. At the same time, Al-Turabi was an avid supporter of foreign jihadists. For example, he had invited Osama bin Laden to Sudan and hosted him there between 1991 and 1996.

I did not know all of this then, and at the dinner, I didn't even remember everything I had read about him on the flight. During the meal, Dr. Turabi asked me, "Can you and your team come to Sudan and train us in media work, especially in television production, at the International University of Africa?" I understood this was an invitation to help them to Islamize Africa, starting with the south of Sudan. So, I replied, "Dr. Turabi, I have such a busy schedule that it wouldn't be possible for a long time."

I am so happy that he didn't know that I was an apostate, an infidel—otherwise, he would have probably made a good kebab out of me!

In Sudan, we also saw my new friend, Mafdy, whom I had met in Cairo just a few days before arriving in Khartoum. He is an Egyptian missionary and had a remarkable ministry in Sudan, with many local evangelists helping him. On one of the evenings, he invited us to participate in an evangelistic meeting. We went there and told our testimonies.

Photo from a course where we trained Sudanese Christians to make TV programs—at a time when we were just learning TV production ourselves.

After the meeting, I asked Mafdy how many people he had on his evangelist team. He said there were about twenty or more. I said, "Bring them, and let's go to our hotel. The government promised to pay my bill." I took them all to dinner. We ordered a lot of grilled chicken, and the poor evangelists enjoyed it immensely.

The trip to Sudan was a new beginning in my life. I would have never guessed this trip would be the opening of a TV ministry for which only the sky was the limit. I don't know why I told the Sudanese Christians I could help them because I didn't know much about TV production then, but I'm glad I did. Later, we trained there more than a hundred people from different denominations for TV programming, and we broadcast our own series on the national TV channel for several years.

New Testaments to Moroccans in Spain

At the beginning of 1994, we continued to make radio programs, but the focus of our work at Keymedia shifted from radio to TV. Because of that, I wanted to learn more about TV production, but finding a Christian organization where someone could be trained took much work. Finally, we found one of the few in the world: the Brussels-based International Media Ministries (IMM) that produced Christian media content itself but also trained people from other churches and organizations in the same ministry. The organization was part of the international Assemblies of God community.

Steven Antturi, Sari, and I went to Belgium, where we were trained in TV programming for three weeks. One thing I was eager to learn was how to act in front of a television camera. Because of my background in radio ministry and as an evangelist, speaking wasn't a problem for me. Even the customer service I had done in my restaurant job trained my communication skills. But acting smoothly on television was quite another matter. A good preacher is not automatically a good TV personality.

I attended IMM's courses several times. Steven also gave me practical lessons. When I had free time, I studied TV production from books I purchased in Belgium and received from Steven.

One day, I got something else to think about. My friend, a British missionary named Graham, had an idea to distribute

Bibles to hundreds of thousands of Moroccans living in Europe, who, in the summertime, would go to visit their families in Morocco. It would be easy to distribute New Testaments to these people while they were waiting in their cars to board the ferry between Europe and Africa. The Bible gift would give them something to read while sitting and waiting.

It was a great idea, and I promised to help him. Graham and I contacted an Egyptian friend of mine, brother Fouad (the name is changed for security reasons), to get permission to print the New Testaments. At that time, he was behind the copyrights of the Arabic–French New Testament we wanted to print.

Graham's team hoped for 40,000 copies, but we didn't have enough money for so many. Another Christian friend of mine, Aki Turunen, who worked at a printing company in Finland, managed to get us a good price for 20,000 copies. They had a batch of paper that could be enough for 20,000 to 22,000 New Testaments, and Aki suggested they use it. The paper was not white but a creamy color, and it was called tobacco paper. It was okay for us, so we made a deal. The covers of the New Testaments would be forest green and the size of a book about 13 x 20 centimeters (5 x 8 inches).

Whenever Graham and I spoke, he told me how much he wanted 40,000 copies. I had also mentioned Graham's wish to Aki, and so on the day the New Testaments were printed, Aki went to the building to bless the Bibles before they were shipped. He prayed that the Bibles could be doubled because the team needed 40,000 copies, but we didn't have the money for so many.

After printing, the Bibles were loaded into the trucks headed for Spain. We had to pay the duty, so the Spanish customs officers counted the books and charged us for 40,000 New Testaments (which I didn't know then). When the New Testaments were unloaded in Algeciras, the evangelist team counted them, and, again, there were 40,000 copies of forest-green New Testaments! (I knew nothing about this either.) Brother Graham only called me and said, "Thank you, they arrived."

One day, the phone rang again. It was brother Fouad. He said to me, "I am a little upset with you. You asked me for permission to print 20,000 New Testaments. Brother Graham called me and said, 'Thank you for the permission, and all 40,000 are now delivered.' It is okay, but please tell me the real number next time."

I said, "No, the order and invoice were for 20,000. What do you mean by 40,000?"

The matter remained pending, but the issue was raised again when Fouad and his family came to Finland later that summer. Then I wanted to prove to Fouad that I was right. So, since we were in Finland, I took us to the printing house. The manager welcomed us and said, "It's impossible that we would have printed 40,000 because that paper was only enough for 20,000 to 22,000 copies." The warehouse manager said the same thing.

Yet the customs officers in Spain had been 100 percent certain that there were 40,000 copies. The distribution team counted the books five times; the result was 40,000 copies each time. I want to believe this was a biblical miracle—God knew the need and provided.

Niilo and I made another trip to Morocco. As usual, we visited some people who had written to IBRA Radio after listening to the programs I made. One of these people was Latif, who had been writing to us for over two years and had accepted Christ. Latif and I became close friends. Afterward, he received support and encouragement also from two godly missionaries working in Morocco. One was Dr. Habeeb Iskandar, now with the Lord, but the other missionary is still in the area.

Later, Latif was the first Moroccan MBB in modern Moroccan history who was ordained as a pastor, and he has become one of the fathers of the MBB churches there. He is married to a great woman of God, Imane. The couple has three children, and they named their youngest son after my name, Harun.

Another example from that period of how God can work in wonderful ways happened in 1995. The Arabic department of Keymedia helped another ministry with a project that turned out to be very effective. The project was based on a simple idea:

to take pages from North African telephone books and have volunteers write the corresponding names and addresses on individual envelopes. Then, into the envelopes, they inserted a short tract of the basic Christian truths about the love of God. Finally, we asked people in mission organizations and churches from different countries to take these envelopes, buy the stamps, and mail them. Thousands of letters were sent from Finland alone.

One of the recipients was a Tunisian police officer who was immensely angered by the message. He contacted a famous local newspaper. They took our tract and published it in their newspaper—word for word!—with a warning that some people were trying to deceive the people by sending this to them. We could not have dreamed of having this simple gospel message distributed so widely. What an awesome God we serve! God works in mysterious ways that can confound our imaginations. We have no idea how many people accepted Christ through the project, but we know that this newspaper's readers have read the entire message of Christ. The rest is in God's hands.

In the same year, the network we had set up in Egypt, the Children of Ishmael, took significant steps forward. We rented an office and set up training schools for churches and local groups to reach out to Muslims. With God's help, we also started to develop a network of discipleship groups for MBBs and began to provide spiritual, physical, and social care to those who needed help. For example, we set up a refuge for those cast out by their families and started a small business project to help those who had lost their jobs because of their new faith. We also had some people on our team who had previously worked for international human rights and religious freedom organizations, so we had a qualified team to monitor the situation of converts from Islam to Christianity and give them the help they needed.

Gradually, all these projects and ministries formed a good model for many who followed us to solve problems faced by MBBs in Egypt and elsewhere.

There is so much more in those years that could be written about that it is suitable to quote Apostle John's famous words,

> *And there are also many other things that Jesus did, which if they were written one by one, I suppose that even the world itself could not contain the books that would be written.* (John 21:25)

The team Ibrahim. In Finland, Sari became my closest colleague.

The Start of Christian Satellite Television

In early 1996, I again attended an IMM course on TV work in Brussels. There I was asked to host a new program based on testimonies of Arabs whose lives were transformed by Jesus. The name of the series was *Oasis*.

Being the host was an enjoyable task for me, and I was able to bring on some additional testimonies of people I knew. This was the first time an MBB hosted an international Christian satellite TV broadcasting to the Arabic-speaking world. We produced five episodes with IMM staff, and they were transmitted for a trial period on a secular European satellite called Eutelsat.

Its channels were seen in the Middle East, North Africa, and Western and Southern Europe.

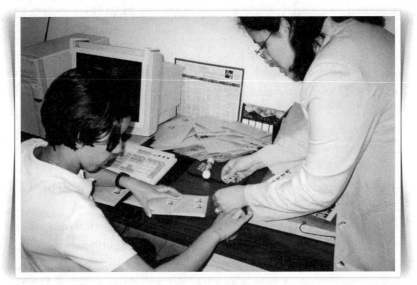

Since the 1990s, we have received feedback from almost every country in the world. A photo of a correspondence center we had in North Africa.

When the first episode aired on April 16, 1996, something interesting happened related to my family in Abu Gosh. As I have mentioned, my conversion to Christianity disappointed my mother and especially my siblings. Later, they got over it, and our relationship became better. When Sari, Ali, Sami, my parents-in-law, and I visited Abu Gosh in 1988, everything went pretty well. But then my mom and siblings discovered I was an evangelist trying to win their fellow Muslims from Islam to Christ, and they got angry with me again. In the spring of 1996, we still had some disagreements and were not talking much. So I didn't know what to expect if they saw these episodes.

On my first broadcast, my brother Ibrahim was watching TV and hopping around from channel to channel. Suddenly, he saw me on TV. He called the rest of the family and said, "Hey everyone, Harun is on TV right now! You need to watch him!"

It was amazing. It was the first time I preached the gospel of Christ to my childhood family via TV. My message was simple and clear. In every episode, I spoke about the power of God that can change people's lives. Each episode also had a song or two that praised Jesus.

When my mom saw me on TV, she was moved in her heart. She immediately called me at home. I wasn't there, but Sari answered. With my sister acting as interpreter, my mom told Sari, "Please tell Harun to call home. We miss him." I had been expecting much more of a negative response, but, praise God, I saw the Bible's promise come to pass: "But seek first the kingdom of God and His righteousness, and all these things shall be added to you" (Matthew 6:33). My appearance on TV brought reconciliation with my family.

A few weeks later, the whole of Arabic Christian media was transformed when a new, interdenominational channel called SAT-7 started broadcasting in May 1996. The story had begun the previous year when English missionary Terry Ascott gathered representatives from more than thirty organizations to establish a satellite TV operator to broadcast Christian programming to the Arabic-speaking world. The meeting was held in Cyprus, and Sari and I were there representing Keymedia.

SAT-7 was the first Arabic Christian satellite TV channel, but in 1997 the number doubled when another channel called Mougeza ("Miracle Channel", now "Miracle Connect"), operated by Norwegian mission organizations, began its satellite transmissions to the region. Before that year, the only Arabic Christian television channel had been Middle East TV, established in 1982 by an American Christian media company CBN. Besides religious content, Middle East TV broadcast other programs, so it wasn't a purely Christian channel, and it also operated only locally in Lebanon. All this reveals how pivotal and significant an event the creation of SAT-7 and Miracle Channel was.

One of our first TV Bible teachers was the well-known Egyptian Evangelical preacher and author Menes Abdul Noor (1930–2015). He was one of the pioneers who had the vision of reaching the Arab Muslim majority with the gospel.

After these channels started their broadcasting, the need for Arabic Christian TV programs grew dramatically. Only a few organizations produced such content regularly then, so interest in our programs increased. From 1996 to 2003, our Arabic media team at Keymedia filmed several TV series and around 1,000 episodes with ministers like Dr. Menes Abdul Noor, Dr. Adel Nosshy, and many others. I hosted around 500 episodes and was the producer for all of them.

The programs included Bible teaching, daily devotion, and Christian theology in layperson's terms. The big theme was the love of God, expressed through the words and actions of Jesus, but the themes of the individual series ranged from the parables and miracles of Jesus to the love of God for all. We wanted to make viewers fall in love with Jesus. In addition, we tried to answer the questions about Christianity that people living in the midst of Arab culture commonly had.

Alongside the teaching, we produced hundreds of musical videoclips with Arabic Christian worship leaders such as Maher Fayez and Fadia Bazzi. Sister Fadia is a gospel singer from a Shia background in southern Lebanon. Brother Maher is a son of an Egyptian Christian evangelist and gave his own life to Jesus in the 1980s after becoming a famous musician. As far as I know, we were the first to produce dramatized Arabic worship music videos, and many of them are still popular today, like "I've Sinned against You" and "Full of Compassion," sung by brother Maher.

In addition to SAT-7 and Miracle Channel, one could see our programs via local cable networks in Denmark, Sweden, Israel, Italy, and the US.

Blessed Journeys to Canada and the US

When the first episode of *Oasis* was broadcast, I was in Canada with Steven Antturi to attend a mission conference. At the meeting, we heard about another conference arranged in Seattle in the U.S. the next week. The event was organized by the Gospel Tabernacle Fellowship, and we decided to continue our trip there.

This conference gathered people from all over the country, and when one of the men in charge heard about my background, he asked if I could share my testimony as an MBB. So I did, and after that, a pastor named Robert Forseth invited me to his church, Smithtown Gospel Tabernacle, in Long Island, New York. They were organizing a mission conference about a month later, and Pastor Robert asked me to come and tell them whatever I had in my heart.

I already knew that when people attend such events, they make new relationships. Still, I felt that Pastor Robert's invitation was like a door opened for us by God. In New York, my speech was the keynote address on the first night, which I considered a great honor. I told the audience how I had become a follower of Jesus and presented my vision to reach Muslims to Christ.

We made friends with Pastor Robert during the conference, and since then, the Gospel Tabernacle has been one of our supporting churches. I love the people there. They are faithful and have been praying for us all these years.

After Pastor Robert retired, Mission Pastor Gary Zarlengo became the senior pastor. Pastor Gary is from an Italian background. He is a great Bible teacher and fun to be around. I am blessed to have these friends in my life. Once, in Morocco, Gary and I went to a marketplace distributing New Testaments to the people. Suddenly we heard a man say to another, "These infidels are distributing the Injil (New Testament). Call the police." I looked at Gary and said, "Pastor, it's time to run!" So, we did. We ran to our car and drove away.

9

A New Kind of Vision — Challenging Islam in Public

When SAT-7 and the Miracle Channel started, many Middle Eastern churches joined the program production, especially for SAT-7. However, it soon became apparent that not all Middle Eastern Christians were happy about the new situation. Several new mission operators had appeared in the area and created their programs from various spiritual perspectives. It seemed to cause disturbance to some local Christian leaders, especially those from the traditional churches who were used to being in charge of the region's Christian content. Some thought we, as evangelicals, had come into this field as competitors. I heard it talked about several times, and it grieved my heart.

When we produced our series for SAT-7, Miracle, and other channels, we had Muslims as the primary target audience in our minds. We tried to determine which Christian themes would benefit them and how we should talk about them so that our programs would lead Muslim viewers to Jesus. However, the programs didn't deal directly with Islamic issues or openly discuss the problems of the religion. That was the philosophy of SAT-7 and Miracle. Officially, their content was for the Arabic-speaking Christian background people in the region. Of course, both channels hoped that Muslims would also watch their broadcast, but they didn't want to take the risk that someone would blame them for converting Muslims to Christians.

So, we produced shows that way for many years. It was a blessed time, but we were dreaming of more. We hadn't seen the major revival in the Muslim world for which we had been praying for so many years. Our shows were planned and filmed mainly by Christian-background believers (I was one of the few MBB hosts for a long time), and officially everything was made for Christians living in the Arabic world. We understood that we had to change all this to see a revival. We had to change our strategy.

Gradually, an idea began to mature in our minds. What if we were to complement the gospel message with straightforward talk that would challenge Muslims with questions exposing the weaknesses in Islam? No one had done anything like that ever before. So, we started to pray that God would open new doors for us to exercise this style of ministry.

Of course, we knew that creating programs like this would be a big challenge and could cause lots of trouble for us—Muslim majorities in Arabic countries would not accept interference in their religion. Islam is an extreme religion that punishes apostates and persecutes those who dare speak up against their prophet or the Qur'an.

We understood there were at least four major challenges we would face:

1. *Fear in the local churches.* At the time, the fear was almost palpable in the churches of the Arabic world because of the pressure from Islamic governments and extremism. Few, if any, Arab Christians would be willing to put their faces on television and speak out against Islam. Where could we get brave enough hosts and teachers for our programs?

2. *Fear in the Christian media.* The same fear seemed to exist among the executives and producers on the Christian TV channels. Would it be possible to find a platform for such content? If the existing channels rejected or censored the programs, where else could they be transmitted?

3. *A need for specialist expertise.* To implement our vision, we needed Christians who had mastered both Islam and Christianity. In particular, there was a shortage of good Christian–Muslim apologists who were able both to defend Christianity against criticism of Islam and to articulate Christianity's challenge to Islam. In addition, the person also had to be suitable for working on TV.
4. *Financial challenges.* Were there sponsors who would share this vision with us? Would our partners remain in ministry with us?

We continued to organize prayer and fasting conferences for Muslim ministry, and we began to pray that God would open the door for us to film and broadcast these new kinds of programs.

One thing was clear: whatever we did, we would need to present the love of Jesus consistently in everything we produced.

Paltalk Ministry

Since our family's return to Finland, I had almost entirely given up street evangelism and had immersed myself in TV work. Yet the evangelist in me also yearned for direct interaction with people.

In 2000, I was introduced to an internet chat platform called Paltalk. I quickly realized that it provided an excellent opportunity to reach Muslims, many of whom had also found the platform. Users could chat via text or audio and, later, video, and anyone could create their own chat room on a topic of their choice. The platform also gave the user an option to appear under a nickname. Many Arab Christians and Muslims interested in Christianity took advantage of this option to help conceal their identity and not face the risk of being persecuted because of their opinions.

So, I started my chat room by sharing testimonies of Muslims who accepted Christ, short Bible studies, some worship music, and prayer. My meeting was scheduled every Tuesday evening for four hours. Later, I got help from my friend, Waheed—an anointed Bible teacher from a Sudanese Coptic background—who became another host in my chat room. We shared the responsibility of preaching the Word every Tuesday. We had hundreds of attendees and even reached an attendance of 2,000 at one point. Many of them accepted Christ.

At the same time, I felt sorry for Sari. I used to minister through Paltalk from home, and the only place I could work was from our bedroom. I was excited, typing on my noisy keyboard while Sari tried to sleep. Despite her using earplugs, I would wake her up frequently. While writing this, I have to apologize even now for the inconvenience I caused her.

September 11 and Father Zakaria

On September 11, 2001, the world experienced a new terrorist strategy with suicide bombers flying their hijacked airplanes into buildings of strategic importance in the US. We now know the event as 9/11.

That Tuesday morning, nineteen members of the militant Islamist network al-Qaeda hijacked four commercial airliners flying from the US East Coast to California. The hijackers crashed the first two planes into the Twin Towers of the World Trade Center in New York City and the third plane into the Pentagon (the headquarters of the United States military) in Arlington, Virginia. The fourth plane they had turned around to fly towards Washington, D.C., but the plane crashed in a field after a heroic passenger revolt. The attacks caused the World Trade Center Twin Towers to collapse, and nearly 3,000 people died. The response to these events was the global war on terror.

Al-Qaeda's name is said to be based on a Qur'anic verse in Sura 9.5:

> *Then when the Sacred Months have passed, then kill the Mushrikun* [idolaters, polytheists, pagans] *wherever you find them, and capture them and besiege them, and prepare for them each and every ambush* [al-qaeda in Arabic, meaning a "place of ambush" and "base"]. *But if they repent and perform As-Salat* [Islamic prayers], *and give Zakat* [the alms], *then leave their way free. Verily, Allah is Oft-Forgiving, Most Merciful.*

The use of terror to achieve the goals of Islam is also taught in the Qur'an, and Muslims are instructed to use it. For instance, Sura 8.60 says,

> And make ready against them all you can of power, including steeds of war to threaten [the Arabic word here is *turhebouna*, which also means "to terrorize," "to torture," and "to frighten"] the enemy of Allah and your enemy, and others besides whom, you may not know but whom Allah does know. And whatever you shall spend in the Cause of Allah shall be repaid unto you, and you shall not be treated unjustly.

Soon after September 11th, God opened one of the most amazing doors for us to launch our new ministry strategy. I met a person on Paltalk who called himself "Servant 13." I heard that behind the nickname was a Coptic Orthodox priest named Zakaria Botros. He was Egyptian but had been expelled from the country by the Egyptian government for his persistent ministry to Muslims. At the time, he was living in England and serving Coptic Christians living abroad, but he also continued evangelizing Muslims.

The Paltalk discussions showed that Father Zakaria had mastered debating with Muslims. He courageously addressed their questions concerning Christianity, but he also asked them challenging questions about Muhammad, the Hadith (the record of sayings and actions of Muhammad), as well as about the Qur'an and other Islamic issues. Many of those who followed Father Zakaria in Paltalk had already accepted Jesus because they had become convinced that Islam didn't hold the answer to their questions and that Jesus alone is the way, the truth, and the life.

I listened to Father Zakaria for two weeks in Paltalk, searching for his contact number until I managed to get it through a friend. I called Father Zakaria, told him about myself, and asked him about his work. It was pleasant to start getting to know him. We shared the same clear vision for reaching the Muslim world for Christ.

Then I told him that I was interested in producing programs specifically for a Muslim audience and in a way that would combine Christian evangelism with straightforward challenging of Islam. I asked him if he might be interested in being a teacher on a TV series like this.

He answered and said he was happy to be asked for the task. Years ago, God had given him a vision to proclaim to huge crowds, but he hadn't imagined how it would happen. He hadn't imagined that God would open the door to international satellite TV for him. My question made him feel the vision might come to fruition after all.

His words made me glad, but I had some further questions for him, so I asked him to answer them before we would book production time.

1. Was he willing to start using his real name? We did not want to have him on the TV with a nickname. It would have been contradictory to speak boldly but still be afraid to use one's real name.

2. Would Pope Shenouda—the leader of the Coptic Orthodox Church at that time—accept that a priest of the church do this kind of TV show? What would happen if we started broadcasting and Pope Shenouda told him to stop being on TV? It was better to know this before spending time, money, and energy and then being told he could no longer continue.

3. Was he willing to co-work with an evangelical MBB and produce a show that would be broadcast on a "Protestant" channel? (Though I didn't know yet which channel we would get on.)

Father Zakaria told me the questions were important and promised to reply in a week. A week passed, and I called him, and he was ready with the answers.

For question 1, he repeated that he was delighted that we asked him to do this, and he was willing to use his real name. He said it would be a pleasure to serve with us, preach the truth, and bring everything to light.

For question 2, he said we didn't need to worry about that. He had asked the Pope to consider him retired, and the Pope had agreed. So, the Pope wouldn't ask him to step down from TV once he was retired. (Father Zakaria was one of the first priests to be granted retirement in the Coptic Church.)

Finally, for question 3, his reply was the biggest blessing to me. He said that he was a follower of Christ and that all those who accept Christ as their Redeemer and King are his brothers and sisters. So, if we at Keymedia believe that God sent His Son to die for us and raised Him from the dead, and salvation comes only through Him, he was ready to work with us to preach the gospel to Muslims.

That was it. We arranged a time to record twenty episodes of a program titled *Questions About Faith—Asela an al-Iman* in Arabic—and started looking for a host to be with him on the show.

We thought it would be good if the host were an MBB. The idea emerged that I would host the program, but I wasn't eager to take on the role. By then, I spent virtually all my working hours managing the team and producing the TV series we filmed. I thought I'd be the host only if we couldn't find anyone else to do it.

Thankfully, we soon found sister Nahed Metwally, who was ready to take the risk and the assignment. She was an Egyptian, and her conversion story was widely known in Arabic countries. Sister Nahed became the first woman from a Muslim background to become a host on an Arabic Christian TV show. She was also the first MBB woman in front of TV cameras without the Muslim veil and with her face and real name. It was a pioneering moment. After her, many other MBB women have done the same.

The first episodes were filmed in Keymedia studio in Kerava, Finland, in February 2002. It was so cold outside that the southern seaside of Finland was frozen at the edges. One day, Father Zakaria and I went for a walk on the beach and walked on the ice. For Father Zakaria, it was a new and even a bit scary experience.

Father Zakaria during a break while filming *Questions About Faith*. Later, many other Christian TV producers also began focusing on Muslim audiences and openly challenging Islam. However, the fruit hasn't only been positive: without a loving heart, criticizing Islam can push Muslims further away from Jesus.

Inside the studio, a new thrill was also in the air. We weren't afraid, but we knew we had stepped onto "ice" that no previous TV team had stepped onto. The show would be the first-ever TV show of its kind—an orthodox priest, wearing a black robe with a big cross around his neck, being interviewed by an MBB about Islam. For the first time in history, a Christian would so publicly—amidst the Muslim community—put Islamic holy teachings under the microscope and question the validity of the Qur'an.

I knew that if we could ever air Father Zakaria's programs on TV, the results in the Muslim world would be both staggering and groundbreaking. In the show, we would ask the same questions Muslims had been asking about Christianity but in reverse: How can one trust in the Qur'an when there are so many differences between the oldest remaining manuscripts? Is it possible to take the Qur'an as the word of God because so many passages in it are clearly at variance with other passages? Is Muhammad a prophet at all because of his immoral and violent actions?

We were sure that the show had the potential to reach millions of people in the Arabic-speaking Muslim world.

After filming, we sent the episodes to the Miracle Channel and asked them to evaluate the program and give us their feedback. Unfortunately, the response was disappointing. One of the channel's staff members urged his colleagues not to accept the series. He was an Arab from a Christian background and feared the consequences the show might cause.

We continued to pray that God would open a new door for us so that we would have the platform to broadcast these programs. At the same time, I was reluctant to tell Father Zakaria about the difficulties we had because I didn't want him to get discouraged at such an early stage of our ministry together.

A Partnership with Joyce Meyer Ministries

Close to the end of 2002, I visited my mom in Abu Gosh. One day, I went to see my friend, sister Catharine, the leading nun at the local monastery of Our Lady of the Ark of the Covenant. I had met sister Catharine, an Irish woman, for the first time some years earlier. Then she had told me how, years before, she had heard that someone from the village had converted to Christianity. She hadn't known who the person was but had prayed for him ever since. Now, it seemed apparent that it was me she had heard about. She also told me then that God had spoken to her about a remarkable Christian ministry that would start from the village.

Later, I also made friends with many other nuns and volunteers who live and work in the monastery—Grace, Maluo, Vivien, Jenny, Rhea, and Nieves. The place and its people are so precious that now I consider the sanctuary my second home in Israel.

One of the blessings the place has brought to my life is that it has changed how I see different denominations. When I first became a Christian, I was sure that the denomination I joined was the most biblical denomination in Finland (and how lucky I was to be a part of it)! I also learned that the Roman Catholics and the Orthodox have very different doctrines than we evangelical Protestants have, so I was very suspicious of them for years. Then, gradually, God began to change my attitude.

At first, He did it in Sudan and Egypt, where I had met many whole-hearted Christians from the traditional churches. Then I came to know sisters of the Abu Gosh monastery. When I first met them, I was not only surprised but impressed by what amazing Christians they were! They constantly talked about Jesus, praised and worshipped Him, and were so dedicated to serving Him. I still can't agree with all the doctrines of their church, but I am sure that they are Christians by the grace of God, saved by the blood of Jesus, just like me.

Over the years, I had also come to know these sisters as genuine people of prayer and empathy. So, when I visited the monastery in 2002, I asked them to pray for the show we were launching with Father Zakaria. Later I heard that they prayed every day for us.

In May 2003, I received a call from Gary Preston, the Middle East Director for Joyce Meyer Ministries (JMM). Mrs. Joyce Meyer is a well-known television teacher and evangelist. Her program is called *Enjoying Everyday Life* and has been broadcast in many languages worldwide since 1993. As I write this, the series is still being produced.

The JMM team had been translating Joyce's books into Arabic and making them into small booklets you could find in the hands of Arab Christians all over the Middle East and North Africa in those days. Now, the organization wanted to translate and dub her TV show into Arabic. Gary Preston had been traveling around the region and had contacts among the Christian churches, ministries, and mission organizations operating there. The problem was that Joyce's program was rejected by the only two existing Arabic Christian satellite channels—SAT-7 and Miracle Channel. One of the reasons for the disapproval was the thought that it was not the right time for Arabs to accept a woman as a screen evangelist/teacher—especially a woman who was sharing her personal life very openly in her programs. It seemed strange to me because, as far as I knew, Joyce was and is one of Christian television's most beloved personalities.

Because there was no opportunity to broadcast these programs on secular Arabic channels either—those operators were all under Muslim control—JMM had started preparing the ground for creating their own channel. By then, they had already translated and dubbed 140 episodes of *Enjoying Everyday Life* into Arabic in Beirut. The dubbing had been done very professionally, with an excellent translation. They also had plans to produce the series in French for North Africans and Arabs living in France. They hoped to start broadcasting on the new channel by September 1, 2003.

When I got the call from Gary, he had already met with most of the Arabic Christian program producers. The available content was limited, and some, if not most, had already been aired on the SAT-7 or Miracle Channel. Gary encouraged producers to film new Arabic programs focused more on direct communication with the Muslim-majority audience and asked if anyone knew of someone currently doing this or willing to work with them to make these kinds of TV series. The response was usually kind but clear that this was not the time to make programs of that nature. Tensions between the Muslim world and the West were still high because of 9/11.

In some of these conversations, my name had come up as someone with the same vision to reach Muslims directly. The message usually had a warning attached to the wisdom of working with someone like me, whom they considered "reckless" and liable to cause "unnecessary harm" to the Christian community. It was no secret that I had a burning desire to evangelize Muslims openly. Those commentators might also know about the *Questions About Faith* project with Father Zakaria.

I disagree with the assessments of me as reckless or liable to cause harm. Yet, I openly admit that I am a pure evangelist and very protective of the calling the Lord has given me. I know that I have received my vision from the Lord, and I have protected it with all my strength despite many attacks, just like I guarded my brothers in my childhood. I knew my vision—to reach Muslims directly—was from God, and I couldn't stand the thought of leaving this task for the next generation.

So, I met Gary Preston shortly after he first contacted me. I was in Frankfurt, Germany, with my good friend Sam Solomon and another friend from the Answering Islam website. We were planning to expand the ministry to reach Muslims on the internet, and Gary came to see us there. He told briefly who he was and how Joyce Meyer Ministries was preparing to start a new Christian Arabic channel. Then he asked us what we thought of their plans and said that if we had any advice or counsel, he would be willing to hear it. He made it clear that he didn't consider himself a media expert. Nonetheless, he desired to see people in spiritual darkness come to know the truth and be saved. Gary said he would not be offended by anything we said.

I was encouraged when he said he would not be offended because Sam and I are very straightforward in sharing our opinions regarding reaching Muslims. Sam is also an MBB and an Islamic scholar with solid ideas and views about the Arab churches and the role of Western churches in the Middle East. We spent the next few hours sharing those opinions while Gary took notes and asked questions occasionally, but mostly just listened. Sam spearheaded the conversation.

I remember Sam telling Gary, "If you start a channel that is the same as any other Arabic Christian channel without challenging Muslims and preaching to Muslims directly, my recommendation is to pack your stuff and go."

I told Gary that we had lots of Arabic series, but one of them was not accepted because of its straightforward approach. It was the program presented by Father Zakaria Botros and hosted by an MBB, sister Nahed. So I said to Gary, "I think I have the perfect program to complement the Joyce Meyer Arabic show."

We agreed that Gary and his wife, Christine, would come to Finland a week later to meet my boss, Mr. Markku Vuorinen, and the Keymedia staff. Gary wanted to see our production facilities and further discuss the possibility of our two ministries partnering on the new channel. It was also important to him to hear our opinions of Joyce Meyer before we went any further. We told him that Joyce Meyer was well-known in Finland and that partnering with JMM would be an honor for us.

During their visit to Finland, we discussed programs and who would be doing what. Gary also repeated that they needed a new and bold Arabic series to speak to the Muslim majority, draw viewers to the channel, and complement Joyce Meyer's programs. I showed him one of the first episodes we had done with Father Zakaria, subtitled into English.

Gary's reaction after watching the episode was remarkable. I wish I would have had a camera with me to capture it. He smiled with amazement on his face; it seemed that God had just answered his prayers. There was no doubt in his mind that this combination of programming—Father Zakaria and Joyce Meyer—was a match made in heaven. Father Zakaria challenging Islam and Joyce preaching God's love for everyone had a tension between them, but simultaneously, they would complement each other just the right way.

So, we made a deal. Keymedia would become JMM's partner on the new channel. It was one of the most remarkable days for our team but also for Sari and me personally. During Gary's and Christine's visit to Finland, Sari and I made lifelong friends with them. Later, Gary would be my closest mentor (besides Sari), and I came to know him as a man of God.

My boss, Markku Vuorinen, told me afterward that while they, as the head of Keymedia, were committed to this major project, they felt it was important to not become a financial burden on the organization. Because of that, he recommended that I start fundraising to be able to fulfill this vision.

Becoming a Grandfather

Over the years, my sons Ali and Sami had grown up to be independent, good men. I am so proud of them both.

Ali married Heidi at the beginning of 2003. In December 2003, I experienced one of the happiest moments in my life—my first grandson was born, Daniel Aaron. I am so glad because of him. He is a kind young man, and I am honored that Ali and Heidi named him after me (Harun is the Arabic form of Aaron). In June 2016, Ali and Heidi had another son named Lukas, a little man full of energy.

Ali is a good husband and an excellent father. I see in his character many things I see in myself, but also qualities I wish I had. For example, like me, he is exceptionally energetic and makes friends quickly. Everyone I know who has met Ali says that it's easy to be friends with him. On the other hand, how Ali deals with his two sons, Daniel and Lukas, is much more mature than how I dealt with him and Sami—maybe he has learned from my mistakes. Ali loves to be at home and play with his sons, and his kids love him.

Ali's wife, Heidi, is a sweet, wise, and devoted mother and wife. Sari and I are happy to have her in our family. She respects us, and we love her dearly.

My younger son Sami got married in 2009 to Tiina, and in 2015, they had a daughter, Ellen, who has brought us much joy. As with all my grandchildren, I love her dearly. Unfortunately, Sami's and Tiina's marriage fell apart shortly after Ellen's birth. Thankfully, they parted on good terms, making it easier for them to care for Ellen.

In July 2018, Sami remarried a girl named Annika. She is a firm believer and has a heart for Israel, as does my whole family. I am very proud of her. Annika has become a second mother to Ellen and a precious wife to Sami. They had a daughter named Linnea in 2021.

Sami is a good husband and a caring father to his beautiful girls. One of Sami's strengths is that he is so well organized. In

2015, he joined our team as a project manager and is meticulous in everything he does. It is a good quality when writing reports for our partners. On a personal level, he likes to choose his friends carefully, so it usually takes a long time before he trusts himself to others.

10

Al Hayat Channel Goes Live!

On September 1, 2003, our new channel, Al Hayat, went live on air. We started to broadcast it on a satellite called HotBird that covers the Middle East, North Africa, a big part of Europe, and the northern part of the Arab Peninsula. This was the same Eutelsat satellite that had previously broadcast our *Oasis* series, but the satellite had since changed its name.

The Arabic word *al hayat* means "the Life." We had asked our Middle Eastern partners to suggest suitable names for the channel, and Al Hayat was one of them. We then looked at how the different names looked when written in Arabic calligraphy. The graphic pattern of Al Hayat looked good and was actually very similar to the symbol of the famous Al Jazeera news channel. We thought that would be a good thing.

Al Hayat logo—
the channel name in Arabic calligraphy.

In addition, Al Hayat ("The Life") was reminiscent of the name of Joyce Meyer's program, *Enjoying Everyday Life*. This also made the name seem appropriate to us. And, of course, the word has a solid biblical background. Jesus said He was "the way, the truth, and the life" (John 14:6), and our mission is to point to the way, the truth, and the life with Jesus. Later, an

Egyptian businessman established a secular TV channel with just the same name in Egypt.

True to its name, our Al Hayat was bursting with knowledge and life from the day it started, preaching God's love for all and boldly questioning Islam on a popular media platform in the Arab world—something that had never happened before in the history of Christian media. After fourteen centuries of the Islamic sword silencing critics of the religion, the time was ripe for God to unsheathe the sword of His Spirit for maximum impact. This was not possible until the dawn of the technological revolution and the advent of Christian satellite TV and the internet. Once Father Zakaria embarked on this journey to respond to questions Muslims directed at Christians and challenge the very foundations of Islam—the Qur'an, Muhammad, his sayings, and other fundamental Islamic issues and practices—there was no turning back.

A little later, we also set up an online radio, which made it possible to listen to the TV channel's programming as audio on the internet. So, some of the long-time dreams I mentioned before—establishing a 24/7 TV channel and a 24/7 radio station—came true almost simultaneously.

The Muslim world was caught off guard and reacted with complete shock when Father Zakaria's programs hit the airwaves. In Arabic countries, people had never heard that kind of public criticism about Islam before. One of the Egyptian newspapers, *Sout Al-Umma* ("The Voice of the Nation"), started writing against our channel, asking the readers to boycott it and warning them of its dangers. However, viewer reactions were just the opposite. We received reports indicating an escalating demand for satellite receivers among Muslims because so many wanted to watch the priest with a black outfit criticizing Islam.

Later, other Middle Eastern newspapers also wrote about the channel. On Egypt's secular TV channels, talk shows discussed how to stop Al Hayat. "Not even all the Egyptian state funds put together can prevent the satellite channels from being broadcast," the Egyptian minister of communications complained on one show.

The interest in our programs was reflected in the viewer feedback we received. The more episodes of Father Zakaria's *Questions About Faith* were broadcast, the more letters and emails we received. Within four months—from September 2003 to the end of the year—the channel received more than 76,000 letters and emails. In 2002, Keymedia's Arabic department had received less than ten percent of that in a whole year.

Among the feedback were many in which the authors wrote about their own doubts about Islam or how the programs had opened their eyes to understand the differences between Islam and Christianity in a new way. Still, the overall tone of the feedback was very negative and critical of us. There were even death threats.

Although Father Zakaria referred in his responses to Islam's own sources, many Muslims ignored the truth. They saw the episodes as nothing more than aggression against Islam. They were not used to seeing anyone—especially *Dhimmis*, the non-Muslims living as second-class citizens in their Muslim-majority countries—questioning Islam. It is even written in the Qur'an that it is not allowed for Muslims to ask questions: "Ask not about things which, if made plain to you, may cause you trouble." (Sura 5.101). That's why it has been so challenging to convince a Muslim of the Christian point of view, no matter how logical it might be. The Qur'an itself had already issued a verdict before hearing the evidence.

Naturally, the fiercest aggression by violent Islamists was directed at Father Zakaria. Some declared him "Islam's Public Enemy No. 1," and radical groups announced they would pay big money to see him dead. Some said the reward was 60 million dollars, but numbers varied. Anyway, close to the end of 2003, Zakaria and his wife Violet decided to move from the United Kingdom to the United States.

In the US, they received help from some brothers who served them in relocating. One of these brothers was Sobhi. I had met him and his family for the first time in Paris in 1989. In 2003, they owned a gas station in their hometown in southern

California, but in 2005, Sobhi started working full-time for Al Hayat, his first main job being to assist Father Zakaria with all he needed. Over the years, Sobhi has become one of the most important people on the Al Hayat team, though he has been working mainly behind the scenes.

"Our Churches Will Be Burned Because of You"

It wasn't surprising to get ferociously attacked by the Islamic media. What I didn't expect was the attack from Christians—criticism which sometimes felt almost as ferocious. In public, many Christians washed their hands of anything to do with us. We received numerous messages imploring us to discontinue our assault on Islam because it would lead to getting Christians in the region killed and churches burned. Some accused us of being savage, hostile, and inciting hatred; others described me with derogatory and insulting adjectives. Our administrative office received letters expressing discontent with Keymedia for allowing Father Zakaria's program to be on air. The writers pointed out that such a movement was instigated by a Muslim-background believer (they meant me) who knew nothing about the ethics of evangelism and shouldn't be permitted to continue in Christian media.

In early 2004, I attended a partnership conference for Christian organizations focused on Arabic ministry in the Middle East and North Africa. The event was held in Europe, and hundreds of delegates came to the meeting—both MBBs and Christian-background believers—from various organizations, churches, and funding organizations from many countries. It was the first such gathering since the start of Al Hayat.

The event's purpose was to tell and hear encouraging news and establish relationships and networks. Because of this, I hadn't expected the reactions from some participants who were deeply concerned about what we do on Al Hayat. Some even refused to shake hands with me, saying, "Harun, you know we will pay the price for Father Zakaria's savage approach on your channel. Our churches will be burned down, and many Christians will be put to death because of what you are doing." Some others said, "It's easy for you to be bold while living abroad, but we will pay the price for your boldness."

Naturally, I was deeply hurt by all these attacks and aggressive remarks against Father Zakaria, me, and MBBs by the Christian Arab ministries. I believe I felt some of the feelings the Apostle Paul had when he was accused before Governor Felix, as recorded in the Book of Acts:

> *For we have found this man a plague, a creator of dissension among all the Jews throughout the world, and a ringleader of the sect of the Nazarenes. He even tried to profane the temple, and we seized him...* (Acts 24:5, 6)

Although I appeared firm in front of the people attending the four-day conference, I repeatedly went to my room crying bitterly because of the criticism. I called Sari to share what I was facing and expressed my desire to return home and abandon my ministry, but she encouraged me to stay. I don't remember how serious I was about my feelings of quitting, but I do remember the pain I carried inside.

"It would be so much easier to just return to baking pizzas," I would often sigh in my mind.

Critical Christian response was also published in the Middle Eastern Arabic media. Some Christian journalists and interviewees said Father Zakaria's programs contradicted the Christian values of tolerance and love: evangelization doesn't mean attacking other religions. The newspapers appealed to Pope Shenouda to stop our channel and excommunicate Father Zakaria.

At some point, I was especially tempted to respond to my critics and vent my anger and frustration. I wrote some responses and was ready to send them. But, fortunately, I first ended up sharing my feelings with Sari and my friend, Gary Preston. As I have said, Sari is a godly and wise woman, and Gary is a man of God. They both advised me to just forget the critics. Gary added that it would be a trap from the enemy to respond inappropriately, which might fuel the impression that MBBs are intolerant and fall short of the heart of Jesus. At that time, only a few MBBs were in a position like mine, and it would have been sad to react in the flesh. Gary always used to ask me the question, "What would Jesus do?"

I truly thank God for Gary, Sari, and all those who prayed for me then. It was one of the most challenging periods in my life. The best lesson I learned amid those storms was to swallow my anger and control my emotions.

Although the letters and emails contained bad words and harsh criticism, many writers did not dare reveal their real names. Some Christian leaders wrote to Joyce Meyer complaining about Father Zakaria and me. Because of our close partnership, Joyce shared the feedback with us—in JMM and Keymedia, we wanted to be open about issues like this.

Thankfully, many critics have since been willing to change their thinking. I met one of them many years later, and he opened the subject with me. He had written to Joyce and said bad things about me and had been thinking that I wouldn't hear about his words.

"By the way, I wrote an email to Joyce about you and the programs, and I was very tough," he told me.

"I know that," I replied.

He was surprised. "Really?" he asked.

"Yes, sir, I knew it on the same day but decided not to reply. However, I am so happy now that you dared to tell me that, and I love it. Thank you so much."

We had a friendly chat, and, since then, we have become friends.

Despite all the criticisms, Al Hayat's breakthrough into the Muslim world continued week after week, and thanks to negative reports undertaken by the Arabic secular media, our channel's influence resounded. Occasionally, local newspapers even published our episode scripts on their pages, and some secular Arabic satellite channels addressed the questions we had raised. Those questions covered topics such as "adult breastfeeding", mentioned in the Hadith, and the Qur'anic and the Hadith's positive attitude towards the taking, keeping, and sexual exploitation of slaves. After our programs, the secular Arab channels tackled the same awkward issues in their shows. As a result, there were messy public debates and embarrassing questions for Muslim scholars.

Of course, not everything the Arabic secular media wrote about us was true. Some said we were a media organization of the Coptic Church; others claimed we were receiving money from the governments of the United States or Israel. Some speculated that Father Zakaria had a link with Zionistic organizations and that they aimed to establish a Coptic state in Egypt. Even though these claims were false, the media reports helped us to become widely known throughout the Arab world. Sometimes everybody in the region seemed to talk about the Al Hayat channel.

And the attention given to Al Hayat by the Arab secular media has continued ever since. One article that sticks in my mind was published many years later in the weekly *Rosa El-Youssef* entitled "Al Hayat is worse than al-Qaeda."

In 2004, Al Hayat and its program producers received more than 247,000 reactions—letters, emails, and phone calls—from the viewers. The reactions included numerous messages indicating that many Muslims received Christ as their Savior.

One of the most painful claims against us was the accusation that Al Hayat was to blame for the persecution and suffering of Christians in the Middle East. As a result, we lost financial support from some Christian institutions because we were believed to be the source of danger. Thankfully, this accusation and fear proved to be unfounded. Religious freedom organizations did not report any measurable spike in persecution in the Arab world as a whole. In Iraq, the situation became much worse than before, but this was due to the US and its allies' invasion of the country in 2003 and the ensuing chaos. In some other countries, the situation got even better. One such country was Sudan, where the peace process between the Islamist regime and the Christian-majority south moved towards the 2005 peace agreement.

So, in short, there was violence, vandalism, discrimination, and pressure against Arabic Christians after the start of Al Hayat, but they had faced all that also before.

In this context, I must mention an interesting phenomenon we heard, especially in Egypt. Since Al Hayat had started broadcasting, it seemed that fewer Christian women converted to Islam than before because they were now more aware of what Islam was really like. In the past, it had been quite common in the country that when a Muslim man and a (nominally) Christian woman married, the woman converted to Islam.

While Father Zakaria was criticized and attacked, the response towards Joyce Meyer was much more positive. Although other Christian satellite channels had been very doubtful about her show, and the Islamist leaders criticized her, too, the audience received her with remarkably warm hearts. To this day, *Enjoying Everyday Life* continues to be one of the most popular shows on the channel. Many of her viewers in the region refer to her as "Mama Joyce," and in the early years of the channel, a North African speaker at a missionary conference even called her "the Billy Graham of the Middle East."

Gradually, the criticism we received from other Christian mission organizations started to fade, and Al Hayat began to become a sought-after partner and program platform. Initially, most of Al Hayat's content consisted of series by producers other than Joyce Meyer and Keymedia, and many of those programs had already been shown on SAT-7 or Miracle Channel before they went on air on Al Hayat. As our channel's popularity grew, we were offered new series first.

As a result of all this, we began to see the accusations we had received from other Christians as the price we had to pay for our success.

Our TV shows have been repeatedly featured in the Arab world's secular media. In the pictures of the article are our hosts, Amani and Farha, and a woman interviewed in our program. Since then, many secular Arab media have also asked critical questions about Islam.

The Fatwa

On a personal level, something very emotional happened in 2004 that changed my approach to dealing with fear. It began when one of my brothers and my cousin called me one day and said that a man named Raed Salah had threatened me.

Raed Salah is from an Israeli Arab town called Umm al-Fahm and has long been one of the leaders of the Islamic Movement in Israel. Now, he had heard that the man producing the programs for Father Zakaria was from Abu Gosh. He had also discovered my name and that my cousin was my relative. So, Raed called him and said that they would issue a fatwa against me, which in my case would mean a decree of death, unless my cousin could make me stop Al Hayat immediately.

The cousin had called my brother first, and now they both were online telling me these things and wanting me to understand that this was a matter of life and death and I must stop. They said Raed had given me three days to think about it and come back with a good answer.

I told them immediately that I didn't need three days—my answer was no. I would not stop what I was doing.

They were very disappointed with my reaction and repeated the threat. The tone of their voice made me feel that it wasn't just that they were concerned about my security but that they also were against my ministry. Of course, I partly understood it because they were Muslims, but still, I would have hoped that, as my close relatives, they would have defended my freedom to live as I saw fit. It was sad to hear such words from family members.

At home, I gathered Sari, Ali, and Sami and told them what had happened. Ali was calm, as usual, and said, "Dad, you do what you think is right, and we are with you."

Sari said, "Remember, you have been an example to many MBBs as someone who goes with his vision and does not let fear control his life."

When it came to Sami, my youngest, his words were strong and touched me deeply. He said, "Dad, we know you love what you do and have never been a coward. I know that if you stop, it would be for us, but we know if you stop, that will kill you—it would kill you to be called a coward. So I think you should just continue, and we should trust the Lord."

Their words were very encouraging to me, and, for sure, the whole situation was very emotional. My heart was full of joy but also full of sadness.

I started to pray for my family in Israel more than ever, and in one of the prayer times, I felt that God gave me a song based on this experience. The song was later recorded, and it became quite famous. Many MBBs thought the song was their song because they identified with the words deeply. Some have even called it "the Hymn of the MBBs." I thank God for this experience of being able to write a song that many people felt was their own. The song is in Arabic, but I hope the translation conveys at least a fraction of what it means to us MBBs.

The song is titled, "This Is My Prayer, My Family," and the lyrics go like this:

> (Refrain) *This is my prayer, my family, and my beloved, that you find salvation in my God. So come to the Redeemer who saved my soul and redeemed me.*
>
> 1. *I announce to you, my beloved, that I now live in security. O my father, mother, and siblings, Jesus died and redeemed me.*
> 2. *I forgive the cursing, and I forgive the insults. Just as my mistakes were forgiven and Jesus forgave me, the sinner.*
> 3. *Mother, do not cry for me. I have not forgotten you or my family. Rather, I follow Jesus, who left glory for me and died instead of me.*
> 4. *I did not deny my origin or my language, and I haven't betrayed my country. Instead, I seek an eternal home that will last longer than the entire earth.*
>
> (Lyrics: Harun Ibrahim, Music: Maher Fayez)

I decided I could not leave the situation with my family in Abu Gosh unresolved. I didn't want to mislead anybody or give the impression that I was not afraid—because I was—but I didn't want to let my fear paralyze me or take control of where I could go or what I could do. That would have been precisely the devil's plan. Many believe that the opposite of fear is courage, but it is not. According to Jesus, the opposite of fear is faith. In Luke 8:50, He says, "Do not be afraid; only believe..." On another occasion, Jesus said to the disciples, "Why are you fearful, O you of little faith?" (Matthew 8:26). Then Jesus got up and rebuked the winds and the waves, and it was completely calm.

So, I had to believe that the God who promised to always be with His followers would be faithful to His word in my case, too.

A month later, I told Sari that I was going to Israel, and despite her reservations, I booked my flight and rental car. When I arrived in Abu Gosh, I did something I did not normally do. I drove around the village long enough for everyone to see me. I rolled down my window to wave and greet many people. In hindsight, my behavior was probably quite foolish and even childish. Still, I was not thinking clearly at that moment because I had only one goal: to be free from the fear of intimidation.

After this, I went to my cousin's place of work and told him that my business was my business and had nothing to do with him. He said, "OK." That was it. Then I drove to my mother's house. She wasn't there, but another brother of mine was. I told him what had happened. He asked me, "Please don't say anything to Mother about this because she will be distraught." It sounded reasonable, and I followed his advice. After that, I have never mentioned the fatwa to my mother.

When the brother who had called me showed up, I hugged him and acted like nothing had happened. His relief was evident, and we went out together to get something to eat. We have never talked about the situation again.

My mom was happy about my coming. Without knowing the reason for my visit, she told the rest of the family that despite my Christian faith, I was free to come and go and that nobody was to interfere. I think the episode revealed, once again, something exceptional about what kind of a woman she is. She is a devoted Muslim woman who lost her husband many years ago, and later, her son became an "infidel." Not only did he convert from Islam to Christianity, but he became a missionary and is converting other Muslims to the wrong religion (from her point of view) and even straightforwardly criticizes the teachings of Islam through the ministry he does. Yet, despite all this, my mom still loves me!

Later, she showed her love when I brought my friends from Al Hayat to see her. They were Muslim-background believers just like me, so they too are apostates and infidels from the Islamic point of view.

When I brought them to her, she welcomed us all. She asked me, "Oh, by the way, are these friends like you?" (She meant converted.)

I answered her, "Yes, Mom, these are Muslim people who became Christians."

"Oh, OK," she responded. "Then I will prepare food for you and your guests."

Once, she even did so during Ramadan, although she was fasting herself. She went ahead and cooked us lunch anyway.

For a Muslim mother to behave in such a way is almost unheard of. It's against the teaching of Islam, and yet she did all of that because of the great love she has for me and all her children. I appreciate her so much for that.

11

Al Hayat into
the Hands of an MBB

When Sari, the boys, and I moved back to Finland in 1993, I parted ways with my friend Niilo. It would become a turning point in my ministry and even personally.

During our years in Sweden, I made many trips with Niilo, mainly to North Africa. I organized most of the trips and arranged the meetings at the destination. Yet, when we arrived there, I spent most of my time acting as Niilo's interpreter because he doesn't speak Arabic. I accepted this role, but often I would have also liked to discuss and preach myself and let the MBBs feel comfortable hearing messages in their language from another MBB. But at the same time, I didn't want to ignore Niilo and cause him to feel like an outsider. I was frustrated about the situation but never said anything about it.

Of course, my frustration was not Niilo's fault, and we could have communicated better with each other about our roles. I love Niilo, and I don't think he stood in my way while I was growing as a believer. Yet, I believe it was God's timing to separate us in 1993. Even after that, Niilo and I made several trips together, but I started to travel more alone or with other Arabic-speaking colleagues. And more importantly, the change gave me more independence in decision-making as a missionary and on the pastoral level. I needed to learn to make decisions by myself and even make mistakes and learn from them.

Niilo and I have very different personalities. He is more gifted in some areas than me, and vice versa. He is also more careful in his approach to things than I am; I am more of a risk-taker. I believe that without taking any of the risks that I've taken in ministry over the past thirty years, it would not have been as fruitful as it was.

So, being separated from Niilo, I was given more responsibilities in a ministry with great potential to grow worldwide. Unfortunately, we still see many mission organizations and churches with MBBs as employees or church members, but not one MBB in any leadership role. Some ministries have had discipleship programs for MBBs for fifty years, and despite that, those disciples are "not ready" to be true leaders. I wonder if it is because of a lack of trust in these people in particular or if it is a deeply rooted underestimating mindset about all MBB Christians. Sometimes it seems that more is required of MBBs than of Christian-background believers before they can be considered suitable for leadership positions.

I remember attending a conference in Cyprus in 2000 with about 250 people from several Arab countries and mission organizations. I was the only MBB at the meeting. One of the participants, a well-known Christian leader, stood up and said, "If a Muslim wants to know Christ, he will not go to former Muslims; he will go to the professionals." By "professionals," he meant educated ministers from a Christian background. I don't know how I was able to sit there and swallow that and remain silent. I think it was only because of the grace of God.

The longer I have been involved in ministry and the more I have read Church history, the more convinced I am that God looks at the heart, not our credentials or degrees. God's grace and the fire of trials make a leader worth following, not just their background or academic credentials. I'm not arguing against studying—I've done it myself and received my MTh degree in 2020 at Martin Bucer International Seminary in Germany (accredited by the Whitefield Theological Seminary). I'm just saying that without a heart shaped by God, any background itself is only smoke and will never produce lasting fruit.

These kinds of thoughts were on my mind in 2006 when Joyce Meyer Ministries wanted to hand over the operation of Al Hayat to me as an MBB—an act that differed entirely from the way such matters had been handled in the Middle East up to that point.

When Al Hayat started its operation, JMM had covered all the administrative and airtime (satellite transmission) costs as the sole owner. At Keymedia, we filmed part of the channel's content and raised the funding for it ourselves, as did all the other program producers. I was also involved, together with Gary, in evaluating the programming of the other contributors. All this time, however, JMM had planned to eventually appoint me as the official leader of Al Hayat, not just from an operational standpoint but also to oversee the spiritual content of the channel.

The plan also included that Joyce Meyer Ministries would no longer cover all the administrative and airtime costs but would instead pay 25 percent of the costs and that Al Hayat would bring on three new partners contributing 25 percent each. JMM said they would reduce their support by 25 percent each year (starting in 2006), giving Al Hayat three years to transition financial support to the new partners. We believed the plan was of the Lord. Through this new beginning, as I heard later, JMM believed that God would confirm the ministry of Al Hayat and my leadership by showing His faithfulness and helping us to implement the plan.

When word about the plan began to spread, many in Arabic Christian media ministry were surprised and confused. Some organizations expressed interest in becoming a partner of ours, but once the reality of the financial commitment sank in, most faded away. Several others expressed their concerns that it was too early for a move like this, and it could severely jeopardize the current and future fruitfulness of the channel. Many mission and funding organizations seemed to pre-judge the plan to fail and didn't want to give an MBB a chance to prove that he could lead this kind of ministry.

To Joyce Meyer Ministries, the risk of delaying the transfer of leadership for too long and not allowing an MBB to develop his gifts and train the next generation of MBBs seemed much more significant.

When the implementation of the plan was about to start, I had questions in my mind I needed an answer to:

1. Do I want to prove the critics right when they say an MBB cannot handle this kind of position?
2. When is the right time for MBBs to step forward and take responsibility and not be kept in the background or supporting roles only?
3. Do I want Middle Eastern Christian-background believers to continue believing that their Muslim-background brothers and sisters are unqualified second-class followers of Jesus?
4. Do I want Western organizations to believe the big lie that all MBBs are still mere infants in their Christianity and still need to be trained?
5. Do I have the faith to do this and to grab the opportunity offered by the JMM?

Being the official leader of the channel was a huge challenge that I needed to work hard to meet. When we started implementing the plan in 2006, we had no substantial commitments to pick up the shortfall caused by the declining portion of JMM funding. Due to that, covering the missing funds for the first year was challenging already, the second year would be a significant challenge, and the third year would be the most arduous of all. As the channel's new leader, I knew the responsibility for finding financing would rest heavily on my shoulders.

Despite the difficulties, I did not want to withdraw from the agreement with JMM. Still, I must admit there were tough moments. One emerged in the first year of 2006 when some of the financial partners we had secured for that year revealed that they could not continue their support after that. Yet, they promised us programs and intercessory support, and we were, of course, grateful for all that. At the same time, however, their decision increased our financial challenges.

Gary and Christine Preston, dear friends of Sari and me since 2003. Gary's godly advice has saved me from many difficult situations.

The situation was not made any easier when a rumor emerged that Joyce Meyer Ministries gave so much money to Al Hayat that I was swimming in a pool of dollars and didn't need anybody's help. I heard this from many people, and for me, it was no surprise—spreading rumors is part of Middle Eastern culture. Often, even the wildest story is considered a fact until proven wrong, and even after that, many people prefer to believe the lie anyway.

One of the people who spread this rumor met me at a conference in Germany. The person worked for another Christian TV channel, and he told me straight-forwardly, "Harun, you do not need to raise funds. Joyce Meyer Ministries gives you everything you need and a little above." Then he informed me that he had also told this "fact" to a German donor who wanted to help us but decided not to help because of this news.

Others spread the claim that we were troublemakers in the Middle East. We fought against such allegations for years. It was tough to forgive them and just let it go, but I had no choice.

New Ministry Partners and Friends

The original plan of having three new owners for Al Hayat, each of whom would have taken over 25 percent of the channel's broadcasting and management costs on behalf of JMM, didn't materialize. However, we got several new ministry partners who helped us with program production, follow-up ministry, special projects, and also airtime costs. Their support helped us to overcome the financial challenges we faced when JMM reduced their contribution in line with our plan.

Here, I want to introduce some of these new friends from 2004 to 2010. They all are precious people and worthy of their biographies. Each has had a remarkable role in the ministry's development, and many have served on Al Hayat's board.

The 2004 conference, where I was heavily criticized and had to retreat to my room several times to cry, also saw positive developments. At the event, I was asked to present my Paltalk ministry to three gentlemen: Paul Schultheis from Strategic Resource Group (SRG), Ben Edwards from Christian Broadcast Network (CBN), and Ron Williams from Cornerstone Foundation. They had already heard about Al Hayat and Father Zakaria, but they were much more interested in how I was working online with my Paltalk chat room. Satellite TV was nothing new to them, but the Paltalk represented cutting-edge technology.

As a result of the meeting, Cornerstone Foundation became our partner organization and blessed Al Hayat very generously. SRG became one of the largest resource partners for Al Hayat from 2005 to 2018—as they have been for many other ministries working in the Middle East and North Africa. With CBN, we began a great, close partnership on different levels. Not only were they strong resource partners to us, but we also learned a lot from their skills in TV production, especially from their Arabic department leader at that time, Dani Sleiman.

Next, I have to mention pastors Dave Gibson and Piers van der Merwe and their congregations, Grace Church in Eden Prairie, Minnesota, and Cedar Springs Presbyterian Church in Nashville, Tennessee.

Pastor Dave and I met through the advice of our mutual friend, Victor Hashweh. I was visiting Israel in 2007 at the same time that Dave was in Jordan, and Victor said we should meet. So, I drove to Amman, met my friend Marwan Qandah, and we picked up Dave together. It was spring, and the weather in Amman was bright and beautiful.

When I saw Pastor Dave, I thought, "What a Nordic-looking man." Dave is tall and blond—like a Viking warrior, but without a beard and with an almost constant smile on his face. He was very friendly, and almost from the first minute, you could sense that he is a man of God and full of love for the mission. Still, what impressed me most was how good an evangelist he is. He is an exemplary evangelist who uses every opportunity to share the gospel. I once thought, "Pastor Dave loves preaching the gospel so much that if there were no one to tell the gospel to, he would look in the mirror and preach the gospel to himself."

Later, I was introduced to his church, Grace Church, in Eden Prairie, Minnesota. Grace Church became a close partner and supporter of Al Hayat, as did Cedar Springs Presbyterian Church in Nashville, Tennessee.

Piers van der Merwe, a pastor at Cedar Springs Presbyterian, I came to know in early 2010 when I planned to attend the yearly partnership conference for Christian organizations on Arabic ministry in the Middle East and North Africa. I had participated in the event many times, and, as always, the meeting place was in one southern European country. Before the travel, I received an email from Cedar Springs from a mission pastor introducing himself as Piers van der Merwe. We didn't know each other before but met at the conference. I came to know Piers as a real gentleman.

Like Pastor Dave, Piers also has a beautiful spirit. Although busy, his heart is driven to reach the unreached people groups. Grace Church and Cedar Springs always make me feel at home.

The same cozy feeling is present when I'm with the Maclellan family and Leslie and Peter Strong—the last partners to mention here. Our path with the Maclellan family started in 2008 when we wanted to create a new discipleship series for Al Hayat. We had approached several organizations for support to cover the production costs but without success. Then, while at a networking conference in Helsinki, we were introduced to the Maclellan Foundation. So we applied for a grant, and, praise the Lord, it was accepted. The series title was *Making Disciples*, and the teacher there was Father Zakaria.

That connection opened the door to one of the most impressive partnerships we have. Hugh O. Maclellan Jr., Robert Maclellan, and their families are wonderful, godly people. I learned that the foundation has dramatically impacted numerous peoples' lives worldwide and encouraged many Christians to donate to the mission. One of the beneficiaries of their blessings was a young man named Billy Graham, who later became one of the world's most famous evangelists. The Maclellans' hearts truly beat for the mission. We are praying that they will be a blessing to many more in the future.

Leslie and Peter Strong came into my life at a mission conference in Arizona where I was one of the speakers. Like all the meetings mentioned above, this proved to be a divine appointment, for which I am grateful to God. Our relationship with Leslie and Peter has become so close that I call Leslie my sister from another mister and Peter my brother from another mother. One thing that especially unites us is our mutual love for Israel. I love to sit at their oval kitchen table in Seattle, sharing our hearts and praying together. Large windows on two sides of the table offer a stunning view of Puget Sound (a Pacific bay off Seattle). I could spend hours there—and thankfully, I have. The Strong's beautiful home has also served as the venue for several board meetings of Al Hayat.

Dreams and Visions

In 2006, a remarkable video production called *More Than Dreams* was published by our ministry partner. The series includes five true stories of Muslims who experienced meeting with Jesus in a dream or in a vision and converted to Christianity.

The high-quality series was created in docu-drama format. The episodes have been dubbed into several languages and broadcast on many TV channels—several times on Al Hayat alone. Millions have seen the series all over the world.

One story is that of an Egyptian man named Khalil (name changed for security reasons). Khalil's story was first told in a book, *Sons of Ishmael,* which I wrote and our Children of Ishmael team published in 1999. In the book, his name is Paul. That's not his real name either, but he has often called himself by that name because, like Paul in the Bible, he persecuted the Church before his conversion. Khalil/Paul was part of our Children of Ishmael team in Egypt for a long time.

Experiencing Jesus in dreams or visions is one of the most exciting phenomena in Muslim ministry. Like Saul of Tarsus, who became Apostle Paul after seeing the resurrected Jesus on the road to Damascus (Acts 9), numerous Muslim men and women have been transformed after following the instructions of a "figure of light" who has identified himself as the Jesus of Christianity. Many of these Muslims have had no previous knowledge of the gospel nor contact with Christians.

I first learned about these cases in Sweden back in the 1980s, and the mission organizations have referred to them more repeatedly since the 1990s. When we read the viewer feedback we receive at Al Hayat today, we see that the supernatural dreams and visions are still there.

One explanation for the phenomenon is the role of dreams and visions in Islam. For Muslims, they are practically the only means by which an individual may expect to hear something directly from God, so they are a useful cultural tool for God to get Muslims' attention. When Muslims see "a figure of light" in a dream, they instantly know what it's about.

When researchers have surveyed the factors behind Muslims' decisions to convert to Christianity, the impact of supernatural dreams and visions has emerged repeatedly. Many of these surveys focus on a particular region or a specific ethnic Muslim group, and the factors seem to vary somewhat by region. However, the following five characteristics are repeated in almost all surveys (wording and percentages may differ):

- Being fascinated by Jesus' personality. A Muslim receives information about the person of Christ and finds his life and teachings attractive.
- Being impressed by the love of Christians. A Muslim meets Christians who witness their faith through words, loving deeds, and respectable lifestyles.
- Experiencing the living Jesus. A Muslim experiences a miracle of healing, receives an answer to prayer, or has a dream or vision, and interprets it as a miraculous act of the living Jesus.
- Disappointment with Islam. It may be caused by the violence of jihadists, Islam's distant God, the religious legalism offered by imams, etc.
- Becoming convinced that the Bible is God's Word. A Muslim reads the New Testament and feels it to be spiritual truth.

In one US survey, 25 percent of respondents said dreams and visions were a crucial factor in drawing them to Christ. That's a lot, but it still means that most MBBs (like me) haven't experienced anything like that during their conversion process. That reminds us of the meaning of gospel preaching. Even when one has had such a supernatural experience, becoming a mature Christian requires hearing the Word and receiving teaching.

To conclude this section, I would like to tell you one of the vision stories I have heard. It happened to a Qatari man who had gone on a pilgrimage to Mecca. He performed the required rituals there but did not receive the peace of God he had come for. So, he left the crowd of pilgrims and went for a walk. He arrived at a large bus parking area (pilgrims in Mecca are transported from their accommodation to the ritual sites by buses). As he passed the line of buses, one bus driver drew his attention.

"What's bothering you?" the driver asked the man. He replied that he had come to Mecca to have God-given peace within himself but had not experienced any. Then the bus driver asked him, "Have you seen any Jesus films? If not, watch one."

When the pilgrimage was over, the man returned to Qatar, thinking about the strange advice of the bus driver. The man had a Christian colleague and asked if he owned any Jesus films. The colleague did, and he brought the movie to the man on a VHS tape.

When the film started, the man was surprised: the actor playing Jesus was the bus driver he had met in Mecca! The man realized the encounter in Mecca had been a vision, and it had been the real Jesus who had appeared to him in the character of the Jesus actor and guided him to watch the film. The miraculous event led the man to learn more about Christianity, and soon he accepted Jesus as Christ and Savior. Later, he told his story to my friend.

New Programs

When Al Hayat was making its breakthrough, my Moroccan friend Rachid moved to the USA. One day in 2005, I called him and challenged him to participate in the ministry of Al Hayat. I thought he would be a perfect host for a TV show. He was a son of an imam, and before his conversion, he had been preparing to follow in his father's footsteps as a Muslim scholar. He had memorized large portions of the Qur'an and was highly qualified to contrast Christianity with Islam. All of this was valuable knowledge to our ministry.

When I told him about my idea, he said he didn't know anything about TV production but would think about the issue. He shared it with his wife and later told me her answer was, "You? On TV?" Others were not very encouraging either. Some said he would have to pay a high personal price if he went on TV. Still, later, he called me and said, "I'm ready."

So, our journey with Rachid continued. I invited him to Nashville, together with a Jerusalemite named Elias, to produce a series called *Unveil the Mask*. There, we recorded the program in our partner organization's studios a few times, each time taping twenty-six episodes. Later, the same partner felt challenged to start a live call-in show for Al Hayat. It would be the first such program in the Christian Arab world. We asked Rachid if he would be willing to be the host. His answer was again positive, and Rachid's ministry in Al Hayat became full-time. A show called *Soal Jaree—Daring Question*—was launched and quickly became a huge success. In addition to the live calls, the show included interviews with MBBs and daily questions about different topics, such as the persecution of religious minorities. The program confronted Islam's deceptions, contradictions, and cruelties but was more practical and less detailed than Father Zakaria's TV series.

The first episode was exciting. The call-in phone system was overwhelmed because of many callers. Since then, people have accepted Christ on-air in significant numbers—a pivotal moment for ministry to Muslims. The show continued for twelve years and became one of the most popular programs on all Arabic Christian television. In each live broadcast, Rachid prayed for callers who wanted to become followers of Jesus. In this way, millions of viewers saw "live" how to become a Christian.

The same applies to our other live broadcasts, such as *The Muslim Woman*, which we started in 2009. The program deals with the relationship of women in Muslim culture to God, family, and society. The episodes have addressed traditionally taboo topics in Muslim communities, such as domestic violence, incest, child marriage, and rape. I had been thinking about a show like this for a long time and had prayed for the right MBB women to host this show. Then the Lord delivered once again. We found four women—sisters Farha, Amani, Nadim, and Mariam—and filmed the first set of episodes in Nashville.

The show started with big potential to become very popular. For the first time in the history of the Arabic world, four MBB women were sharing testimonies, revealing the deceptions of Islam and bringing to light the treatment of women in Islam.

The hosts' teachings about the Bible, conversations with viewers who call in, prayers with and for them, and discussion of the lives of Muslim women touched both women and men. These women have become some of Al Hayat's best-known program makers and role models, especially for women from Muslim backgrounds. The show, broadcast live on Friday evenings, has become one of the most commented shows on the channel, and it is still ongoing.

Sister Amani hosting *The Muslim Woman* live show. Al Hayat's popular live broadcasts are usually made on the West Coast of the US at local time in the morning, conveniently the prime time for evening viewing in the Middle East and Europe.

A little later, we began producing another significant series with another friend, Waheed, who had helped me in my Paltalk ministry. He had served as a Bible school teacher in the Netherlands, and I decided to challenge also him to join Al Hayat. He is a Christian-born believer but has a heart for Muslims.

When I told him about my idea, he agreed but asked if it was possible to wear some make-up to disguise his appearance. I said, "Do you want the short answer or the long answer? My short answer is, 'No.' My long answer is, 'No, definitely no.' Either you go in front of the camera as you are or not at all."

Then I boldly told him, "Brother Waheed, what if an MBB calls you and tells you that he is afraid and worried that his family will find out he is a Christian? What would you tell him? Wouldn't you tell him to read Psalm 23 and Romans 8:31: 'If God is for us, who can be against us?'"

We agreed to pray over the issue for two weeks. Less than two weeks had passed when Waheed called me, saying, "I'm ready. Your last question in the discussion was terrible, but I thank you for it. You woke me up."

So, we started taping a series called *Doubts and Answers*, for which we filmed 204 episodes. Then we began a new program with Waheed and his wife Fadwa, a live call-in show called *Al Daleel*, meaning "The Guide." It is still produced, and it is one of my personal favorites on Al Hayat. If you compare TV shows to eating a meal, there you have a good, healthy, tasty, and satisfying meal. Brother Waheed knows the Bible and has wisdom and maturity of character. In my opinion, he has become one of the best apologists in the Arab world. He acts godly with the Muslim callers even if they attack and sometimes curse him.

One of my gifts, which I thank the Lord for, is identifying people with talent and giving them the opportunity to develop their gifts.

Although we are an Arabic channel, we also kept in touch with organizations reaching Muslims in other languages. In 2007, some ministries from the Nordic countries and others from different parts of the world came together and decided to start a Christian satellite channel for the Turkish-speaking world. The channel's name was ETC TV. They also approached Al Hayat and asked if we could produce some Turkish programs for it. So Gary Preston dubbed Joyce Meyer's and Father Zakaria's episodes into Turkish. Later, we were asked to join the ETC TV board. We suggested the channel's name be changed to Kanal Hayat, which means "the Channel of Life" or "Life Channel" in Turkish. Other board members liked the idea and made the change.

Father Zakaria's shows were on Kanal Hayat for two years. Then some Turkish brothers said Zakaria's Islam criticism was too much for the Turkish-speaking world at that time, so we removed the programs from the 24/7 stream and made them available only on social media. Nevertheless, we continue to be a part of Kanal Hayat, which has proven an effective means to reach Turkish people with the gospel.

Reaching New Audiences

One day, we received word that Nilesat and Arabsat, two famous secular Middle Eastern satellite companies, would be able to broadcast Christian programming soon. However, both channels had reported one exception: Al Hayat was not welcome because of our approach.

When I heard about it, I had an idea: what if we tried to get to these satellites under a different name? We started with Nilesat, and the plan worked: we got in. Soon, however, the satellite company executives discovered the content was the same as Al Hayat and dropped us after only 95 hours. It was still quite a long time to be on Nilesat, the most popular satellite provider in the Middle East and North Africa, which had a larger audience than the HotBird satellite we were using.

We were not discouraged and tried again, now to Arabsat. This time they dropped us off after only 22 hours. I called my friend who had informed us about the opportunity and said, "You can call the other Christian channels [since 2003, many new Arabic Christian channels had started] and tell them about Nilesat and Arabsat. That way, if not through us, at least Jesus will be preached on those satellites."

In 2009, one of my dearest friends, Abu Yehia, a German missionary in the Gulf who worked for a mission organization called Hilfe für Mensch und Kirche (HMK), told me that the brothers and sisters in Yemen were so disappointed that Al Hayat was not broadcasting on a satellite that could reach them.

I have seen many Western, Christian-background missionaries working in the Middle East and North Africa. Some of them have become very well integrated into Arabic culture and can communicate the love of Christ effectively to Muslims. My friend Abu Yehia, "My Yemeni German" as I like to call him, is one of them. One of the compliments that we MBBs use when we meet someone like him is to say, "You are an MBB, but one that was just born in the West."

After what Abu told me about Yemen, I started looking for a way to broadcast there. Then I found out about the ABS-1 satellite that reaches Yemen and the very south of Saudi Arabia. So I called my Israeli friend Lior Rival, who is in the TV business, and asked him for advice. He promised to investigate the issue. At the time, I was traveling in Israel, and two days later, at 9 p.m., while driving from Samaria back to Jerusalem, I got a call from Lior.

He said, "If you want to be on ABS-1, there is a free spot right now, but you have to give me a deposit of two months, and the price for the year is $250,000."

That was exceptionally expensive to reach only one country. Still, I had a burden to do something for believers there. They felt neglected, and Abu Yehia was such a good friend that I wanted to help him reach the people God had put in his heart.

I called Abu and asked, "Do you have faith?"

He replied, "Yes." I informed him that we had to come up with $250,000. After hesitating and speaking for a while, we decided to go forward, even though we didn't have approval from either of our boards.

Sometimes, I have heard it is better to ask forgiveness than for permission. I must disagree, but this time it worked. The board of HMK informed Abu that it was not good that he had made that kind of decision before coming to them, but they were still happy about the decision. The board of Al Hayat said much the same thing. HMK is one of the best mission organizations I've ever met. They are prayer warriors—kind and godly people. Our relationship has grown stronger and stronger throughout the years. I feel as if we are one family.

In autumn 2010, Lior Rival approached us with a new opportunity to broadcast on Nilesat, and this time permanently.

Satellite owners' attitudes to Muslim evangelism had not changed, but they had leased some of the satellite's transmission capacity to independent European contractors. After that, the owners had no say in whom the contractors leased that capacity to. One of these contactor companies was run by Lior, so he was able to help us get Al Hayat on Nilesat. Our potential audience grew remarkably, which we took as a gift from God.

Although online TV and TV apps have increased significantly in Arabic countries, one can still see satellite dishes everywhere—on top of buildings in cities and the roofs of huts in the desert. A photo from Algeria.

As the Yemeni example showed, satellite broadcasting is extremely expensive. Later, with the proliferation of mobile devices and the growing popularity of the internet and social media platforms, we decided to leave HotBird and some other satellite operators we had been using to focus on internet TV and mobile applications. Currently, we broadcast Al Hayat on Nilesat for Europe, North Africa, and the Middle East and on the Optus D2 satellite for Australia. However, the potential audience for Al Hayat satellite broadcasting is still more than 300 million, as Nilesat can reach the entire Arabic-speaking world.

A Controversy and a Reconciliation

One of the most painful events in all my ministry happened in the winter of 2009–2010 when, unfortunately, another Christian channel abused our trust. Without going into the details, they accused us of taking a big check meant for Father Zakaria and putting it into the Al Hayat account, and they told Zakaria this. The rumor was a big lie. We had never received such funds and will never use any funds designated for others. Such an accusation was a classic thing that happens to ministries; when the devil's attacks from the outside don't work, he attacks from the inside through other Christians.

What made it even worse was that the accusations were echoed by many Christian leaders in the Middle East, blaming me, saying, "How could you do this to this man of God?" Some even volunteered to help Father Zakaria take me to court, and one of the leaders wrote a letter to our Finnish leaders telling them how bad I was. The content of his letter was something that almost sounded like it came from Hollywood movies—so imaginative and wild was it. These same people had forgotten that only six years earlier, they objected to seeing Father Zakaria on the air, claiming that it was improper to use this style in Muslim evangelism. Now they were behind him but against us one more time.

To resolve the matter, we had an audit. Fourteen people representing different organizations came together, and I sat in front of them and answered questions. I remember those moments as if they happened yesterday. All I had in mind were the words I had heard many times, especially from my dear friend Gary Preston: "Don't defend yourself; just let God work." He told me I should just shut my mouth when I am attacked because if Christians defend themselves, they say to God, "We don't need an advocate." If we close our mouths instead, He will fight for us, as it says in Exodus 14:14: "The LORD will fight for you, and you shall hold your peace." So, at the audit, I tried to keep my answers short—just giving them the information they asked me without any accusations.

In the end, Al Hayat and I were found to be clean, but the process had left a wound in the relationship between our team and Father Zakaria, and he decided to separate from Al Hayat in May 2010. He went to another channel, but was there only for three weeks because they could not be faithful to their promises. Later, he chose to start his own channel.

All this turmoil we had gone through turned out to be a blessing. After Father Zakaria left, some people expected Al Hayat to be negatively impacted, but it was the exact opposite. All other programs on Al Hayat began to grow in popularity. Viewer responses for *Daring Question*, *The Guide*, *The Muslim Woman*, Joyce Meyer's *Enjoying Everyday Life*, and other shows grew daily. So, God turned the painful things into a better plan. And best of all, we had a sweet reconciliation with Father Zakaria three years later. He is very dear to my heart. I bless him, and so does the entire Al Hayat family.

Every day we received responses from viewers. One of the most memorable responses during that period came from a Syrian man. He sent it as a letter, which had become rare. Most viewer responses at that time came via email.

The letter was written in beautiful handwriting, and the author told us he was 93 years old. In addition, he wrote,

> I have been doubting Islam for many years. Then I found your channel, Al Hayat. I have watched your channel since. I watch all the programs. I like them all and am convinced I know the true God now. I know that the Lord Jesus Christ died for me, and He is my Redeemer.

> I made this decision almost at the end of my life. It makes me very happy but, at the same time, sad because I wish somebody could have told me about God's love in Jesus earlier. But instead, I spent almost all my life following a false god that handles his people with an iron hand, writing their deeds and destiny in advance, and still, he punishes them when they are doing what he already planned for them to do.

I hope that no one experiences this terrible disappointment as I did. Please continue telling Muslims and the whole world about my beloved Jesus. I will be praying for you. Thank you again for opening my eyes to come out of the darkness into the light.

Whenever I remember this man's response, two thoughts come to my mind.

First, this is what it is all about!

Second, are we really doing all we can to reach people and bring them the word of life?

12

Internet:
A Tool in the Right Hands,
a Weapon in the Wrong Hands

By around 2010, the global media sphere was changing rapidly. People worldwide had become increasingly aware of the power of the internet, and the Muslim population was no exception. People started communicating with others beyond their borders, and many were searching for the spiritual truth. Over the next several years, streaming television through the internet (IPTV, Internet Protocol Television) became popular in many regions. Social media was taking off.

In this situation, many Muslim preachers also started using the internet and social media to spread their interpretations of Islam. Even terrorist organizations such as al-Qaeda and ISIS found the new media platforms to be an effective tool. These organizations began uploading horrific videos to the web, using them to communicate with fanatics and give orders for action. In some cases, these jihadist groups even published the exact locations of Christian missionaries so they could be persecuted or even killed.

One of the platforms that Muslim extremists have particularly used is Telegram. This communications program was founded in 2013 by the Russian-born brothers Nikolai and Pavel Durov. ISIS, for example, has used Telegram to hold meetings, publish videos, and send out their newsletter titled *The Harvest*. I was not surprised when I saw the newsletter for the first time. It was well-presented with nice graphics, and it reported how many killings or attacks on Christians had recently been carried out. But I have been surprised that the intelligence organizations of the West haven't been able to interfere with this.

If I tell the truth, I think Islamic terrorist organizations have taken way more advantage of the internet and social media than most Christian organizations have.

It is a strange coincidence that the name of the ISIS media wing is "Al Hayat Media." Even their logo is very similar to ours. I wonder if they did this purposefully or just by chance. As mentioned above, the word *al hayat* means life, but in their case, it is all about death.

Exposed to the Internet

At the beginning of 2010, I was contacted by an Egyptian man who said he was a Christian but who most likely was not. He told me, "I heard you are the treasurer of the MBB Fund. I heard you pay $3,000 a month as support to MBBs." Then he continued, "My wife is an MBB, and I would like to take her share."

With a straight face, I tried to explain to him that there was nothing called an "MBB Fund" and that we never bribe people to come to Jesus. (Later, this gave me a good idea for a song I wrote, which says, "People think we buy people for Jesus with money, but the price is much higher. It is the blood that Jesus shed on the cross.")

The guy didn't believe me, and in revenge, he wrote an article about me for a well-known Egyptian newspaper. He knew who I was through my meeting him on Paltalk. In the article, he revealed my real name, Sari's name, that we live in Finland, and that I was an Israeli Arab. He then added the magic words that work in every Muslim country, "Harun Ibrahim is a captain in the Israeli [intelligence agency] Mossad, and the Mossad pays him $75,000 a month to convert Muslims to Christianity." (I did not know the Mossad pays that well. I can assure you I've never seen a check like this.)

I tried my very best to keep calm, and I forgave him. But a year and a half later, on November 15, 2011, one of the jihadi websites wrote about me. The author of the article was a Palestinian living in Finland. He had taken the information from the article published in the Egyptian magazine. In addition, he or the website staff had done an excellent job of hacking into the computer of one of our program hosts and got a hold of many emails between the program team. With the article, the website published the emails, a picture and address of Keymedia's facilities in Finland, pictures of Niilo and me, and the fact that Sari and I lived in Kerava, Finland. Then they indirectly asked people to kill me.

This was not good news. We called the Finnish National Bureau of Investigation and got advice from them. We installed security cameras in the Keymedia building, and some of our friends recommended to Sari and I that we should move. One of them was Victor Hashweh's wife, Maha, a great woman of God. She offered to sell a piece of land she owned and give us the money to buy a house and change our address. Sari and I prayed and felt it was not the right move to go and hide.

A photoshopped humorous picture of me, Father Zakaria, and my "twin brother." A jihadist website got hold of the image and thought it was real. On the right, the original photo of me, Father Zakaria, and Dani Sleiman.

The funniest thing the website published was a picture my friend Dani Sleiman had photoshopped a few years before. He had taken a photo of him, Father Zakaria, and me, put my face onto his body, and wrote the subject, "Here is Harun, Father Zakaria, and Harun's twin brother Abu Ali." The jihadi website published the photo with the text. At the time, it was not funny, but now I think it's funny that I can look in the mirror and say hello to me and my twin brother.

Arab Spring — Hopes and Disappointments

In 2011, anti-government protests and armed rebellions spread across the Arab world, and for a while, it seemed that the whole region was coming apart at the seams. The movement quickly became known as the "Arab Spring."

The events began in Tunisia after the self-immolation of a poor street vendor named Mohamed Bouazizi in mid-December 2010. His act of desperation won the sympathy of local people fed up with corruption and repression, and massive protests around the country ensued. After widespread international coverage, the demonstrations spread to Egypt, Libya, Syria, Yemen, and Bahrain, and—on a smaller scale—more than ten countries, from Morocco to Oman, Lebanon, and Sudan. People everywhere hoped the movement would finally end corruption, bring true democracy, increase economic justice, and improve human rights.

The Arab Spring was an example of the political role that social media and the internet can play in today's world. Activists used Facebook to plan protests, Twitter to coordinate demonstrations, and YouTube to share video footage of the protests worldwide. The rapid and real-time communication of internet bloggers and mobile phone users proved to be crucial in challenging the existing regimes. Al Hayat also covered the movement in its programs—the avalanche of events touched the lives of Christians in the region, who hoped for greater tolerance and freedom for themselves. All other religious minorities had the same hope. Many from these minorities participated in the protests.

As a result of the demonstrations, rulers Zine El Abidine Ben Ali (Tunisia), Muammar Gaddafi (Libya), Hosni Mubarak (Egypt), and Ali Abdallah Saleh (Yemen) were deposed. Still, in most countries, only a few, if any, of the demonstrators' original aspirations were realized. The demonstrators faced violent responses from authorities, counter-protesters, and militaries. Things turned into a mess. Civil wars started in Syria, Yemen, and Libya. In Egypt, the radical Islamic group, Muslim Brotherhood, took over for a while.

As I'm writing this, Tunisia is the only country where the uprising resulted in a transition to constitutional democratic governance, and even there, the social situation has since deteriorated again. Many have started to call the Arab Spring the Arab Winter.

The turn of events caused much confusion, especially among the young people, who started to ask questions like, "Is this what we fought for?", "Do things never change?", "Why should we go back to the past?" Some began to reflect on the link between Islam and the collapse of the protesters' dreams. Later, the mistrust of Islam was reinforced by the brutal violence of ISIS and other extremist groups. As a result, many young Arabic people have moved from Islam to another religion—especially Christianity—or atheism. Arab atheist groups have gained popularity in the region, though the number of non-religious Arabs is unclear. In many countries, abandoning Islam is illegal, which means that most do not dare to reveal their new non-Islamic identity to pollsters. In addition, because of the awkwardness of the phenomenon, governments try to conceal such information.

The Message Safely through a Mobile Phone

Since the days of the Arab Spring, the use of social media in Muslim-dominated countries has continued to expand, coinciding with the rapid growth of mobile phone subscribers. In 2013, the world's highest percentage of Twitter users lived in Saudi Arabia! At the same time, the internet penetration in Bahrain, Qatar, and the United Arab Emirates exceeded 90 percent of the population—reaching this number earlier than in countries such as the US, Canada, Germany, and Australia (Statista, Internet Live Stats). Since then, Arab countries, especially in the Gulf, have been among the global trendsetters in internet and social media use.

All this had a tremendous effect on the Arabic Christian TV ministry. One can imagine the empowerment viewers feel when all they have to do is pick up their mobile device to interact with the ministry whose content they've just watched. Mobile applications also offer users more opportunities to search for information and watch programs safely, even with their non-Christian family members around—an option that traditional television doesn't have. TV is a family affair, but mobile devices allow people to watch the content independently at any time.

All this led Al Hayat to make a strategic decision in 2010. While we had used the internet from the beginning, in 2010, we began to develop shorter program formats particularly well suited to social media. This was followed by creating our own mobile apps, live streaming, and podcasting MP3 audio. We also wanted to move the follow-up—answering viewers' questions— to these platforms as much as possible.

At the same time, technological developments offered us many new ways to collect and analyze viewer feedback. The most notable were the Facebook and YouTube engagements, likes, dislikes, comments, shares, and video views. The new audiences and feedback categories rapidly multiplied the total number of viewer responses, as the following figures show:

- In 2011, the channel and its program makers received around 393,000 responses—emails, phone calls, letters, text messages, voicemails, etc.
- In 2012, after we started to count the Facebook and YouTube reactions, the total number of viewer reactions was almost 2.76 million.
- In 2013, the number rose to 8.74 million.
- In 2014, the figure was almost 13 million. At that time, more than 97 percent of the responses and reactions were received and collected via social media.

Later, we stopped counting social media page "likes" as feedback when it became possible for anyone to buy them. Even so, as I write this, the latest feedback figure (for 2023) was more than 109 million viewer engagements and interactions and around 236 million downloads and streams on our internet and social media platforms in one year.

I feel that God has given us modern technology as a tool. How complicated and expensive global communication was just a few decades ago! Communication technology has become central to proclaiming the gospel among all nations.

Poisoning in Spain

One of the things people must know is that the devil never gives up. He tries to attack the Christian community from the outside and inside, and if that doesn't work, sometimes through Christians' health.

In 2014, while traveling in Spain, I was writing at my desk when I felt a prick in my left arm—probably, there was some splinter on the table's surface. I looked at my arm and saw that I had a small cut. Despite the cut's size, my hand soon became painful, so I saw the doctor. He said it was a minor infection and gave me a shot. The next morning, however, I had terrible pain, and I booked an earlier flight home.

After arriving in Finland, I went to the health center, and the doctor there said the same thing—it seemed to be a small and harmless infection. But as I was leaving the room, he stopped me and said, "Wait… you need to go to the hospital and have a blood test."

In the hospital, after a blood test, a specialist came to see me. He looked at my hand and told me that he suspected a more severe bacterial infection and that the situation was worrisome.

"You need to stay here. We may have to open your hand," he said.

So, I spent the night in the hospital. In the middle of the night, I felt so much pain that I rang the bell. I told the nurses about my agony, and they called a doctor to see me. When the doctor came and saw that my arm was getting vast and red (it had been swollen and red before, but now it was almost glowing and looked more like a pumpkin), she decided to operate on it immediately. All the operating rooms were occupied, but my situation couldn't wait, so they brought the equipment into my room. They didn't even have time to give me an anesthetic, and when the doctor made the incision in the skin, blood sprayed out of my arm.

They told me it had been a bacteria called *Staphylococcus aureus*. It's a common bacterium that causes a wide range of skin and soft tissue infections, some of which are very serious. Later, one of my doctor friends told me I had been fortunate. If the cut on my skin had been only 0.04 inches (one millimeter) closer to a vein, the infection would have gone straight to my heart, and my heart could have stopped.

Praise the Lord; through prayer and knowledgeable doctors, I made a complete recovery.

13

Dialect-Based Programs and Other Innovations

When my Egyptian MBB friends and I started the Children of Ishmael organization in 1991, one of our dreams was to have a publishing ministry. Yet it took almost ten years to release our first book, *Sons of Ishmael*, in which I collected several MBB testimonies. This was followed by *Kāfir* (Infidel), *Son of Kāfir*, *Evangelist's Guide*, *Dialogue with a Muslim Friend*, and many more, as well as evangelistic tracts like *Everlasting God*. Most of the authors were MBBs. In addition, we translated numerous books into Arabic, such as *The Call of God*, *The Heavenly Man*, and *Messiah of the New Testament and Messiah of the Old Testament*.

Of course, Arabic Christian literature had been available for years, and we had been using it since the 1980s. Still, the number of titles was very limited, and we felt that many books available were not best suited to the needs of MBBs and Muslims.

For MBBs, we saw a need for gospel-centered, Bible-based materials that would introduce them to the good news, the teachings of Christ, and the transforming power of His love—recognizing the specific challenges Muslim-background people have in understanding these things.

For Muslims and spiritual seekers, we wanted to produce apologetic books and booklets that would present the truths of

Christianity and expose the deceptions of Islam. The viewpoint was the same we later took with many programs on Al Hayat.

When we started the book production, we quickly encountered a problem: how to finance, market and distribute our literature. Although we found publishers for our books, in many cases we had to finance the printing costs ourselves because the publishers didn't see how to market and distribute such controversial books. The magazine *Awraq-leltanweer* ("Pages of Enlightenment"), which we produced from 1991 to 1995, was available in some Christian bookstores in Egypt, but these bookstores didn't want to help us with our books and tracts. They thought our books were too controversial and it would be too dangerous for them to distribute them.

We understood that. Rejecting Islam is a red rag in Muslim culture, and it's hard to avoid criticizing Islam when discussing Muslims' decisions to convert to Christianity. Distributing such literature in a Muslim-majority country could jeopardize or even end one's bookstore business. This was an eye-opener for us, and we began considering setting up our own distribution system. Later, it became a reality with the Al Hayat channel. We set book production as one of the goals of Al Hayat Ministries, and we started to publish books ourselves using the name Water Life Publishing.

In 2007, we took a step forward with Islam-analyzing books. We put together a team to research and produce literature that examines Islam in a way that is highly academic in its methodology but focuses on the questions appropriate for our audience. The team's biggest challenge to date is a three-part Qur'an commentary series, *Qur'an Dilemma: Former Muslims Analyze Islam's Holiest Book*, published in Arabic and English between 2011 and 2021. The series analyzes each Qur'anic verse and offers special articles on many topics related to the Qur'an and Islam.

The next phase began in early 2016, when we joined forces with the European Institute for Islamic Research, Inârah. The

Arabic word *inârah* means the "Enlightenment." This highly respected institute is dedicated to the scientific, historical-critical, and philological study of the Qur'an, the origins of Islam, and its early history. The establishment of the Institute was a response to new research findings in the historiography of Islam. Modern analysis by the Inârah scholars and others had shown that the standard Islamic account of Muhammad, the Qur'an, and the emergence of Islam has little or nothing in common with historical reality and the well-established parameters of late antiquity in the Middle East. Previously, even academic research had uncritically accepted the traditional narrative of the rise and spread of Islam.

Inârah's research group includes internationally renowned professors such as Dr. Claude Gilliot, Dr. Markus Gross, Dr. Karl-Heinz Ohlig, Dr. Gerd-Rüdiger Puin, Dr. Elizabeth Puin, and Dr. Robert Kerr. The cooperation with these scholars has been rewarding, for which we at Al Hayat are very grateful. Over the years, the Inârah team has published more than ten books, and every year we release together a new volume in the *Entstehung einer Weltreligion* (Origins of a World Religion) series.

As I write this, Children of Ishmael and Al Hayat's Water Life Publishing has produced over a hundred titles. All these books, booklets, and tracts, primarily written by former Muslims, are uniquely designed to communicate Christ's message to Muslims and people from Muslim backgrounds. In addition, the materials are excellent tools to educate Christian churches and believers about Islam's true nature and assist them in their evangelical outreach to Muslims. The products are available in Arabic, English, and some other languages, and in recent years, they have increasingly been delivered to readers also in electronic format. In addition to Muslims, MBBs, traditional Christians, and churches, we enable other ministries to get books and reference materials cheaply, helping them to fulfill the Great Commission to the Muslim world.

A Language with Several Words for Love

I told above how I struggled with my Arabic as I started my ministry in Sweden in the 1980s.

As I mentioned, there were several reasons for my challenges: I hadn't studied Arabic since primary school, and I had mainly used other languages in my daily life. In addition, the Christian vocabulary I needed for my ministry I had learned in Finnish. So, my first Christian speeches in Arabic were full of grammatical and vocabulary mistakes—as my friend Sonia so bluntly informed me.

Of course, Arabic has its linguistic difficulties. The Semitic language system differs from others, and some sounds in our language are difficult for foreigners to pronounce. Some non-Arabs say that Arabic sounds like the speaker has a sore throat, and I can understand this kind of humor. Still, in my ears, Arabic is a beautiful, expressive, and versatile language that, for example, has several graceful words for different aspects of love. So, probably needless to say, today I'm proud to be able to preach the gospel of God's love in Christ in my dear mother tongue.

One pronunciation peculiarity in Arabic is that it does not have separate 'p' and 'b' sounds—there is only one 'b.' As a result, the 'p's in other languages are difficult for us to pronounce. For example, some Arabs pronounce English words such as 'peter' and 'people' as 'beter' and 'beoble'. (In the Arabic Bible, Apostle Peter is named Boutros.)

I remember how I was driving in America with two Arab friends one day, looking for a parking space. When we finally found a spot, my driving friend said in English, "Let's bark here." The other two of us responded—simultaneously—by imitating the voice of a dog. Then we all had a good laugh.

In church meetings, I have often smiled when I have heard an Arab believer say, "Let's bray."

According to linguistic statistics, there are more than 300 million native speakers of Arabic in the world. It is an official or co-official language in more than twenty countries, from

Mauritania in the west and the Comoros in the south to Iraq in the northeast. Because its speakers are spread over such a large geographical area, Arabic has been divided into over thirty spoken varieties, differing vastly.

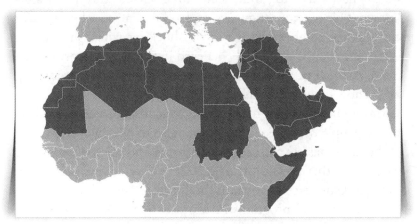

The Arabic countries. The map is missing the Comoros, located in the Indian Ocean, southeast of Tanzania. (A photo: Wikimedia Commons)

The most widely spoken of these dialects is Egyptian Arabic (called Masri), which is well understood throughout the Arabic-speaking world due to the success of Egyptian music, films, and TV series. Another well-known dialect is Levantine Arabic (called Shami), spoken in Lebanon, Israel, Turkey, and the western parts of Jordan and Syria.

It is important to note that all of these varieties mainly concern spoken language. The written form of Arabic, known as Classical Arabic or Modern Standard Arabic, is virtually the same everywhere and is taught in schools throughout the Arab world. The official media in Arab countries also use a more restrained form of speech than the dialects used by ordinary people, and this "evening news language" is also often called Classical Arabic. When we started Al Hayat, the program hosts and teachers mainly used this official style of speech. If they used dialects, they were Egyptian and Levantine Arabic. Gradually, however, we saw great possibilities in using local varieties—especially among particular ethnic groups.

Shocking Is Our Style: The Saudi Magazine

As anyone familiar with Bible translation knows, hearing God's Word in your mother tongue touches your heart in a special way. That's easy to understand, but there's another, lesser-known point here: languages and even dialects always carry cultural connotations that can be shocking when shaken up. For example, it is still widely believed in the Islamic world that a Saudi Arabian or a Moroccan is always a Muslim, so producing a TV show in which a Saudi or a Moroccan MBB talks about his Christian faith in their mother tongue sends a powerful message to the people of those countries, but also to Muslims elsewhere.

Shocking has always been a part of Al Hayat's style, so when we realized this effect of using dialects, we wanted to put it into practice. Our first step towards this kind of approach was filming some testimonial programs in Moroccan and Algerian Arabic. But we produced the first real, ground-breaking, dialect-based TV series in Khaliji, one of the varieties spoken in Saudi Arabia. The first episode of it was aired in January 2015.

Over the years, we had prayed a lot about being able to preach the gospel to the Saudis effectively, and we even met with some other mission organizations to discuss and pray about this enormous task. Gradually, we got a solid vision to produce a special TV series for these people living in the birthplace of Islam, and we wanted to do it in the local dialect and in a way relevant to their culture. The problem, however, was that we didn't have suitable Saudi believers to recruit for the program.

I remember the Al Hayat board meeting in the Strong family's living room in Seattle in 2014. We had once again been praying for a show focusing on Saudi Arabia, and suddenly, a Saudi MBB living in Australia came to my mind. His name was Dr. Khaled Al Shammari, and I had met him a few years earlier when we were filming some MBB testimonies for the channel. Among them were Dr. Khaled and his Syrian wife, Rana.

I had come to know Khaled as a very spiritual man, and when I now remembered him, I wanted to call him right away to introduce him to the board and to ask him to the show. We got him on the line, and that day, we decided to grab this opportunity. The Strong family—Leslie and Peter—promised to finance the project along with the Maclellan Foundation.

We called the project *The Saudi Magazine, Al Majalla al Saudiya* in Arabic. It was the first Christian TV series produced in the Khaliji dialect, hosted by Saudi Christians dressed in Saudi clothing. The first season was filmed in Israel in the footsteps of Jesus in biblical locations. On one filming day, we were driving down to the Dead Sea when we stopped to buy gas and have coffee. I lost sight of Khaled, and when I spotted him again, there he was amid twenty Israeli soldiers sharing his testimony with them.

He said to the soldiers, "Shalom, my name is Khaled, and I am from Saudi. Can I hug you and talk to you?"

They looked at each other and said, "What for?" Then he shared his testimony briefly. After that, he told them that as a believer in Yeshua (Jesus), he started to love the people of Israel. He knows salvation came through them and that the Bible teaches the followers of Jesus to love Jews.

All that Khaled said is very true. When Muslims accept Christ, they usually don't have a problem with accepting the Jews or Israelis theologically: by reading the Bible, they understand that God made specific promises to the Jews and that the Messiah was Jewish. Most MBBs also seem to reject those forms of the so-called replacement theology, which states that since the birth of Christianity, the Jewish people no longer have any unique, collective role in God's plans. At the same time, MBBs know from the Bible that Jews also are saved only by believing in Jesus.

So, if Christian ex-Muslims have problems with Jews, they are mostly about other, non-spiritual things, such as the Arab community's experiences of injustice perpetrated by the Israeli state against the Arab population. Yet, you can see a change even here. The people who used to be strongly influenced by the political views of their Muslim society have now experienced a new faith that is changing them and giving them new perspectives on things.

Once the decision to produce *The Saudi Magazine* was made, we knew that we also needed some music for the episodes. As far as we knew, there hadn't been any recorded Christian music in the Khaliji dialect before, so we needed brand new songs. We also wanted them to be so high quality that we could produce them as karaoke-style video clips and PowerPoints with lyrics and chords for the region's underground church. I called my dear friend Naser Musa, a talented musician involved in the music production for the Mel Gibson film *The Passion of the Christ* and challenged him to pray to the Lord for songs in the Khaliji dialect.

Besides dozens of music videos, Al Hayat has published over 50 worship albums with many artists. I have had the honor to be part of this music production by writing lyrics to 32 songs, most composed by Naser Musa (in the picture) or Maher Fayez.

Naser initially rejected the idea, thinking, "Who am I to do this?" but then prayed anyway. Later, he told me that God had encouraged him to accept the task and even given him words for the first Khaliji song.

Brother Naser is one of the wonderful people I have the privilege to work with. I first met him around 2011, when he was already a world-famous musician. Born in Jordan in 1964 to a Palestinian Christian family, he had concentrated on music at an early age because his poor eyesight limited his opportunities for other hobbies. He had developed as a player of the oud, a Middle Eastern lute, and later, when the family moved to California, USA, he continued his music studies there. Since then, he has toured the world with renowned ethnomusicologists, appeared on the albums of world-famous pop stars such as Beyoncé, performed at the 60th anniversary of the United Nations in 2004, and received praise from the Arab media in the Middle East.

In my opinion, Naser is the best oud player in the world.

The Saudi Magazine made us ministry partners and started a new phase in his life by making him more known as a Christian artist. Since the beginning of 2015, he has been in full-time ministry with Al Hayat, and to date, he has produced over 200 Christian worship songs, over a hundred of which are in the Khaliji dialect. On Al Hayat, he has also been hosting two series, *The Hymn and Lute* and *Let's Worship Him with Joy*.

"Moroccan and Christian"—MBBs Praying for the King

We aired the first *Saudi Magazine* episode in January 2015 and uploaded it to YouTube. Soon the episode caught the attention of one Saudi Mufti—a local Islamic cleric. He posted a YouTube video where he vented his anger at our claims, which he called infidel, and warned people not to watch the program.

Again, the effect of the warning seemed to be precisely the opposite of what was intended: people got hooked on our content, and the first episode has been viewed over 770,000 times on YouTube alone.

The Saudi Magazine confirmed our view about the need and possibilities of such region-specific programming, and the series was followed by others, such as *Good Morning Saudi* and *Friendly Talks*. These also touched the lives of Saudis in the Khaliji dialect and in a way relevant to their culture.

The next dialect we picked up was Kuwaiti Arabic. The program was called *Kuwaiti Enlightenment*, and the hosts were two precious Kuwaiti-background MBBs living in Northern America—Adel and Laila.

As I mentioned earlier, the varieties of Arabic are very different, and one of the most significant differences is between the non-Egyptian North African dialects and the others. In particular, Moroccan Arabic (called Darija) is difficult for Arabic speakers living east of Libya to understand. We had already filmed some testimonies in the Darija dialect, but in 2016, we started producing a whole new series with CBN called *Moroccan and Christian*.

The idea was born at Sari's and my summer cottage, where I was visiting with some Moroccan friends. There, in the sauna's warmth, we ended up talking about the Arabic Christian TV programs. (I have introduced so many Arabs to the joys of sauna bathing that I think I deserve an award from the Finnish Sauna Association.) During the discussion, we became convinced there was a need for a program where Moroccan Christians talked about their lives, their faith, and what it is like to be a Christian in Moroccan society—and the program should be in their dialect, Darija. Later, we formed a group of Moroccan believers who began to work on the concept under the supervision of Al Hayat. The show's primary host became sister Imane, a Moroccan MBB I mentioned earlier in connection with her pastor husband Latif. The show is still being produced.

The series has always had especially two audiences in mind: the local Moroccan MBBs and the country's Darija-speaking majority. For the first group, the idea for the show came from the fact that when Muslims accept Jesus Christ as their Savior, not only do their beliefs change, but the entire way they function in society changes. However, if you have lived in an Islamic culture all your life, learning the Christian way of life is not easy, and you need help and guidance to follow in the footsteps of Christ in your everyday life. In the episodes, we have, for example, answered many of the ethical questions Moroccan MBBs encounter, such as, "Is it Christian to obey the laws of Morocco and pay taxes?" (It is common in Arab countries for people to cheat on their taxes.) "Should a Christian pray for the local non-Christian authorities?" And, "How should Christians deal with those who persecute them?"

These are relevant questions for all Arab MBBs, but this time, the questions were put firmly in the Moroccan context.

To Morocco's Darija-speaking majority, the series explains who Moroccan MBBs are, what they believe in, and how they practice their faith. The program team wanted their fellow citizens to know that the decision to follow Christ wasn't driven by emigration intentions, money, or other benefits—except for eternal life with God. The local MBBs desired to belong to the country even after changing their religion. The team wanted to challenge Moroccan Muslims to accept and tolerate the presence of other faiths.

When we started broadcasting the episodes, it felt as if the whole of Moroccan society had been shaken up. Many of the country's Muslim majority changed their judgment and opinions, and Christians gained much respect. Even several secular Moroccan news platforms in Arabic and English covered the series. One of these was the *Morocco World News* website, where the headline of the story read: "I, Iman, a Moroccan Christian, love you all." One issue that attracted particular attention from the local secular media was that MBB Christians pray for the King of Morocco. The Arabic editions of the international news services Sky News, CNN, and the BBC also covered the program.

This was big in a country where more than 80 percent of the population still identifies as religious or somewhat religious, primarily Muslim.

Of course, the believers who appeared in the episodes also received threats, insults, and anger. Perhaps the most dangerous situation in Al Hayat's history occurred in the first year of the series (2016) when a group of men armed with knives tried to break into the home of an MBB from the series. Fortunately, the attempt was unsuccessful.

Amid hardships, the team encouraged each other to keep their eyes on the Lord and how He had cleared the way for them through these trials.

The popularity of the series is reflected in the number of viewers. Even though the primary target audience is quite small—around 38 million Moroccans—individual episodes have received up to 100,000 views on social media platforms, which I think is a good number. Moreover, the feedback shows that many have watched the show on the Al Hayat satellite stream, too, and not only watched: numerous persons have come to the Christian faith due to the program. Last year alone, we received about 250 such testimonies. Only God knows how many there are who will never tell us about their conversion. We have even heard of marriages of people who have come to faith through *Moroccan and Christian*.

Later, we launched specific programs in several other varieties of Arabic, such as in the dialects of Tunisia, Sudan, Yemen, Libya, and Iraq.

Closely related to this theme is the media ministry in the Somali language, which we have supported since 2016. It is the ministry of a Somali MBB couple, Shino and Shania Gabo. My friend Niilo met them at a conference in Malaga, Spain. The Gabos were reaching out to Somalis using Facebook and other platforms. Niilo encouraged them to develop their media skills, and when he returned to Finland, he told me about them. I shared their story with another friend of mine, Abu Yehia, who represents our partner organization HMK. Al Hayat and HMK wanted to help the Gabos, so we contacted them and offered them the opportunity to come under the Al Hayat umbrella.

Somali is not a dialect of Arabic, but Somalia is considered an Arab country, so the move was natural for us.

The Gabos thanked us for the opportunity and the support we could offer them in TV production. For us, it was one of the best decisions ever made. The Gabos' program, *Jidka Janada* (*The Way to Heaven*), can be seen on social media and the Ethiopian Christian channel El Shaddai, whose satellite broadcasts reach much of Europe and Africa. We also helped the Gabos to set up a Somali-language website, *jidkajanada.com*. The site features their programs and, among other things, a Bible in Somali, which is difficult to find in book form.

Somalis have been one of the least evangelized people groups in the world, but by God's grace, the Gabos have received around 8,000 reports of salvation decisions in the last seven years.

Shorter Programs and Sharper Viewpoints

When Al Hayat first started, we were attacked especially for two shows that the Arab world was not used to seeing: Joyce Meyer's *Enjoying Everyday Life* and Father Zakaria's *Questions About Faith*. The very personal way in which Joyce taught about the Christian life and the way in which Father Zakaria challenged the credibility of Muhammad and the Qur'an shattered public perceptions, including those of Western media broadcasting organizations, of what Arabic Christian television content should and could be.

Because these programs were controversial, they created an image for the whole channel. In particular, Zakaria's *Questions About Faith* led many people to believe that Al Hayat's content consisted mainly of Islam criticism. However, series focusing on the problems of Islam have always accounted for less than ten percent of the channel's total content. Currently, we have five or six series out of seventy-one that critically analyze this religion. Of course, almost anything you say about Christianity challenges Islam in some way. For example, if you say that Jesus is the Son of God, it is an attack on the teachings of the Qur'an and the Hadith because they teach otherwise.

The themes that have always been most prevalent on Al Hayat are evangelistic preaching, Bible teaching, personal testimonies, Christian music, and Christian life issues—things that help the viewers to come to Christ, grow as believers, and live out their faith in their daily lives. For example, not many people from a Muslim background know how Christians pray or how to arrange a Christian home group, so we need to teach them.

When something special happens in the Arab world, we also cover these things in our programs. The fact that we have teams and studios in eleven countries around the globe helps us to do this and react quickly when needed. For example, if something dramatic happens in the Middle East during the day, content preparation can start in Finland, the program can be shot live in the US later that day (when it is still morning in the US), and the Australian studio can do the post-production, which means, for example, posting video clips on social media. This is how we have dealt with events such as the turning points in the Syrian war, the earthquake in Turkey and Syria in February 2023, and some lethal terrorist attacks. Such events affect Christians and Muslims alike, allowing us to both address the day's issue and advance the gospel at the same time. We have also reported on the persecution of former Muslims.

A moment before the camera starts rolling. Al Hayat's staff comprises nearly 200 paid and voluntary workers. Here we are in Kerava, Finland.

More than the changes in content, the last twenty years have seen transformations in program formats. The most significant factor for this change has been the increasing shift of media consumption to the internet: in the Middle East and North Africa, only those over fifty still mainly watch traditional TV. Most people under fifty have switched to online TV and mobile video apps. People under twenty are even more engaged with various social media applications. Only in rural areas do younger people still watch quite a lot of satellite TV.

We have reacted to these changes by filming new, shorter program series more suitable for YouTube, Facebook, Twitter, and other mobile platforms. For example, suppose we do a half-hour show on satellite TV about a particular subject. In that case, we'll cut the same material to three ten-minute episodes on the online site. For the youngest viewers, we need to make video clips that are only a few minutes long—or even less.

All this makes program production more challenging. The shorter the format, the harder it is to squeeze in all the content. And that's not the only difficulty: on social media, the video must also quickly capture the viewers' attention. The analysts have calculated that you have around seven seconds to do this, or the viewer will move on to the next video. In TV production, this is known as the seven-second rule. In fact, even middle-aged people are more demanding with these things than before. I think most of us know this from our own lives as well—if a program doesn't seem attractive or the presenter spends time on idle chatter, we're quick to switch to another channel.

One of our most popular short video series is *What is Behind the Turban*, hosted by sister Farha. In the program, she shows clips from videos of Muslim teachers and then comments on the ideas they present. Once, for example, a Mufti was saying in a video that Islam has always respected women, and because of that, when the Qur'an tells a man to beat his wife, he should not beat her hard—only with a small stick, not a big one. After showing this clip in her show, sister Farha asked what on earth it meant to hit a woman lightly or with "a small stick"—was it a joke? Didn't the mufti understand that all talk of hitting is offensive to women, and all hitting is wrong and a crime? Mitigating the severity of the beating does not nullify the crime itself.

What makes TV ministry difficult for all Christian channels is that many people look to media primarily for entertainment. In this situation, movie-style Christian content is one option. As I write this, we plan conversion testimonies produced in this way, even though drama productions are much more expensive than most other formats.

As mentioned above, at Al Hayat we count several categories of viewer reactions, such as social media comments, video views, and shares of our posts and videos. Their sheer volume gives us a good indication of what topics people are interested in. This, in turn, helps us to develop programs, websites, and applications. That's why, for more than ten years, we have had a specialist on our team whose main task is to analyze people's viewing behavior.

The Al Hayat Board—More Than Colleagues

Throughout the years, one of the most stabilizing factors we have enjoyed at Al Hayat has been the wise overseers on the channel's board. The projects and developments mentioned above have been possible only because of them. And they are not just ministry partners to us: all those who have served us in this role are close friends of mine and the whole Al Hayat team. I am so grateful for all these godly servants and want to thank them all for their prayers, love, and care for the ministry, me, Sari, and my family.

As I write this, the Al Hayat board includes Hani Bushra, Dave Gibson, Latif El Qochairi, Ali Kalkandelen, Veli-Matti Kärkkäinen, Leslie Strong, Dagnaldo Pinheiro, Gary Preston (advisor), and Sam Arra (secretary).

Most board meetings have been held in members' homes, and we have received such generous hospitality and beautiful memories. But sometimes we have met elsewhere. In 2015, for example, we traveled to Israel, and I showed our board the Holy Land from my perspective as an Israeli Arab. We also had meals with Al Hayat's Israeli follow-up team and visited our local partners.

One day, we made a trip to the Dead Sea to see the Qumran caves where the Dead Sea scrolls were discovered in the 1940s and 1950s and to swim. It was early spring, and at that time there were only a few other people swimming there because the water was still a bit cold. When we got into the water, I noticed a couple swimming close to us and said to Sam, "I bet that couple is Finnish." We listened for a bit, and sure enough, I was right. They spoke Finnish, and we laughed at my successful guess. For the Finns, the water is always warm enough in the Dead Sea.

There was also an elderly Russian woman swimming nearby, but she obviously wanted to get out of the water. The beach was uneven, and she struggled to return to dry land. I wanted to be a gentleman, so I offered to carry her out of the water, but I hadn't realized how heavy she was. But since I had offered to help her, I felt obliged to do so. So, I took this babushka (the Russian word for grandmother) in my arms, slowly lifted her, and carried her onto dry ground. Everyone in our group had a good laugh and took pictures of me heroically carrying this woman to safety. To this day, whenever Pastor Dave Gibson gets the chance, he will pull out the photo he took that day of the man he calls Harun Hasselhoff.

The boards of Al Hayat and Keymedia in a joint "class photo" from 2018.

14

Facing the Fanatics

In 2015 and 2016, around two million refugees from the Middle East and Central Asia arrived in European Union (EU) countries. The news was filled with images of overcrowded boats arriving on Greek islands and endless queues of people on Balkan roads. Millions more made it as far as Turkey, but not further. Most of them are still living there in refugee camps and elsewhere.

For many Europeans, the mass migration was stressful and unsettling. They criticized the EU for allowing it to happen. Even the media called it the "European migration crisis" or the "European refugee crisis." As I mentioned earlier, prominent Muslim immigration has often led to some negative consequences in the West. Muslim "ghettos" have sprung up, and in most countries where Muslims have become significant minorities, their willingness to integrate into society has diminished. There have even been calls to restrict the religious freedom of others and to change local laws. Perhaps this was the reason for the negative attitudes of so many Europeans in 2015. Yet that's not the whole picture.

For us as Christians in the West, this massive influx of people from Muslim-majority countries turned out to be a tremendous opportunity to reach these people with love and welcoming hearts. As a result, many Muslims who came to Europe at that time have come to know Christ as their Lord and Savior.

While it is impossible to know the total number of converts, in Finland, for example, the numbers have been astonishing. Of the approximately 38,000 asylum seekers who arrived in the country during those years, 2,000 to 3,000 of them have since confessed Christ as their Savior. We know, of course, that some of the conversions were fake—some people just wanted to be baptized in the hope that it would improve their chances of staying in Europe. Still, I dare say that such cases were in the minority.

When the movement started, many of us in the Finnish churches began organizing ourselves to handle these new non-Finnish-speaking attendees coming to our small and big congregations. These new believers and people interested in Christianity mainly spoke Arabic, Kurdish, Dari, and Farsi. We held conferences for them and often saw as many as 300 to 400 people, primarily MBBs, in a single meeting. This was the first time anything like that happened in a small country like Finland.

Once, we had a host from Al Hayat, sister Farha, as a speaker at one of these conferences. One of the participants in the event had traveled around 600 kilometers (380 miles) from Northern Finland to be there. He was a refugee from Iraq.

After the event, the man approached Farha and said, "I have seen your programs and cursed you a lot. Then I started to think about what you say in the episodes. I began to read the Bible and finally became a believer in Jesus. Can you forgive me for cursing you badly?"

Farha looked at him with a smile and said, "Of course. If you want, I can also pray for you and declare your sins forgiven."

Similar situations have happened elsewhere when our hosts have given their testimony or preached. People come to them saying they even had the plan to kill them, but then they came to faith in Jesus themselves.

Most refugees from the Middle East and Central Asia, however, stayed in Turkey. When they arrived there, some were already followers of Christ but had been hidden believers. Now, in Turkey, they began to evangelize other refugees. New congregations and small Christian groups were established throughout the country.

Many missionary organizations also started to work in Turkey's refugee camps, and some did excellent work. Others, however, did more harm than good, seeing the work among the refugees as an opportunity to attract donations from their supporters in the West. Christian media, eager to report on the Christian ministry among the refugees, helped them in this fundraising effort. In some cases, only a tiny proportion of the donated funds have been used for the refugees.

Apart from that, there is so much to be thankful for. Once again, we have witnessed how God allows such things to happen that don't make sense to us when they occur, only to understand them later. As the Apostle Paul stated so clearly,

> *And we know that all things work together for good to those who love God, to those who are the called according to His purpose.* (Romans 8:28)

God has His ways of fulfilling the Great Commission, and His ways are not our ways. I pray that one day, many of these new believers will return to the Muslim world and start new Christian revivals there.

The Jihadist Logic

The world has seen the rise of several Islamic groups in recent history, starting in 1979 when Ayatollah Khomeini returned to Iran from exile and took over the country with his companions. To this day, Iran's Islamic leaders form the most fanatical group in the Shia Islamic world and rule the country with an iron fist. However, due to this heavy-handed treatment and strict interpretation of Islam, many Iranians have turned their backs on the religion. Some have converted to atheism, others to other faiths, mainly Christianity. As I write this, several experts estimate there are around one million MBBs in the country, making the Iranian church one of the fastest-growing churches in the world. In addition, there seem to be many Iranians who, although they continue to act like Muslims to avoid problems, have abandoned Islam in their hearts.

Beyond their homeland, Iran's ruling Islamist social class has sought to spread its ideology abroad and has been fighting the West for years. The West, for its part, has tried in various ways to undermine the country's leadership—mostly in vain.

In the same year that Ayatollah Khomeini returned to Iran, events with far-reaching consequences took place in Afghanistan as well. Soviet troops invaded the country, occupied the major cities, and were confronted by the local Sunni Islamist freedom fighters, the Mujahideen rebels. The war attracted many Islamists from other parts of the world to join the Mujahideen, and a new group called the Taliban emerged. Some years later, in 1988, al-Qaeda—another Sunni Islamist group—formed in neighboring Pakistan.

At one point, the West thought it had defeated the Taliban, and al-Qaeda was also weakened after the death of its leader Osama bin Laden in 2011. However, the ideology was still vivid and boosted another even more fanatical organization called ISIS. The Taliban returned to power in Afghanistan in 2021 after the withdrawal of US troops from the country. Both in Iran and Afghanistan, we have seen that the real war has to be waged against ideology, winning people's hearts and minds. That's why I think that fighting violence with violence is not the answer to the deeper problem, which is spiritual and ideological.

To understand jihad, the holy war against non-Muslims, one must perceive two things:

- Islam is not only a religion but also a political system aiming to subjugate the whole world under its regime.
- According to the Qur'an and Hadith, even the most devout Muslim cannot be sure of his salvation. No amount of prayer, fasting, or almsgiving can guarantee it. The most robust promises of salvation are given to those who sacrifice their lives to promote Islam. Martyrdom is the only sure way to heaven.

That's why jihad seems so attractive to many. In a context where you don't have any other way to be sure whether your destiny is in heaven or hell, fighting and giving your life for Islam is an attractive option, especially if your life is full of misery and bitterness. I think this is one of the main motivations behind suicide bombings against non-Muslims.

Of course, most Muslims are not fanatics but moderates who follow only part of Islam's teachings or seek to interpret the Qur'an's violent injunctions in a new, non-violent way. They believe that jihad has only a spiritual meaning and that Sharia law should not be the rule of life for the community. There are many wonderful and highly respectable people among these Muslims—like my mother. But the problem is that traditional Islamic theology teaches precisely the opposite: calls for violence are particularly prevalent in those Qur'anic verses Muhammad received during the last years of his life. Because of that, Islamic theology considers those verses to be the most binding.

Therefore, all those who say that the actions of ISIS, al-Qaeda, and the Taliban do not represent the fundamental teachings of Islam are wrong. To me and other MBBs, to numerous Islamic scholars, and from a careful reading of the Qur'an, the actions of these groups are precisely what Islam is all about.

Unfortunately, many people in Western societies don't understand this inner dynamic of Islam. Especially since the Second World War, it has been difficult for Western countries to speak out against Islam, even when they can see what is happening in the region. The Arab countries control the global oil market, which is too big of a business. There seems to be too much at stake.

But on Al Hayat, we cannot keep silent. Due to that, during the last twenty years, we have seen hundreds of Muslim fanatics become entirely different persons after experiencing the love of Jesus Christ. Some of them are now serving God with the Al Hayat team. At Christian conferences, I often see these people—who used to hate Christians and wanted to kill all the Jews in the world—hugging Messianic Jewish believers and American brothers, whom they used to call representatives of "the great Satan." Some of them have even visited Israel to see the places where Jesus walked.

The strategy of Al Hayat is to deal with the ideology at the root, which is why we try to recruit people with a vast knowledge of Islam and Christianity to be in front of the camera. We hope that, in the future, we will have more MBBs with fanatic backgrounds to tell the whole Arabic world how Jesus has changed their lives.

I believe one of the first of them is my friend Mohamed, a converted Salafi.

A Salafist's Jesus Hashtag

In early 2017, after ISIS had already lost a significant part of its territory in Syria and Iraq, I heard about a person who had published a live broadcast on Facebook from Masjid al-Haram, the Great Mosque of Mecca. In the broadcast video, he revealed two Arabic hashtags written on his hand: "#Jesus is the solution" and "#The Convert Salafi." The Kaaba building at the center of the Great Mosque could be seen in the background.

Many individuals and ministries shared his post on their Facebook pages because this kind of act was unheard of. The video showed it was a man's hand, and the word "Salafi" revealed that he belonged to a very conservative revival movement within Sunni Islam, Salafism. The movement emphasizes "the pure" doctrine of the first generations of Islam, rejects religious innovation, and supports the implementation of Sharia law. Questions and rumors flew: Who was this person?

In 2018, a member of the Al Hayat follow-up team told me about a young man from a Salafi background who had contacted our channel. The man's name was Mohamed, and he had been an active member of one of the most prominent Islamic organizations, the Muslim Brotherhood, while being a hidden follower of Christ. Now, he had escaped to Latin America and wanted to get in touch with other MBBs. He was the man in the Facebook video.

So, I set up an online meeting with Mohamed, and when I heard his story, it sounded almost too incredible to be true. He was arrested and imprisoned several times on charges of terrorism or violence in several countries. In 2013, he was imprisoned again, this time in Egypt for one and a half years, and during that stint in prison, he learned about Christianity through reading the New Testament and other texts. Gradually, he became convinced of the gospel and Jesus and became a Christian.

"Jesus is the solution." A Facebook video where an unknown person revealed his faith in Jesus in Mecca stunned Arabic Christian media organizations in 2017.

So far, his story was a familiar Muslim conversion story, but then he made a surprising decision. After his release from prison in early 2015, he feared that his Salafist friends and other Islamic jihadists would discover his new faith. To avoid the danger, he decided to stay close to the fire and joined the Muslim Brotherhood. He was sure that if his new faith became known, it would have meant his death.

After the Muslim Brotherhood lost power in Egypt in July 2013, thousands of its members moved to Turkey. So, Mohamed also moved there, became involved in the organization's activities, and soon was chosen as a deputy to one of the leaders, Dr. Yahya Hamed. Dr. Hamed had been the Minister of Investment in Egypt during the Muslim Brotherhood regime.

Then Mohamed got a job at the Muslim Brotherhood's main media center in Istanbul, where he became the deputy of Dr. Talaat Fahmy, the media spokesman for the Muslim Brotherhood's international organization. Mohamed was also elected as the youth spokesperson for the Egyptian Revolutionary Council in London and appeared in the Arab media.

All this he did hiding his faith in Christ. In 2017, he even made a pilgrimage to Mecca, acting like he was still a Muslim but published his confessional hashtag video on Facebook. He felt he had to go to Mecca because he still did not want his Salafist friends and other Islamic organizations to suspect his loyalty to Islam. In addition, he wanted to meet his family, who were going there for the pilgrimage.

Then, after Mohamed had returned from Mecca, some of the Salafist leaders who still were in an authority position towards him commanded him to join them and come to Syria as part of ISIS. It was too much—Mohamed decided to flee and hide from everyone, and moved to Latin America. There he began studying at a Baptist Bible college and started openly sharing his Christian faith on social media.

During the online meeting with him in 2018, I found Mohamed to be a friendly and sincere young man searching for the Lord's will for his life. He told me that he would graduate from the Bible school later that year, and after that, there would be a ceremony where he would be ordained as a pastor for the local Baptist church. However, he also planned to return to the Middle East one day and start a Christian ministry to Muslims there. During his Bible school studies, the courage and desire to share the gospel with Muslims had grown in him regardless of the risks.

As he told me these things, many thoughts came to my mind. I know how hard it is for MBBs to be outside of the previous community they enjoyed as Muslims. Sure, Mohamed had friends in the Baptist church, but he still seemed to feel alone and like he hadn't yet found his place in a Christian community where he could share all his joys and sorrows. That's why it's so important for MBBs to have other believers from similar backgrounds walking alongside them. I sensed that this was a call from the Lord for me to be a family for him so that he would not feel so alone. That was my desire at the time, based on Christ's commandment, "Therefore, whatever you want men to do to you, do also to them, for this is the Law and the Prophets" (Matthew 7:12). And if Mohamed were to return to the Middle East one day, he would certainly benefit from our networks there.

I told Mohamed that I would like to visit him during his ordination ceremony. He said, "Really? That would be so special." I don't think he believed I would come, but I did. When I arrived, he was at the airport with his pastor and the pastor's wife. They welcomed me with very warm hearts. I also met another pastor from the same church who had served in Egypt for about ten years as a missionary. He surprised me by speaking such fluent Egyptian Arabic. He told me of several people he baptized in Egypt who had become Christ-followers through the Al Hayat channel. I was also informed that he had continuously told Mohamed that he wished for him to have a future in ministry on Al Hayat. If that were to happen, he would reach millions of people through media, the pastor had said.

I had come there to accompany the young man on this significant occasion so he wouldn't feel alone. Later, however, when I got to know him better, I had a suggestion for him to consider: what if he joined the Al Hayat team instead of going physically to the Middle East? He said the idea sounded great and that he felt comfortable being with us. So, we have been blessed to have him as a part-time staff member since 2019. He has continued his pastoral work in his new home country in Latin America, but at the same time, we have been preparing him for TV ministry. As I write this, our plan is to launch a new live call-in program, which he will host. We expect broadcasting to start in 2024.

When I think of my former life as a secular Muslim, and many other stories that are similar to mine, and then of my Salafi friend and the many who used to be very devoted Muslims but are now serving the Lord, I can see that we all experience John 1:12:

> But as many as received Him, to them He gave the right to become children of God, to those who believe in His name...

Non-Arabic Missions

During the 2015 European migration crisis, among the migrants were numerous Afghans and Iranians, and, for some reason, they seemed particularly interested in Christianity. This created a desire for increased media ministry in the languages spoken in Iran and Afghanistan, especially Farsi (also known as Persian, the official language of Iran), Dari (a variety of Farsi), and Pashto, the main languages in Afghanistan.

At Al Hayat, we had already worked with Iranian brothers and sisters who produce Farsi-language programs for organizations such as Heart4Iran and Mohabat TV. So, when the need for Christian Farsi content grew in 2015, we helped them by giving them free studio time in Keymedia's facilities in Finland. Later, they broadcast those programs via satellite and the internet.

As the Taliban grew in power in Afghanistan and the withdrawal of US troops in 2021 approached, we received several calls from missionaries working in Afghanistan, asking if there was anything we could do to help the MBB Christians there. In particular, the missionaries asked us to produce programs analyzing Islam in the main languages of Afghanistan. So, we decided to translate some of the shows we had made earlier and dub them into Dari and later into Pashto and Balochi (Balochi is a minority language in Iran, Afghanistan, and Pakistan).

The missionaries asked us to send these dubbed programs via satellite to Afghanistan, but so far, it has not been possible, and we have only been able to distribute them on the internet and social media. Still, the shows have found their audience. For some reason, Afghan viewers have particularly liked our animated series *Dr. Sam and Islam*, in which Dr. Sam performs health checks on a patient called Islam. Perhaps the ironic style has appealed to the hard-pressed Afghans, or maybe the exploration of religious issues in animation form has been new to them.

As I write this, our collaboration with Mohabat TV and Heart4Iran is deepening even more. We have set up a joint studio in the Middle East to co-produce evangelistic programs and dub them in Arabic, Farsi, Dari, Kurdish, Turkish, and Hebrew. The shows will be broadcast on Al Hayat and Mohabat TV, other organizations' satellite and online channels, and social media. It is beautiful to see the MBBs on the Al Hayat team, mainly from Sunni backgrounds, and the MBBs of Mohabat TV and Hear4Iran, who are from Shia backgrounds, working so well in harmony. We really are one family in Christ.

Since 2017, our programs have also been dubbed in Russian in cooperation with TBN Russia. By the time I'm writing this, they have translated more than 200 episodes of several series. Russia and many other parts of the former Soviet Union have a significant Muslim population, and I'm delighted that TBN Russia has the desire also to reach them with the gospel.

Shelanu TV — Taking Jesus Back to His People

In May 2020, we found ourselves in the middle of a storm that we had not hoped for but which came as no surprise to us. The situation was reminiscent of the start of Al Hayat, but this time the venue was Israel. The Jewish media was abuzz, and petitions to stop our programs were flying. Even some secular magazines in the West wrote about the storm.

A reason for all this was a Messianic TV channel that Al Hayat, GOD TV, and the Messianic community in Israel had started together. The local cable TV operator had accepted our channel, Shelanu TV, as part of their channel package. This meant that the population of Israel heard about Jewish Jesus,

Yeshua the Messiah, for the first time from local cable TV in Hebrew. Things went well for a week, but then the orthodox Jewish community woke up and began to demand that the channel be taken from the airwaves.

We tried to defend ourselves, but the pressure was too much. The cable TV operator gave in to the pressure and shut us out.

The story had started more than ten years earlier. The media ministry to Israel had been on our hearts for a long time; Israel was one of the countries I wanted Al Hayat to reach. The Arabic programs we produced had already been broadcast on Israeli cable TV in the 1990s, and later, Al Hayat's satellite broadcastings covered the region, but we wanted to do something also for the Hebrew-speaking audience. So, in 2009, Gary Preston and I made a trip to Israel and tried to find partners to start something in Hebrew in the country.

That was not a successful trip, but a year later, I got connected with some local ministries in Israel and discovered that there were less than 100 hours of Messianic, Hebrew-speaking TV content available. On a 24-hour channel, one hundred hours of programming would be broadcast in less than a week unless we repeated the playlist several times, so we made it our goal to produce more programs soon. I had also hoped that many Messianic and evangelical ministries and congregations in Israel would be more than willing to partner with us in evangelizing TV ministry in the country. Unfortunately, it became evident that getting contributions for any social project within the Jewish community was much easier than getting support for evangelizing the Jewish people.

We started the Hebrew-speaking online channel anyway in 2012 with the partners we had found and with the name *Israel Chai* (Israel is Alive). At first, we operated it from Keymedia's facilities in Finland, but soon we took the operational activities to Israel. In addition, we began to hand over the ministry to our Messianic partners, such as Revive Israel, Dugit, Oded Shoshani, and several others who became the channel owners. The channel's name was changed to *Yeshua Chai* (Jesus is Alive). Our partners gave their own productions to use on the program stream, and at Keymedia/Al Hayat, we continued to film part of the content.

The channel operated that way for several years, but we felt it was not going forward as we wanted. Then something happened that made it much more effective.

In 2019, Israel's largest cable TV company contacted a Messianic pastor, Ron Cantor from Tel Aviv, who represented GOD TV in Israel. GOD TV is an internationally renowned Christian media operator, and the cable company wanted GOD TV to have its English station on its network. Ron said he was not interested in broadcasting an English channel to a Hebrew-speaking country but would be very interested in a Hebrew channel. Unexpectedly, the cable TV company said it was also okay for them. When I heard about their answer to Ron, I wondered if these guys knew what they were saying yes to.

Ron gathered Messianic Jewish leaders from all over Israel to tell them about the idea, and some representatives of our Yeshua Chai team were there, too. The cable company representative told them how historic it would be to have the first Hebrew-speaking cable TV gospel channel ever! The astonishing thing was that the representative, so enthusiastic about the issue, did not seem to be a Messianic believer himself.

The decision of the new channel was made, and by the grace of God, we were able to merge Yeshua Chai into this new partnership. Now we had more opportunities to upgrade our Hebrew program production to a more professional level. Ron Cantor became the channel's president, and we hired another person to manage the channel's practical activities. The name was changed to Shelanu TV, which I was delighted with. The Hebrew word *shelanu* means "ours." We were telling the Israelis that Yeshua came from them, from Israel. He was not a foreigner or imposter—He was a Jew from Galilee.

GOD TV got involved with the channel in a beautiful way. We never felt that, because of their size, they were arbitrarily trying to take over the reins. It has always been a fruitful partnership for which we are very grateful.

So, Shelanu TV went live on April 28, 2020, Israel's Independence Day that year. A week later, all hell broke loose against us. The orthodox Jewish community had a great outcry, and the Israeli government was also pulled into the quarrel. The Shelanu team, led by local Messianic Jews and me as an Israeli-Arab Christian, issued a press release explaining that Shelanu was not a foreign company—it was governed by Israelis. Because of that, we, as Israeli citizens, expect the same freedom of speech, religion, and expression as every other citizen.

Our plea seemed to fall on deaf ears. After some incredibly intense days, the government of Israel realized that legally they could not shut the channel down, so it appears they pressured the cable company to drop Shelanu.

But we were ready! Within three hours of being taken off the air, our Shelanu TV website was live and has been ever since. We are also on Facebook, Instagram, and other social media platforms. We have seen many Israelis accept Yeshua as their Savior and Lord and enter the waters of immersion, a Christian baptism. In 2021, our first full year of operation, we received 350 requests from Hebrew-speaking Israelis asking for the New Testament and a gospel book called *Identity Theft*, which explains the Jewish roots of the New Testament. In Israel, 350 requests are a good number, and in 2022 the figure was even higher. We receive contacts from all branches of the Jewish community: secular, orthodox, and even ultraorthodox Jews.

When writing this, the social media statistics show that our pages and applications have over 350,000 visits per month.

In my opinion, Shelanu TV is an authentic witness to how Arab and Messianic believers can work together and prove that we are one family. As I have said, when Muslims accept Christ, they usually don't have theological problems with accepting Jews or Israelis, and the same goes for the attitude of Messianic Jews towards Arab Christians. As a Gentile MBB, I have never felt that I am an outsider among the Messianic Jews or less important than anyone else. I feel respect and love from their side.

Apostle Paul says in his letter to the Romans:

For there is no difference; for all have sinned and fall short of the glory of God, being justified freely by His grace through the redemption that is in Christ Jesus, whom God set forth as a propitiation by His blood, through faith, to demonstrate His righteousness [...] Where is boasting then? It is excluded.

(Romans 3:22–27)

The apostle's message is clear: there are no first-class and second-class sinners. Both Jews and Arabs need God's healing influence and an opening of eyes to the reality of the kingdom of God, where there is neither Jew nor Gentile, but all are one in Christ. As with Sunnis and Shias, so it is with Jews and Gentiles: what unites us is not our background but our present life in Jesus Christ, the life that has passed from darkness into light.

The Apostle Peter speaks of the same thing when he reminds all followers of Jesus—Gentile and Jewish believers alike—

But you are a chosen generation, a royal priesthood, a holy nation, His own special people, that you may proclaim the praises of Him who called you out of darkness into His marvelous light...

(1 Peter 2:9)

15

Persecution
and Other Hardships

"Islam is a religion of peace!" The man's voice was angry, and the words came out of his mouth almost in a shout.

My friend and I were on the street in a Turkish town and had spontaneously started a discussion with a man we met there. As usual, the conversation quickly moved on to religious matters.

"Do you believe in Christ?" the man asked my friend after we had talked for a while. The man had discovered that we were ex-Muslims.

"Yes," my friend replied.

"Why did you leave Islam?"

"Because Islam is a violent and bloody religion."

Immediately after hearing this, the man lost his temper and hit my friend in the chest, saying, "Don't say that, you...!" Then he continued with the words about Islam being a religion of peace.

I believe I'm right when I say that the people who feel the aggression of Islamic fanatism most acutely are former Muslims who have publicly said that they have converted to another faith. In a Muslim society, they are considered *Murtads*—renegades or apostates—and *Kafirs*, infidels. Such people are legal enemies of Islam who are to be punished and prosecuted under the regulations of Sharia law.

The Qur'an mentions apostasy several times and how those who commit it will incur the wrath of God and be punished. According to the Qur'an, it is even permissible to kill an apostate:

> *They* [people who have fallen back into error and disbelief] *wish that you reject Faith, as they have rejected (Faith), and thus that you all become equal (like one another). So take not Auliya' (protectors or friends) from them, till they emigrate in the Way of Allah. But if they turn back (from Islam), take (hold) of them and kill them wherever you find them, and take neither Auliya' (protectors or friends) nor helpers from them.* (Sura 4.89)

Also, a hadith quotes Muhammad saying, "Whoever changes his religion, kill him" (Sunan an-Nasa'i 4059). In a culture where the whole world is to be made obedient to Islam, rejecting Islam is the ultimate crime.

As I write this, there are about ten Muslim-majority countries where apostasy is a crime punishable by the death penalty. In several other countries, it is punishable by fines, imprisonment, or losing custody of one's child. Fortunately, capital punishment is rarely carried out—there are only a few cases where the authorities of Muslim countries have imposed the death penalty in recent decades. When someone has been killed, in most cases, it has happened at the hands of relatives or some local jihadist group.

The radical step of rejecting one's previous faith and confessing Jesus as the Son of God can, of course, meet with resistance everywhere: within the Hindu culture of India, in Buddhist Sri Lanka and Japan, in the tribal religions of Africa, and even in the secular West. Still, I dare say that the challenges are most significant within the Muslim culture. There are several reasons for that, including:

1. The conquering nature of Islam, mentioned above, which commands Muslims to subjugate the whole world to Islam
2. The harshness against apostasy in the Qur'an and Hadith
3. The way the whole legislation reflects Islamic principles in many Muslim-majority countries, which exposes the adherents of other faiths to structural violence and lowers the threshold for Muslim citizens to cause harm to non-Muslims.

Because of all this, security challenges are very familiar to MBBs everywhere in the Muslim world. The situation has been the best in the most moderate Muslim-majority countries, such as Kazakhstan and Malaysia, but in regions like Eritrea, Yemen, Somalia, and Afghanistan the circumstances are extremely challenging.

In the Middle East and North Africa, not only MBBs, but also followers of Jesus who grew up in a Christian family, face persecution. The latter, however, have certain rights and obligations derived from Sharia's *Dhimmi* (non-Muslim) law which apply to practitioners of other religions. For example, a Christian-born believer can belong to a government-recognized church, participate in the political process, or open a business. Among the most notable restrictions faced by Christians are the restrictions of non-Islamic mission work, the prohibition of the teaching of Islam by non-Muslims, and the prohibition of criticizing Islam (so-called blasphemy laws). Under these laws, for example, pastors have been imprisoned for being willing to baptize a person of Muslim background. Sharing the gospel with a Muslim on the street can lead to prosecution or violence. In practice, dhimmi laws relegate people of other religions to a second-class status.

In addition, all Christians face persecution that is not based on national law. Christian churches have been burned and bombed in Muslim-majority countries even in the 2020s.

In the case of MBBs, the challenges are multiplied, and they start from home. Their family practically always opposes their conversion. Of course, the intensity of this opposition can vary significantly between families and at different times. In my case, it was certainly on and off. I had several uncomfortable situations with my family members—at first, they were unhappy about my conversion and later about my ministry. Still, in other families, a family member's decision to leave Islam may even cost that person their life.

Here, women are particularly vulnerable. Many Muslim-background women have been tortured or raped by close family members (even fathers and brothers) for becoming Christians. Some families will lock up their MBB daughters. An MBB woman may disappear for years or forever with little or no explanation from the family because, in Islamic countries, it is not culturally acceptable to talk about women from other families. Such disappearances are more common in countries where there is total segregation between men and women, such as Saudi Arabia, Yemen, Libya, and even the countryside of Egypt. We have heard so many testimonies of that kind of situation.

Even if a family allows their MBB son or daughter to continue in social life, the family may still punish them by taking over their property, throwing them out of the family and home, leaving them without inheritance, or denying their educational opportunities. In most Middle Eastern countries, financial support from the family is required for vocational training and, especially, university studies.

If a female Christian convert is married, her husband often uses pressure, isolation, or violence against her. If it's a husband who accepts Christ, the Muslim wife or wives are sometimes the first to expose him to his family or the authorities as revenge for their honor. In Islam, it is forbidden for a Muslim woman to live with a Christian man.

The situation is, naturally, much better if both husband and wife have found Jesus. Still, being isolated from relatives causes insecurity and loneliness, and it also affects the couple's children. In Arab culture, children usually have good relationships with their extended families, everyone hugging and kissing them and giving them presents. When the parents have converted, no uncles, aunts, or grandparents may come to children's birthday parties or other family events. And the isolation is not just limited to family members; Arabs typically have a very active social life, and unrelated guests often come over. Suddenly, there may be none of that.

All these things apply to most Muslim-majority countries. And when MBBs living there go outside their homes and

families, the situation is usually no better. The following is a list
of real-life scenarios I know of. Most of them are from Arabic
countries:

- Although authorities rarely carry out the death penalty, they may
  arrest and imprison MBBs on charges of religious blasphemy or
  hold them in pretrial detention for long periods. Believers whose
  new faith has been revealed can also be banned from traveling
  abroad. Muslim converts to Christianity who work in the public
  sector are likely to lose their jobs and students are likely to be
  expelled from their educational institutions.

- If a wife accepts Christ and her husband wants to divorce, she may
  lose her children, and vice-versa. If both parents become Christian,
  they both may lose their children to the authorities because the
  kids are still seen as Muslims, and it is illegal in many Muslim
  countries for a Christian to raise Muslim kids. In several cases, the
  biggest challenge has come when the children of an MBB family
  have started to share their Christian faith with other kids. The
  school has kicked them out, and in some cases, the school has
  informed the police. I know of a family that went through this
  kind of challenge, and the situation ended with the police raping
  the wife before her husband's eyes.

- In some Arab countries, like Egypt, a person's ID states the
  individual's religion, and changing the religion listed on the ID
  from Islam to another faith is illegal. (Changing one's religion *to*
  Islam is legal.) The appearance of Islam on identity documents
  results in many consequences for MBBs, such as registering their
  children as Muslims on their birth certificates and later enrolling
  them as Muslims in school. When the children are taught as
  Christians at home and forced to identify as Muslims in the wider
  community, it often causes them to struggle with various mental
  health issues, such as anxiety.

- Neighbors of MBBs may persecute them and try to make them move
  out of their homes. I know cases where neighbors have persuaded
  the landlords to evict converts, leaving them homeless. Neighbors
  and relatives may also pressure a believer's employer to fire them.

- Even going to church is also often a security matter for MBBs, as
  most traditional churches in the Middle East and North Africa
  have Muslim security guards at the doors. They may reveal MBBs'
  Christian faith to the authorities or their families.

Thus, whereas a Christian-born believer can belong to a government-recognized church, participate in the political process, or open a business, an MBB whose faith is known usually cannot. Instead, they face prosecution and persecution. Every week, we hear reports of how a Muslim-background believer somewhere has been arrested, abandoned by their families, or otherwise persecuted for their faith. Even in the most moderate Muslim countries such as Tunisia, Algeria, and Turkey, MBBs and their congregations still face difficulties once their faith begins to have an impact on local society.

A Christian service in a Muslim-dominated country. Attending a Christian congregation or even a house church is still not always possible for MBBs. For them, Christian TV and radio channels function as the only "church" where they can feel fellowship and receive Bible teaching.

Most of these challenges are personally familiar also to the MBB staff of Al Hayat. Brother Emad, who appears in *The Saudi Magazine*, was imprisoned and tortured while living in Saudi Arabia. Sister Amani, one of the hosts of *The Muslim Woman*, was arrested in Egypt and suffered at the hands of her Christianity-hostile husband. In Morocco, knifemen tried to break into the home of an MBB from the *Moroccan and Christian* series. Recently, a member of our Egyptian staff was detained for two years without a trial before being released. Some others have been interrogated at the police station.

Sister Amani's words, spoken when she left Egypt and moved to the US, summarize the experience of many MBB believers. She had her daughter and son with her on the flight. As they sat on the plane and it took off, Amani took off her Muslim veil. The act was an outward symbol of everything she had experienced on the inside.

When her son saw what she was doing, he said to her, "Please, mother, don't take off the headscarf because, without it, you will go to hell."

Amani looked at him and said, "Listen, son. We have just come out of one."

Shadows in Safe Haven

For Amani, moving abroad meant freedom from the pressure, verbal abuse, and violence she had faced in her home country, but even in America, for a period, she continued to face persecution from her husband's family. So, moving to another country often does not eliminate all persecution, at least not immediately. In fact (and unfortunately), the more Muslims there are in the new environment, the more likely it is that oppression will continue in some form.

Looking at the situation of MBBs living outside their home country, the first thing to note is that those who live abroad with their Muslim families—whether they are first- or second-generation immigrants—often face family members' anger and disappointment in the ways described above. Even being in the secular or nominally Christian West does not guarantee security and religious freedom from their family.

Here are some of the other challenges MBBs face in non-Muslim countries:

- Some are persecuted by their family members, who travel from their home countries to find them. Several women have faced honor killings or other horrific persecution by their family members who have come into the West after them for revenge. To prevent this, many threatened with violence must live in hiding or move repeatedly.
- If MBBs end up living in an area with a Muslim population and their Christian faith is exposed, the local mosque clerics and some fanatics may indirectly incite people to persecute or even kill MBBs—despite the laws of the country where they are. Due to pressure and hostility, it may not be easy even to go to cultural grocery stores to buy cultural foods.
- If an MBB tries to join an immigrant church from their home country (many traditional Middle Eastern churches have diaspora congregations in the West), the believer may be rejected and accused of being an agent of the homeland security agencies. (This is rare, but I know of cases where it has happened.)

Numerous converts have to experience all this in addition to the "normal" challenges most immigrants face, such as cultural shock, inability to speak the new country's language, lack of employment opportunities, and the pain of losing friends and community.

Like the difficulties mentioned in the previous section, most of these challenges are familiar also to the MBB hosts on Al Hayat, who have publicly announced their Christian conversion and are now living abroad. They must be careful not to expose their home addresses and working locations to their families in their home countries. Even shopping in malls and grocery stores in Western countries with significant Muslim populations has often been difficult because people easily recognize them.

So, there are numerous stories of persecution, and we and several of our partner organizations track and document them and try to act on behalf of the persecuted. At the same time, however, it is worth raising the following point: when we look at the whole body of messages we receive from Al Hayat viewers, the oppression and violence experienced by converts has never emerged as a significant phenomenon. I have wondered why that is. Are MBBs such mature Christians that they don't want to complain about the hardships other people cause them? Are they so numbed to social isolation and verbal slander that they are not moved by these kinds of "soft persecution"? Or is there less persecution than we used to think?

After thinking about it, I'm leaning toward the last two options. The situation is bleak, but if you compare the number of reported instances to the whole number of converts, it may not be as grim as is often thought.

To conclude this section, I would like to return to the children of the MBB families. When the escape abroad goes well, and a family doesn't face persecution in their new environment, the first months are often a honeymoon period for the parents who have borne all the worries and pressures in their home country. For the children, however, the same period is typically a time of great misery. Their loneliness is acute because the extended family has cut off all contact, and they have yet to make new friends. So children usually become very dependent on their parents at first. Even later, when they already have friends, they continue to miss the community of the extended family and the love they used to receive from them.

Understanding this, every time I'm with MBB families in the West, I try to pay attention also to their children. Many of them have started to call me Grandpa, so I have many grandchildren. Some send me videos and presents, and others draw pictures of me and send them to me (although kids often politely draw me with more hair than I really have). They are also happy when I send them a video, call them, or send them a quick text. MBB families need love and lots of it, and if we have the heart to give it to them, I am sure that many of these kids will become the most active evangelists later on. They are God's shining stars.

A Word for Western Christians: Remember, God is in Control

Although not all MBBs suffer active persecution in their daily lives, the previous pages have shown that Muslim-background believers go through difficulties that much of the Western

Church cannot identify with. Many of these difficulties are caused by Muslims who are zealous for their faith. Therefore, many readers who have grown up in the midst of Christian culture may now be thinking, "Oh, this is too much! I should be scared to death of Muslims." Creating such feelings has not been my intention.

Instead, I have wanted to talk about these things for two reasons. First, to gain some appreciation for what it is like to walk in the shoes of an MBB. Second, to get you to pray for them but also for Muslims who hurt others in the name of their faith. Those Muslims probably haven't heard the good news about the love of God and are as much in need of Christ as you were when lost in darkness and sin.

So don't be afraid to share the love of Christ with these people through witnessing with words and your life. God can change anybody. If God has changed the lives of ISIS fighters, al-Qaeda recruits, and many other Muslims—and mine, which once was so deep in sin and worldly desires that Sari considered my salvation an absolute impossibility—for sure, He can change your Muslim neighbor's life, too.

I know an Algerian man who used to live in Switzerland. He was a Muslim but deceived a local church by telling them he was a Christian. He did this for three years, and the Swiss congregation took care of him all that time, and many families showed him love and hospitality.

Finally, the Swiss government refused to give him asylum status, and the man was sent back to Algeria. After a year back there, he was thinking about the love he had experienced in that congregation in Switzerland. He missed the people there and felt miserable for what he had done to them. He began to read the Bible, and God spoke to him through the Word and the love he had received from the Swiss Christian community. The man started to struggle and process things in his heart, and finally, he confessed Jesus as the Son of God and his Master—this time, with a sincere heart. Later, he became an active member of the MBB community in his home country.

God did not make a mistake by making this Muslim man a friend and neighbor to these Swiss Christians. God is in control. He can protect you also. The worst place is where God does not want you to be.

As Christians, we need to remind ourselves from time to time of what Jesus says in Matthew 5:11, 12:

> *Blessed are you when they revile and persecute you, and say all kinds of evil against you falsely for My sake. Rejoice and be exceedingly glad, for great is your reward in heaven, for so they persecuted the prophets who were before you.*

I pray that you, me, and all Christians can live in peace and security. Yet, whatever happens, let us remember that if we have Jesus in our hearts, there is no need to be afraid.

MBB Marriage: Searching for a Spouse

I conclude this chapter with a challenge experienced by many Muslim-background believers, which is so intimate that I hesitated before writing the following lines. It is about finding a spouse.

On a personal level, every MBB, like every human person, is looking for love and acceptance. Getting married is integral to most people's lives, and Muslim-background Christians are no exception. However, in their lives, this issue can have extra difficulties for several reasons:

- In many Muslim-majority regions, the number of possible Christian spouses is very limited because there are only a few MBBs and Christian-background believers in the area, or they are challenging to find because they hide their faith.
- The family of a female MBB may force her to marry a Muslim man so that the family can "cover up" the shame her conversion will cause them.
- In most Muslim-majority countries, it is illegal for female Muslims to marry a Christian man, and because MBB women are still officially seen as Muslims, it restricts their freedom to choose a husband. (Muslim men, on the other hand, are allowed to marry Christian women, which makes the situation easier for MBB men who are still listed as Muslim in the population register.)

Since I know the Middle East and North Africa better than other parts of the world, I will now look at this issue from the perspective of these regions in particular. Because of the similarities in culture, these challenges are a reality in all countries in the region, but there are also remarkable differences between countries. Let me explain what and why.

A particular feature of North Africa (except Egypt) and the countries of the Arabian Peninsula is that these countries don't have a long tradition of churches. That means there aren't many Christian-born women for an MBB man to fall in love with. So, to find a compatible marriage partner, converted men must look for one among other MBBs or among moderate Muslims. The same is true for women who have converted from Islam to Christianity, but in North Africa and the Arabian Peninsula, it's still common for Muslim families to arrange the marriage of their daughter who has converted to Christianity, and the family usually has no will to choose an exceptionally moderate husband for a woman—often quite the opposite. Thus, finding a like-minded spouse in these regions is often difficult for all Muslim-background believers, but it is particularly difficult for women.

In Egypt, Lebanon, Syria, Iraq, and some other Middle Eastern countries, there are several traditional churches, so there are many more potential Christian marriage candidates, and relationships between an MBB and a Christian-born believer are also quite common. For converted men, there is not even a legal barrier to such marriages, and ex-Muslim women can circumvent the law, for example, by marrying abroad. Unfortunately, however, in many cases, traditional Christian families aren't happy with their child's plan to marry a person from a Muslim-background. The result may be that an MBB whom his or her own family has already cast off will also be rejected by the family of the one they love. I know more than twenty MBBs who have experienced this kind of situation. Of course, the family's rejection doesn't always prevent a couple from getting married, but it does put an extra strain on their life together.

Sometimes a marriage between a Muslim man and a Christian woman succeeds, but too often, it doesn't. In my case, after Sari and I got married, I became a follower of Christ. Some would take this as an example, but I recommend caution. Sari and I had a special story, and it is not an automatically recurring scenario. I would not recommend any Christian woman or girl to marry even a secularized Muslim man. It is not wise to think it is OK to marry a Muslim man because God will soon bring him to know the truth in Christ. The hope that he will become a missionary, minister, or apostle for his country may be just wishful thinking and not from God.

Let's imagine that a "young Sari" was to ask me, a sixty-four-year-old man who has been a Christian for more than three decades and has seen a lot in life, if she should marry a twenty-year-old Muslim Harun. I would say, "No, definitely not." The truth is that when we mess up our lives, God can change and turn them back towards His will, but we shouldn't give Him the script of our life in advance and expect Him to follow it. The Bible gives us good guidance that we can also apply to choosing a spouse, such as: "Do not be unequally yoked together with unbelievers" (2 Corinthians 6:14–18). Let God do it the way He sees fit.

Over the past twenty years or so, some ministries and churches have tried to help Muslim-background believers find suitable spouses by organizing special meetings or conferences for single MBBs to meet each other. While these ministries and churches are compassionately trying to help these believers fulfill their dreams, sometimes there is also another motivation at work: in many countries, establishing an MBB family provides a natural meeting place for other converts in the neighborhood and thus serves as the beginning of a house church.

I am not saying that organizing such single meetings is wrong. Still, when you have only five or six single men and five or six single women, it seldom works. In my experience, more than 80 percent of couples whose spouses have met in such a meeting or conference end up divorced. Some of my close friends have gone through that. Even if there are limited options, we can't force love. This is one of those issues where we have to trust God that He will provide. I don't have the answer to this problem, but what I see happening is not working.

I know one case where the marriage of a couple from a small church succeeded. 1987, I attended a conference where the pastor revealed how he and his wife met. He was from a small congregation in a small village. He told us, "I wanted to marry. I was twenty-one years old, and in my church, we had only two single women, a sixty-year-old and a twenty-year-old. So, I made my choice, and I took the twenty-year-old. I had no other choice." The story may be funny, but everything went well. When I write this, they're still happily married.

16

Yes to the Contextualization of the Gospel — No to "Messianic Islam"

If you've been reading this book from the beginning, you've encountered the acronym "MBB" more than a hundred times. The three-letter initialism is a handy way to shorten the expression "Muslim-background believer," and it is widely used when talking about us who have converted from Islam to Christianity. Some others call us "BMBs"—believers from a Muslim background.

Despite the convenience of these acronyms, I believe none of us MBBs are especially fond of them. These kinds of expressions always have a risk of over-simplifications and mis-generalization within and between people groups. Still, these titles have stuck for now, and we have even started to call ourselves by these names for lack of better terminology. Of course, they have their advantages: they give quick information about our shared background—if one knows what words the acronym represents.

Yet, "MBB" and "BMB" are not the only special terms used to refer to former Muslims. In 1998, the pseudonym John Travis, a Western missionary and missiologist working in a Muslim culture, developed "the C1–C6 Spectrum" to describe the various types of Muslim-background Christians and groups he saw existing in the Muslim world. The scale recognizes six models of contextualization differentiating by language, culture, worship forms, religious identity, and willingness to worship with others. According to Travis, the "C" here stands for the "Christ-centered community," but it could just as well be seen as referring to the "contextualization" of the gospel. The term refers to using local practices and ways of thought in Christian teaching and worship.

Travis' scale has also been used for other religions, but here, I apply it only to Islam. Travis intended the classification to describe the contextualization of MBB believers, but I will also use it for missionaries when describing the categories C1–C4.

Here is a summary of the scale:

- *C1: Users of non-indigenous language and cultural customs.* This group includes MBBs and the Christian communities who practice their faith in a non-indigenous language—say, English—and their church meetings resemble a foreign Christian culture and church structure. Congregations following model C1 are like islands amid the Muslim community, totally removed from the local culture.

- *C2: Those who use indigenous language but maintain foreign Christian traditions.* These MBBs and congregations use the local language, but all other aspects of their religious life follow foreign traditions and methodology. The result is a Christian culture that stays very separate from the local Muslim-majority culture and the life of the people.

- *C3: Users of indigenous language and non-religious indigenous cultural forms.* Here, the MBBs, congregations, and missionaries also adopt local non-religious cultural traditions and habits, such as regional musical and artistic styles, in their religious practice. In addition, the worship service can take into account, for example, whether people traditionally sit on the floor or benches. At the same time, these Christians and congregations still attempt to break from all spiritual elements of Islam, like observing Islamic dietary laws, Ramadan, religious holidays, and Islamic religious terminology.

- *C4: Users of Islamic religious language and biblically acceptable Islamic spiritual forms.* Members of this group also adopt Islamic religious practices and terminology that are not considered to be in conflict with the Bible. This means, for example, that MBBs and missionaries call Jesus by the Qur'anic name Isa, do not keep dogs as pets (in Islam, dogs are seen as ritually impure), do not drink alcohol nor eat pork, and—in some cases—fast during Ramadan, follow Islamic holidays, and even observe Islamic prayer postures. Many "C4s" prefer to call themselves "followers of Isa" rather than "Christians."

- *C5: "Messianic Muslims" continuing within the Islamic community.* This group means converts who follow Jesus as Lord and Savior but also continue to participate in the mosque prayers, recite the Islamic creed (Shahada), and thus remain part of the Muslim community. Many of these believers see Muhammad as similar to the Old Testament prophets and accept the Qur'an as a holy book except where it conflicts with the Bible, or at least see some Qur'anic principles as a small light directing people to the broader truth. Besides attending Muslim worship services, these believers may have their own gatherings where they study the Bible, pray together, and experience fellowship. Some call the converts following the C5 model "Messianic Muslims."

- *C6: Secret/underground believers.* These MBBs also act in their everyday life like Muslims around them, but they do so not in an effort to reconcile Christianity with (parts) of Islam but out of fear of the consequences of revealing their new faith amidst the Muslim community. These believers are typically isolated from any larger Christian community, but some have their own small, scattered groups.

When I became a Christian in Finland in 1985, I was C1, for sure. I used Finnish as my spiritual language and joined a congregation following the Finnish-Pentecostal tradition. There was nothing Arabic in those church services besides the Arabic numerals used to indicate the songs in the songbook.

Later, when I began my ministry in Stockholm, I started participating in the Arabic Christian group and using Arabic in my prayers and Bible study. This took me into the category of C2. Soon I became rooted also in Arabic-style Christian music, art, and other cultural forms, so I became C3, which I still am.

For me, safe and fruitful contextualization adapts the Arabic culture's positive aspects but rejects Islam's rules and spiritual elements. Following the New Testament, I can eat pork, and I do not consider it a problem for a Christian to drink a small amount of alcohol at a meal or on some special occasion. I could also keep a dog as a pet (though Sari and I have had only cats). I don't call Jesus by his Qur'anic name Isa.

Most of my MBB friends belong to groups C3 and C2, but I also know some belonging to C4. The C5 "Messianic Muslims" I haven't met. In fact, I would say that the C5 is quite rare in the Arabic world—it seems to be more common in some Asian Islamic societies.

Looking at Travis' spectrum from a missionary perspective, I believe my words carry weight when I say that "the C3 method" has proven to be the most fruitful way to present the gospel to Muslims. That's why most Al Hayat content represents this category—only a minority is C2. We don't have any programs that represent C4. While we have taken the local Arab cultures into account vividly in many of our series, we do not want to compromise with Islam. We love Muslims, but we hate Islam and don't see any reason why we should submit to its rules. The other popular channels, such as SAT-7 and Miracle Channel, also operate in the C2 and C3 categories. C4 Arabic Christian satellite channels, I don't know.

Saying this doesn't mean I would consider the C4 model dangerous. However, I think some of its aspects, such as following Islamic prayer postures and holidays, can obscure essential differences between Christianity and Islam. If someone says that biblical theology should be contextualized to fit the Middle Eastern context, I remind him that the Bible is already a Middle Eastern book—not a Western one.

The "safety line" goes between C4 and C5. I cannot endorse any believer to retain their Muslim identity or attend religious services in mosques as secret believers who follow Jesus in their heart but continue to revere Muhammad as God's prophet. It endangers their own faith and is also misleading to others.

In Al Hayat's programs, contextualizing the gospel means adapting the Arabic culture's positive aspects but rejecting Islam's rules and spiritual elements. Here are the hosts of the *Kuwaiti Enlightenment* series, Adel and Laila.

Let me explain more deeply why I think so.

Irreconcilable Conflict

The problems I see in the C5 and C6 models are threefold:
1. Confessing the Qur'an as a holy book
2. Confessing Muhammad as a prophet of God
3. Continuing to participate in the ritual prayers in the mosque

Confessing the Qur'an as a holy book. While the Old Testament points toward the new covenant expressed in the New Testament (Jer. 31:31–34, cf. Hebrews 8–9) and the New Testament confirms the Old Testament's authority (e.g., Luke 24:27), neither the Old nor New Testament points toward the

Qur'an, nor does the Qur'an confirm the Bible as the true, reliable word of God. More than that, the New Testament especially warns of teachers who come after the Apostles and teach about Jesus, God, and salvation differently than Jesus and the Apostles did (cf. 2 John 7–11, Romans 16:7, etc.). The Qur'an, if anything, is such a book because it straightforwardly denies many central New Testament teachings, such as Jesus being the crucified (Son of) God who died on behalf of our sins.

This means Islamic and Judeo-Christian faiths do not share the same scriptural taproot. We can't say that both the Qur'an and the Christian Bible are the accurate Word of God: either one is true, or neither is true, but both cannot be right and holy. A Jew is considered "Messianic" when they recognize Jesus of the New Testament fulfilling the Old Testament messianic prophesies. Because the Qur'an directly conflicts with the Bible regarding these things, no amount of faith in the verity of the Qur'an nor calling Jesus *al-Masih* (Messiah) in the Qur'anic meaning will ever render a Muslim "Messianic." Recognizing the Qur'an as a holy book places the verity of Scripture, God's character, and the Messiah's identity in question.

Confessing Muhammad as a prophet of God. By the biblical definition, a prophet is a person who hears and expresses the words of God to others (e.g., 2 Samuel 23:2; 2 Peter 1:19–21). This includes several dimensions, of which I will here mention two.

First, expressing the words of God means loyalty to the revelation God has given before. By denying several basic teachings of Jesus and the Apostles, Muhammad (or anyone else) doesn't fulfill this Christian criterion of a true prophet.

Second, in Judeo-Christian tradition, the genuine prophetic ministry is reflected in specific supernatural knowledge of events that shall come to pass (e.g., Deuteronomy 5:18, John 13:19). A true prophet has "shall come to pass" foresight. So, to attribute the status of the prophet to Muhammad, the words of the Qur'an should also verify the author's supernatural knowledge of (at least some) future events. However, unlike the Old and New Testaments, the Qur'an does not contain predictions in that sense. In the Qur'an, there are only general references to the future, such as that there will be a day of judgment. This means that Muhammad doesn't meet this criterion of a true prophet, either.

So, the reputation of Muhammad as a prophet is in question, and due to that, the recitation of the Shahada ("There is no god but Allah, and Muhammad is his messenger") becomes an instrument of deception of the most heinous sort. This means that if you are a secret Muslim-background Christian but continue confessing "Shahada," you—whether you believe its words or not—reinforce the belief of others in this theological error and encourage its proliferation.

Continuing to participate in the ritual prayers. If the confession of the Shahada strengthens the heresy in others, attending the mosque and participating in the ritual prayers (Salat) can only fuel this unholy fire. These activities not only establish the practitioners as "good Muslims" in other Muslims' minds but also place the participants on the anti-Christian front—whether they like it or not.

One reason for the latter fact is two verses from the opening Sura of the Qur'an, which Muslims pray in each of the five daily ritual prayers:

> Guide us to the Straight Way. The Way of those on whom You have bestowed Your Grace, not (the way) of those who earned Your Anger nor of those who went astray. (Sura 1.6, 7)

Interpreting these words, Muslim scholars usually agree that "those who went astray" refers to Christians and "those who earned Your Anger" are the Jews. This means that every person who prays in the Islamic way asks God several times daily that He wouldn't make them a Jew or a Christian.

For me, this attitude speaks clearly about the dark spiritual forces lurking behind the Islamic religious system.

Here we come to the last argument against the C5 model: people attending Islamic worship expose themselves to the demonic spiritual power wrapped up in these observances. The Apostle Paul did not say in vain, "Evil company corrupts good habits" (1 Corinthians 15:33). One cannot remain in fellowship with the messengers of deceit and propaganda for very long without being threatened by the ideology they represent. Therefore, in the lifestyle described by the C5 and C6 models, there is a high risk that the converts relinquish their Christian faith and revert to Islam.

So, avoid these Islamic practices, and you will do well.

"This Is Not My House"

One of the most powerful things to inspire a Muslim to benevolent change is the clear difference between Christian and Islamic life. Paul's admonition is apparent in the second letter to Corinthians 6:14–18: We should not be unequally yoked with unbelievers. I have previously referred to this passage in the context of marriage between Christians and non-Christians, but it also applies here: Righteousness has no fellowship with lawlessness. Light has no communion with darkness. Christ has no accord with false gods. The living temple of God, which we are, has no agreement with idols.

Instead, since God dwells in us and walks among us, we ought to come out from the midst of unbelief, lawlessness, darkness, and fellowship with demons. That doesn't mean that former Muslims or anyone else should separate themselves from Muslims in general—quite the opposite, if possible—but that no one should join Islamic religious practices. For Muslims to be touched by the gospel, they must see a clear and inspiring distinction in how Christians live. Without this lifestyle distinction, Christianity offers little hope to Muslims forcefully embedded in their religion and Islamic culture. As followers of Jesus, we are to be involved in the world, but we are not to represent the world (cf. John 17:14–16, 1 Corinthians 5:9–11).

All this may sound harsh in a situation where a convert may—at worst—be subjected to brutal physical violence. So that my words are not misunderstood, I want to clarify that when I'm warning about the C5 and C6 models, I don't mean a new ex-Muslim who is afraid to reveal his Christian faith and is struggling with what to do. Sometimes it is necessary to continue in the mosque for a while to avoid discrimination and mistreatment and to grow in the Christian faith. Sooner or later, however, a convert must confront the truth and either remain a Muslim in the mosque community or follow Christ and leave.

I want to emphasize that these are not only my opinions. I don't know any MBB theologian who recommends the C5 or C6 model as a permanent solution for a Muslim-background Christian. Despite this, some Christian-background missiologists and priests in the Muslim world think that a Muslim who becomes a follower of Jesus should continue their religious practice in the mosque. Such thinking is often accompanied by downplaying of the importance of Christian baptism. The idea is that because baptism may cause hostile reactions by Muslims, the whole sacrament can be bypassed.

This happened to one of my close Egyptian friends, Hussein, many years ago. When he accepted Christ, he went to a traditional church in Cairo, met a priest there, and told him about his conversion. The priest, however, was afraid to admit him into the congregation and did not want to baptize him.

Instead, the priest told Hussein, "Well, I would like you to consider going to the mosque. When you pray there, you can pray in your heart to Christ."

Hussein wondered about the instructions but did as he was told. The next day, he went to the mosque and stood in the line of the praying Muslim men. Suddenly he heard a voice saying in his mind, "What are you doing here? This is not my house; I want you to be a part of my family. I want you to go and worship among your brothers and sisters in my house."

Hussein understood what it was about. He left the mosque, returned to the church, and told the priest what he had heard. Despite Hussein's experience, the priest still did not want him to join the congregation. Thankfully, Hussein later found his place in a small group of evangelical Christians in Cairo. He was also baptized.

According to the Bible, whoever believes and is baptized will be saved (e.g., Mark 16:16, Acts 2:37–39). One meaning of baptism is to create a barrier to protect and strengthen the new believer in their faith. For Muslims, especially, the act of baptism demonstrates that the person has left Islam and become a follower of Jesus, the Son of God, whose true majesty Islam denies. So I consider baptism a crucial step on the path to Christianity—so crucial that if a Muslim-background person claiming to be a Christian does not want to be baptized, I become nervous. Does the person have some secrets?

Often, a baptism ceremony of former Muslims includes an outspoken renunciation of Islam, much like it was once a common practice in Western churches to renounce all the works of the devil in a baptism.

17

A Dream about *Ummah*, a Community

When I tell Christians or journalists about our work, I am repeatedly asked for different figures. One of the figures that raises the most interest is the number of converts from Islam to Christianity worldwide.

The question is important but tricky to answer. In fact, I'd also be happy to know the number myself. The estimates presented vary a lot. Some say higher numbers, others lower. When writing this, most appraisals are between 10 and 30 million.

Personally, I think 15 to 20 million former Muslims following Jesus today is the safest and best-justified figure. In uncertain cases like this, my principle is to avoid the most optimistic statistics. If it should happen that, despite all the consideration, that number turns out to be wrong, it is more comfortable to be corrected upwards than downwards.

In any case, the most significant MBB populations seem to live in Indonesia, Ethiopia, and Iran. In Muslim-majority Indonesia, there is a long history of mass conversions to Christianity. Many years ago, it was already estimated that there were more than six million Muslim-background Christians in the country. In Ethiopia, the number also seems to be counted in millions. (The latest figure I heard from a local church leader was five million, but this may be too optimistic.) In Iran, as noted in the

"Jihadist Logic" section above, there are estimated to be around a million ex-Muslims following Jesus.

Remarkable MBB populations also exist in countries like Algeria, Burkina Faso, Nigeria, and Tanzania—in all of which live hundreds of thousands of Muslim-background Christians. In the West, the most significant number of converts live in the US, around half a million.

This statistical uncertainty reflects the exceptional difficulties in counting MBBs accurately, including the following:

- There are different definitions for "MBB." For instance, do we count converts' children into the number?
- Many MBB groups still have no contact with any denominational or missiological structure.
- The traditional churches seldom make exact statistics of the converts' backgrounds.
- The number of hidden Christians among Muslim communities is believed to be significant, but it is only possible to make rough estimates of that number.

When we looked above at the persecution and oppression faced by former Muslims, a key theme was abandonment and isolation from one's former social network, most notably one's own family. A fear of this kind of rejection is probably the main reason why some converts find the C5 and C6 models attractive. Their family and Muslim community have given them security, met their social needs, and provided them with a sense of belonging and identity—all significant parts of most Muslim cultures. A public conversion from Islam would probably result in, at least, a temporary loss of all these.

For me, the most significant struggle before my conversion was whether it would cause a permanent loss of relationship with my immediate family, especially my mother.

Knowing all this, one of my biggest dreams from almost the beginning of my ministry has been forming a community where all of us who have turned from Islam to Christianity can meet our need for belonging, express our new identity in Christ, and get help to survive in a hostile environment. In the

Bible, the Christian congregations are described as mothers (2 John 1, 13), and Jesus and the Apostles describe their care for the believers with motherly expressions (e.g., Matthew 23:37, 1 Thessalonians 2:7, 8). Using that kind of vocabulary, I have dreamed about a community that would take the new MBB Christians into her arms like a mother and be their Christian *ummah*—the Arabic word for society, based on the word for mother, *um*.

Over the years, this community-building project has sometimes taken up even more of my time than running Al Hayat. As I write this, I'm happy to tell you that we now have an officially registered MBB denomination called Communio Messianica, serving as a spiritual family for millions of ex-Muslims. The project would hardly have succeeded without the help of the World Evangelical Alliance and other Christian-background friends and advisors, to whom we as a whole MBB community express our gratitude.

I believe the story is worth telling from the beginning.

Towards the end of the 2010s, more MBBs were willing to publicly reveal their faith and, for example, share their baptism photos on social media. This makes conversion a more familiar phenomenon in the Arab community. Yet, many still do not dare to speak about their faith for fear of retribution.

Searching for a Fellowship

When my friend Niilo and I traveled to Morocco, Egypt, and elsewhere in the 1980s and early 1990s to meet Muslim-background Christians, we became familiar with the joy of discovering Jesus these people felt. At the same time, however, we also became familiar with the many unique challenges they faced. The greatest of those seemed to be rejection by their immediate community and the loneliness that caused them.

In regions with a Christian presence, this situation usually led new MBBs to contact traditional Christian communities if the person felt it was safe to do so. However, as we have seen, joining those churches often proved complicated. Sometimes traditional Christians saw MBBs as "Muslims" and were cautious in their interactions. Even more often, those churches couldn't accept Muslim-background Christians as members because of the constraints of society and the national legal system. Baptizing a person who has left Islam could bring persecution upon the church by the local community. As uncomfortable as it is to say, for these churches, MBBs were a stress factor.

Sometimes joining a traditional church succeeded, but MBBs still experienced feelings of alienation within the community because they were unfamiliar with the Christian terminology. The same applied to congregations in the West, where it may have been easier for ex-Muslims to join the church, but even there, the different cultural backgrounds typically slowed down the process of getting to know and trust a new member from a Muslim background. Hidden racism and xenophobia, which unfortunately exist even in many Western churches, often had the same effect of preventing the deepening of relationships.

Because of all that, many MBBs found their place in house churches with other ex-Muslims—if such a group existed nearby.

The more I saw these challenges, the more convinced I became that Muslim-background believers should have their own grassroots spiritual movement. I learned that some such movements and alliances had been formed here and there, but they all functioned nationally, regionally, or within some smaller ethnic group. No global MBB community existed.

So I started to speak about the issue to people I met—missionaries, local MBB leaders, traditional church pastors in the Middle East, and leaders of mission organizations. For a long time, only a few seemed to have the same desire to develop that kind of international MBB fellowship. In fact, it seemed that many Christian-background people did not like the idea at all and perceived forming such a group akin to creating a new competitor to their community.

Finally, after more than ten years of ministry, in 1996, I managed to convene the first group to promote our vision of a global MBB community. There were fifteen people present, and the meeting took place in Finland at Keymedia's facilities. It was a small start, but a start, nevertheless. Later in the same year, we met in Egypt with a partially different lineup. Many of the people in the new group belonged to the *Children of Ishmael* team we had started in Egypt in the early 1990s, so Egypt was a natural place to meet with this aim also.

In 1998, I told my communal vision to my friend Victor Hashweh. I met him in 1989, and even though he is from a Christian background, he has a real heart for MBBs. He was lit up about the idea. Victor and I started identifying MBB leaders with the same vision, and it turned out that Victor knew many people I didn't know, and I knew many that he didn't. So together, we were able to gather a group of twenty-five people to attend the next conference in the summer of 2000. This meeting was also held in Finland.

After that, things started to move faster. Later in the same year, eleven of us met again in Egypt. There we initiated a formal MBB network and established an executive board with Victor as the president. I was selected as vice president and media consultant, and Stephen Kelley, an ex-Muslim who emigrated to the US, was nominated as treasurer and training consultant. Jordanian MBB pastor and missionary Marwan Qandah became secretary and human rights and counseling consultant. This was the first time Muslim-background Christians from across the Arab-speaking world had formed such an organization. We named it "the United Family."

In 2001, we met in Istanbul with 60 attendees and added "International" to our name, making our group officially known as United Family International (UFI). The following year, the executive board traveled to Switzerland and registered the organization as an official entity.

In 2002, we convened a conference in southern Spain, and the attendees rose to around a hundred. Then, in the Netherlands, we were even more, as well as in Malta and other places. It was a blessing to meet many new people and leaders of MBB communities and groups from different countries. We brought people together to have visions and strategy sessions to reach the Muslim world and link more MBBs into the fellowship. We also decided to support eleven Muslim-background Christians on their mission trips.

The meeting places varied a lot. Sometimes we gathered on the grounds of a theological college, other times in a quiet seaside hotel or a Christian conference center in the countryside. Everywhere we went, we had to take safety considerations into account. In those days, the early 2000s, it was very dangerous for MBBs to gather like that. There was always the risk that some participant would turn out to be a traitor and later cause us trouble—or that someone would stupidly take a photo and it would fall into the wrong hands. You couldn't always even rule out the possibility that some outsider present, such as a member of the hotel staff, would have contacts with Muslim fanatics and expose us to them or—when we were meeting in Muslim-majority countries—the local authorities. There were also risks associated with travel, especially if the participant came from a very closed Muslim country.

The latter risk materialized after the UFI meeting in southern Spain in 2002. One of the attendees was a Saudi man named Abdul. This was the first time a Saudi believer had joined a larger group of MBBs face-to-face, and we saw strong symbolism in his presence—Saudi Arabia is, of course, the cradle of Islam. In addition, Muslim-background Saudi Christians were extremely rare at those times, and Abdul knew some others, too. So, it seemed that we could later contact the wider Saudi MBB community through him. For us, his presence was like a lottery win.

I had invited Abdul to the conference after meeting him a few years earlier in Egypt. When we started talking there, he asked me suddenly, "Do you believe in dreams and visions?"

I told him I did. So he continued, "I had a vision that I was in Mecca, but I sat there in a church meeting in a basement where there were about sixty-five to seventy people."

At that moment, I interrupted him and asked if he would let me continue the story. He was surprised.

I said, "Brother, I saw the same or similar vision. The room had small windows close to the roof, and the chairs were crimson, with golden metal legs. The curtains were also crimson."

"No way!" Abdul said. "This is it… the same room!"

I told him I had seen this vision a year before and kept it in my heart.

We rejoiced and praised the Lord for this. I believe God confirmed this vision by showing it to both of us, and one day, there really will be churches in the holiest city of Islam.

After the conference in Spain in 2002, Abdul traveled back to Saudi Arabia. When he arrived, the airport officials detained him. He called me right away, close to midnight, and said, "Harun, I am at the passport control now, and it looks like I will be arrested. Please pray for me."

I was worried. After a while, I called him, but there was no answer. I understood that they had taken his phone. About an hour later, I received a call from his number. I answered, but no one replied. I was certain that he was arrested. Later, I heard from our mutual friend, a missionary working in Saudi Arabia, that the officials had taken Abdul's Blackberry and found a digital Bible on it. He had been sent to prison for five years.

After serving his sentence, Abdul was released, but our dream of contacting the wider MBB community in Saudi Arabi did not pan out quite as we had hoped. The authorities' suspicions about Abdul have forced him to be very cautious. Still, I regularly hear through the mutual missionary friend that Abdul still lives in Saudi Arabia and is OK. A strange detail is that I receive a missed call from his number every year. Every time it happens, I am reminded to pray for him and about our mutual vision concerning the Christian church in Mecca.

Home, Umbrella Organization, and Voice for the Voiceless

When we formulated a vision for UFI in 2000–2001, we included five elements:
- To be a voice for the voiceless
- To be an umbrella organization for smaller MBB organizations
- To be a gathering point
- To be a home for converts from Islam to Christianity
- To deal with human rights

Being the "voice of the voiceless" meant that we wanted UFI to speak on behalf of MBB believers who, under threat of violence, are forced to hide their faith or are belittled in their present Christian community because of their background. We included "umbrella organization" and "home" because we saw UFI as a community where individual MBBs and their communities could gain support and understanding from others of the same faith and background. By "gathering point" we meant that we wanted UFI to be a body that both Muslim-background believers and external actors, such as foreign missionary organizations, could contact if they needed information about the life of MBBs or, for example, were searching for partners from the same field of action. In the arena of human rights, UFI focused mainly on promoting religious freedom.

In practice, these objectives were implemented via counseling, fundraising for relief efforts, mentoring, networking, organizing conferences, pastoral care visits, producing media content for Al Hayat, and providing guest speakers and worship leaders for Christian events. We also provided monthly support to more than twenty Muslim-background leaders in the Middle East and North Africa—and some others who worked among MBBs in the region and did not have any other source of income. In 2010, we helped to establish a center for MBBs in Beirut. At one point, we even planned for an online church.

Some of these projects we did as UFI, some with other ministries. The latter was helped by the fact that many members of the UFI board also served as board members of other organizations.

Brother Victor was our chairman until 2012 when he decided to retire at 70. After that, I became the chairman. Between 2000 and 2019, we had four UFI chairs/presidents: Victor Hashweh, me (2012–2015), Jordanian Marwan Qandah (2015–2016), and a Sudanese-born MBB pastor, Yassir Eric (2016–2019).

Despite the word "international" in our name and the phrase "MBBs wherever they may be found" in our vision statement, our emphasis was practically only on the Arab world for years. It was only in the 2010s that we started to think more about expanding internationally and creating a home for Muslim-background Christians from all continents, languages, and ethnic groups. The first non-Arabs—some Somali, Turkish, and Iranian believers—joined UFI in 2014 and 2015.

So, over the years, UFI developed into a pretty good service organization. Still, our goal for it to be a spiritual home for Muslim-background Christians had yet to develop as hoped. For several years, we did not have the money to organize big MBB conferences, which had been an effective networking tool, especially for leaders. Also, some of our prominent figures were very cautious, fearing how the rest of Christendom would react if we raised our cause more visibly.

We needed help.

18

Rebooting the Community — Communio Messianica Becomes Reality

In 2015, my dear friend Abu Yehia, mentioned above, told me that those of us on the UFI leadership should have a conversation with the World Evangelical Alliance (WEA). He had some friends there, and he thought that we should meet them and vice versa.

The meeting took place in Malta in early 2015, and it surely was a blessed gathering. Our new friends in WEA encouraged us to be bolder in bringing UFI to the public and to work harder to make it global. It strengthened our resolve, and we tried to act on the advice we received. At the same time, we continued our prayers for God to guide us and open a door for us. And that's what happened.

For that, we had to travel to Bonn, Germany.

In mid-January 2017, the highway from Frankfurt to Bonn was slippery. The temperature was below freezing, and it had rained a little. Part of the UFI board had flown to Frankfurt, but our meeting place was in Bonn, where a religious freedom specialist of WEA, Thomas Schirrmacher, had kindly invited us. We rented a minibus, and I was asked to drive; others knew I was used to driving in icy and snowy conditions in Finland.

In Bonn, there were five of us from the UFI board: Dr. Yassir Eric, Shino Gabo, Dr. Mike Ansari, Latif El Qochairi, and myself. In addition, our "Yemeni German" friend, Abu Yehia, was also invited. We visited the house of the famous composer Ludwig van Beethoven (1770–1827), ate German food (pork knuckle with sauerkraut and potatoes is my all-time favorite), and enjoyed each other's company. Still, the most remarkable moments of our trip were spent on the local church premises, where brother Thomas had arranged a place to gather.

We came to Bonn because we had asked Thomas—the future Secretary General of WEA—if he would be our adviser in developing UFI. He had not attended the Malta meeting in 2015, but had heard about us and was willing to help. Upon his recommendation, we also invited Archbishop William Mikler from Communio Christiana, an Anglican-background international denomination.

William and Thomas are both great personalities. Archbishop William is charismatic and mission-orientated, with a solid evangelistic heart, and Thomas is very familiar with the challenges religious minorities face in Muslim-dominant environments. We soon noticed how much they both love and care for MBBs.

In the meeting, we told them that, as UFI leaders, we were searching for a path forward to develop the organization to be more communal and effective. William and Thomas listened to our stories and the challenges many of us had faced when trying to find our place in traditional Christian denominations and mission organizations. Because of those challenges, we hoped that UFI would be a place for MBBs to belong and serve.

After listening, William and Thomas had two recommendations for us:

1. We should form our own self-governing communion—a denomination—with our indigenous leadership.
2. We should join the new communion to the World Evangelical Alliance, primarily to defend the religious freedom of MBBs (with the WEA, we would have a louder voice) but also to help us identify with the broader Christian community.

They promised to help us if we wished to take these steps. They said they recognized our apostolic gift, but at the same time, they thought they might have some valuable experience to share with us when we're developing our community.

Among the UFI board, we held a short discussion and felt the recommendations to be solid and worth implementing. We had learned to appreciate the WEA's work. Thomas's and William's help was also very welcome. It was good to have people with experience to guide us in this formation process and show us what it would look like.

Then someone asked what name we would give the new communion. After a short chat, we decided on "Communio Messianica" (CM), the Community of Messiah. We thought the two words best expressed the heart of the movement and organization we had in mind. The name was also easy to translate into other languages; the Arabic name, for example, is *Ummat Al-Masih.*

Later in the same year, another meeting was convened between us, the World Evangelical Alliance, some missionaries, and others who shared the same vision.

After two years of preparations, Communio Messianica was formally registered in Switzerland in 2019 and replaced the previous UFI. Later in the same year, at a big mission conference in Mainz, Germany, we introduced Communio Messianica to a broader range of MBB- and Christian-background church leaders, NGOs, and mission organizations focused on the Muslim world.

As I write this, I am in my fourth year as the chairman of the CM Board of Council. For me, the change from UFI to Communio Messianica was relatively small—the central vision and the board members remained the same—but the Mainz conference was still a significant step forward. I felt the gridlock we had been in with UFI had finally broken. This time, we managed to package our vision so that also others experienced it how we wanted.

When Sudanese Yassir Eric's (left) family learned about his conversion to Christianity, they held a funeral in his memory—he became like a dead man to them. Since then, Yassir has become a well-known MBB theologian and leader. Here he is with American Messianic Rabbi Jason Sobel.

The most remarkable change was that while both the MBB majority and external actors had seen UFI primarily as an NGO, with Communio Messianica people began to see our community as we wanted it to be seen: as a spiritual home. This became clear in the feedback we received.

For MBBs, Communio Messianica seemed to be a long-yearned-for response to their needs—a door of hope at the end of a dark tunnel and a home to replace the one they had as Muslims within the Islamic ummah.

For many from Christian backgrounds, the move looked like creating just another schism within the body of Christ. From the minute we announced that Communio Messianica would be established as an entity, many mission organization and traditional church representatives reached out, wondering why such a movement was needed.

They feared Communio Messianica would become another club that thought itself too big.

Not to Replace but Complement

With these fears in mind, we tried to write the Communio Messianica Constitution and other documents carefully and pay attention to the concerns we had heard, still remembering our original vision.

For example, in the preamble of the CM Constitution, we state:

> In belonging to the universal body of Christ as integral and accountable members of His body—while prioritizing the meeting of needs specific to our own community of Christ followers—we have of necessity formed a new jurisdiction (i.e. denomination), not to separate from any existing jurisdictions, but rather to facilitate the formation of a new contextualized identity, a home within the global body of Christ, to provide pastoral care including supervision and accountability by leaders who understand the unique challenges and discipleship needs of those coming out of Islam to Christ. This jurisdiction is expressed in local church bodies which are grounded in biblical faith and truth, and are united and administered locally and regionally through the auspices of CM.
>
> This distinct but integral jurisdiction will allow CM to better meet specific needs in serving those within the emerging multitudes of MBBs who, for various reasons, cannot be integrated into existing churches either within their own countries of origin (if indeed there be any) or within the Diaspora.
>
> CM recognizes and celebrates her debt and vital connection to historical and current Christian missional entities and seeks continued and increased cooperation and fellowship. Thus, CM will vigorously pursue this goal through existing as well as new alliances and advisory capacities....

The Communio Messianica's English website presents the same themes grouped into three facets:

1. *Pastoral Care Facet.* In order to meet the MBB needs for identity, community, and belonging in their newfound faith, CM is formed as a new ecclesiastical movement of Christ's one Church, not to separate her from any existing jurisdictions, but to establish a well-ordered ecclesiastical body of the emerging multitudes of MBBs who, for various reasons, cannot be integrated into existing local churches (if indeed there are any). CM recognizes and respects other jurisdictions of the Lord Jesus Christ's one Church and seeks cooperation and fellowship with them.

2. *CM Missional Facet.* The CM missional facet manifests itself in training, equipping, and commissioning of MBBs to be effective missionaries within the context of their own countries, and in the Diaspora.

3. *CM Community / Cooperative Facet.* CM is a canonically organized part of the one holy universal missional Church of the Lord Jesus, the one household of God which is built upon the foundation of the Apostles and Prophets, with Jesus Christ as the Chief Cornerstone (Ephesians 2:17–22). As such, we seek communion, inter-communion, and partnerships with other churches and Christian institutions.

I quote these documents at such length because I hope they will allay the concerns that Communio Messianica was set up to create a new dividing line among Christians.

First, both texts underline the fact that we do not see ourselves as an exclusive club, special people, or in any way elitist. Instead, we are only meeting the specific needs of our people, MBBs, and especially those who struggle to find a spiritual home and family. As mentioned, traditional churches in Muslim-majority countries often cannot accept them as members of their churches. We want to be able to do what they cannot do.

Second, Communio Messianica does not intend to recruit Christians from other churches. Where Christian congregations already exist and can welcome Muslim-background converts, Communio Messianica will seek to support the integration of MBBs into them. You'll never hear our leaders whispering to anyone that they should leave their present Christian community and join us. Christian-background brothers and sisters don't even need Communio Messianica. Anyone from a Christian background in Cairo, Khartoum, Casablanca, or Qatar will have no problem integrating into an existing church because it is written on their ID card that they are a Christian. Nevertheless, we want to work with these communities and be in touch with all denominations across the Muslim world.

Third, it's time for MBBs to learn to give and care. One of our aims is to guide Muslim-background Christians to lead their lives with a deep sense of responsibility. Within Christendom, we have been on the receiving end too long, and the time has come for us also to give and serve. We believe the Lord has called us to this purpose. And this should not be limited to just the spiritual or social needs of the believers.

For example, the earthquakes in Turkey and Syria in early 2023 also affected MBBs living in the region. There were many of them among the victims, and many of those who survived lost their homes. Church meeting places were destroyed. In the crisis, as CM, we organized support for those brothers and sisters—to do otherwise would have been immoral. The missionary ministry does not end with answering the converts' first questions and sharing their conversion testimonies in our newsletters.

Finally, we are convinced that Communio Messianica is needed to defend human rights. MBBs know the shortcomings concerning these issues firsthand. When someone faces persecution for their faith, we try to help in the most concrete way possible. Sometimes, for example, when converts have been arrested in a Muslim country, we have hired lawyers to help them. In the West, we connect with politicians and remind them that religious conversion is a fundamental human right and should apply to all religions everywhere.

This mission to defend human rights and religious freedom is especially important in Muslim-majority countries where MBB Christians and communities are lacking legal status. If a congregation or individual does not belong to any officially registered denomination, Communio Messianica offers them the opportunity for such belonging. Membership allows them to tell the local authorities that they belong to the international Communio Messianica denomination. Sometimes, simply stating this fact may give them more freedom to operate.

We hope that one day we can also legalize Communio Messianica in Muslim-majority countries. We know that it would require a fundamental change in the influence of Sharia law in those countries, and if that happens, it would be nothing short of a miracle. But assuming that it could happen, the result would also be the liberation of the traditional churches from the rules of dhimmitude, the second-class status Islam gives them. This, in turn, would clear the way for celebrating an amazing unity among all followers of Jesus in the Muslim world— whatever their background.

If it isn't already on your prayer list, I challenge you to adopt this dream as your intercession topic!

Part of the Communio Messianica's Board of Council with Thomas Schirrmacher (front left) and Archbishop William Mikler (front right).

Focusing on the Primary Doctrines

When we looked at the constitution document above, some might pay attention to the odd-sounding expression, "[we have] formed a new jurisdiction (i.e. denomination), not to separate from any existing jurisdictions." How should this expression be understood?

The idea in the sentence is, in short, that if some congregation or individual believer wants to join Communio Messianica, this does not require resigning or ceasing to participate in their previous Christian home community.

Of course, other churches may have their rules restricting the congregations' and members' possibilities to join other denominational structures. For us, however, the overlapping membership is possible because Communio Messianica focuses on the central doctrines of Christianity shared by most Christians in different denominations. When we founded CM, we decided to adopt as its official doctrinal document the Lausanne Covenant, a well-known evangelical document including the basic principles of the central theological issues, such as the purpose of God, the authority and power of the Bible, the uniqueness of Jesus Christ, the power of the Holy Spirit, the Church, and evangelism. The document was formulated by the world's leading evangelical theologians and released in 1974 in Lausanne, Switzerland. Since then, the covenant has become the basic doctrinal document of numerous Christian organizations.

So, all who commit to formulations of the Lausanne Covenant and the values of the Communio Messianica are welcome to join and serve in it. And many have come. At the time of writing, over a hundred church networks and congregations from dozens of countries have joined the community, and the number is growing. As individual members, we have Pentecostals, Lutherans, Baptists, Anglicans, Presbyterians, etc.—even MBB members of the Roman Catholic Church, Coptic Church, and some other Oriental Orthodox churches regard our community as their other spiritual home.

We treat all these people as our members, even though most who identify with Communio Messianica have not formally joined it. Sometimes it may be because they already are official members in some other denomination, which can prevent them from formally belonging to another. Still, most often, the reason seems to be that these people don't see official membership as meaningful. For most from the Global South, belonging to the religious community is something other than a name in a register. We involved in the CM leadership think the same way.

So, how many members does Communio Messianica have? We don't know, but we would venture to say that the figure of those who feel CM is their spiritual home and family (or one of them) is counted in millions. The estimation is based on the fact that Al Hayat and its partners, such as Mohabat TV, openly identify with Communio Messianica and regularly speak about it as an "MBB denomination" in their programs, and the number of viewers and friends of those programs is counted in millions.

In addition to MBBs, Communio Messianica is a spiritual home for many from non-Muslim backgrounds. We have, for example, Christian Kurds and converts from some other Middle Eastern people groups, such as Yazidis, who are sometimes regarded as Muslim by outsiders but who don't consider themselves as such. After coming to Christ, these brothers and sisters face many similar challenges as we do, and they are warmly welcome to participate in Communio Messianica if they like. Furthermore, many of us are married to spouses with a Christian background, making us a diverse community.

Because the Lausanne Covenant covers only some theological topics, we have had to consider how to reconcile people's different views and practices that they have learned in other churches. These include, for example, baptism and the Eucharist, which are essential to the Christian life but which the Lausanne Covenant doesn't mention.

Regarding baptism, we have decided not to baptize the babies of MBB families but to bless them. Still, if the family belongs also to a church with a custom of baptizing infants and the parents want to baptize their little one there, we respect their decision.

Regarding the Eucharist, the Holy Communion, we have decided to celebrate it together even though we come from different denominations, and many of these denominations do not have official theological agreement on the Eucharist and shared sacramental life. I know that some may now call us "theological rebels" because we don't feel the need for such agreements. Maybe so, but we don't want the current situation to deprive our new sisters and brothers of possibilities for the shared Eucharist as an MBB family. We want to take the Eucharist as a genuinely unifying gift of God for all followers of Jesus—as we see it in the Bible.

At this point, I must say that we respect the theological discussion that takes place in and between churches and want to learn from it. Still, from the Muslim-background converts' point of view, some of those doctrinal disagreements look—excuse my strong language—like useless pedantry. We understand the differences that have been a part of the churches, but please don't bring those issues to us. Come with Jesus' spirit and leave your differences at home. I love how MBBs from North Africa reply to the question, "What church do you belong to?" Usually, the answer is, "I am a Christian, and I am one of the Moroccan/Algerian/Libyan, etc. Christians."

At the risk of sounding over-optimistic, I firmly believe that we don't need to be a part of the split within the Church.

Where community governance is concerned, I already mentioned that we have the Board of Council, which exercises the highest strategic decision-making power in the community. On the Board, we have members from several denominations. Most members are ex-Muslims, but we also have some Christian-background believers who have a long history with MBBs and in the Muslim ministry.

Up to this point, many practical management tasks have been carried out by the CM General Manager, who has also represented the community in public and in various networks. However, in March 2024, that role and title were phased out, and Dr. Yassir Eric, mentioned above, was consecrated as the first Bishop to serve Communio Messianica. The consecration ceremony was held in Kigali, Rwanda. Archbishop Dr. Laurent Mbanda of the Anglican Church of Rwanda officiated the ceremony in the presence of the CM's Board of Council and Archbishop Dr. Thomas Schirrmacher, Secretary General of the World Evangelical Alliance. Later, we plan to consecrate other bishops from among the members of the Board of Council.

The move to episcopal governance was the result of a lengthy reflection by the CM board. After much discussion, we were convicted that the episcopal leadership model would be the best way to clarify the community's leadership, care for the faithful, and cooperation with other denominations. For ordinary members, the title "bishop" is also more informative and familiar than the "General Manager" of the church. Despite this episcopal step, we aim to keep Communio Messianica's governing structure simple. Suppose you draw a line from a "Christian fellowship" type of community to the Catholic or Coptic Church with a massive administrative apparatus. On that continuum, Communio Messianica stands, and will continue to stand, nearer to the first end.

In addition to a bishop, we have CM pastors. Some of them have previously been ordained in a pastoral role in their background community and still minister there. This means the same person can simultaneously be a CM pastor and, say, a Baptist pastor. Nor do we have a problem of principle with the female priesthood. However, it can be a problem in some countries or cultures, and we do not appoint female pastors in such areas.

On the current issue of same-sex relationships, we follow the traditional Christian view we see clearly stated in the New Testament.

What delights us is that today, most of the traditional churches in Muslim-majority countries seem to be backing us up, recognizing Communio Messianica as part of the body of Christ. Relationships are good, for example, with most Orthodox churches in the Middle East, and the Roman Catholic Church has also expressed its positive attitude towards our community. In addition, many Christian mission organizations operating in Muslim-majority regions have expressed their willingness to stand with us. Their previous fears about us have faded out. Today, they pray for us and praise the Lord for our community because, as they say: "Finally, the Lord has provided a new generation of people who will take care of the MBBs that we cannot care for."

An excellent, recent example of this partnership is from Upper Egypt. In early 2023, a representative of a local Coptic diocese called me to ask for help because more than 400 Muslims had converted to Christianity in the area, including several entire families. Some of them had contacted the Coptic Church, the only Christian community they could think of, and the church workers started to help them—and still do. However, the church was not in a position to help them much, and they felt they had limited expertise in teaching MBB believers. So we started supporting these new Christians, and three Al Hayat follow-up workers have been visiting the area weekly to teach them. The converts live in poor rural villages without internet access, so online meetings are not an option.

It was touching to hear one of them say that he had become a Christian eight years ago but had not been taught since then and had had no contact with other ex-Muslims or local Christians for years. Still, he had gotten hold of the Gospel of Matthew somewhere and had read it repeatedly until he finally knew it by heart. It had been his study material!

The Most Difficult Conflict

To conclude this chapter, I would like to give an example of the unique theological debates and controversies that may arise in MBB communities and in those with a mix of Christian-background and Muslim-background believers. The debate in question started among the Al Hayat family in 2018 when two of our hosts, Maher Fayez and brother Rachid, expressed different opinions regarding Christian mysticism and mystic worship. At the core of the debate are, quite naturally, one's definition of "mysticism" and one's approach to ecstatic spiritual experiences.

The debate started after brother Maher said that he sees mystic worship as a natural and positive phenomenon in Christian spirituality. He is from an evangelical Christian background, knows church history, and is used to experiential spirituality. For him, Christian mysticism, rightly understood, is the safe focus on and experience of God's presence. Maher also sees this being a part of Christianity since the days of the Apostles.

Brother Rashid, on the other hand, is from a Muslim background, and he strongly linked the idea of mystical worship to Islamic Sufism and the Dervish ecstasy. Sufism is an Islamic movement that emphasizes direct personal experience of God, and the Dervishes are members of Sufi fraternities known for their ecstatic practices through which they believe to reach the divine. So when Rachid heard talk of Christian mystic worship, he conflated it with the ungodly aspirations and even evil forces he saw operating in Sufism and the Dervishs' practices.

During the conflict, Rachid and Maher expressed their theological arguments, and the stakes got high. In the end, both made me feel that the board or I had to decide who stayed on the channel and who left. Rachid stated clearly, "It's him or me."

It was a tough season. On a theological level, I understand that sometimes such a discussion may be necessary. However, I am sure that in this particular case, it had more to do with personality differences between the opponents than about theology. Rachid and Maher are very different in nature. It made the decision-making even more difficult for me. The decision would have been much easier in a secular company; in ministry, it is a nightmare.

I had met both Rachid and Maher in 1989, and they had become dear to me. When the debate started, I decided to follow the advice I had learned, in particular, from my friend Gary

Preston: despite attacks by opponents and their supporters, I tried to remain impartial. The board of Al Hayat also decided not to choose a side. We discussed the situation at length with both hosts, and in the end, they both decided to leave Al Hayat. We sent them off regretfully but in peace, blessing them in their future endeavors. We discovered once again that when we bless others, we are blessed. This turned into an opportunity for the channel, and we were able to bring new people into the spotlight.

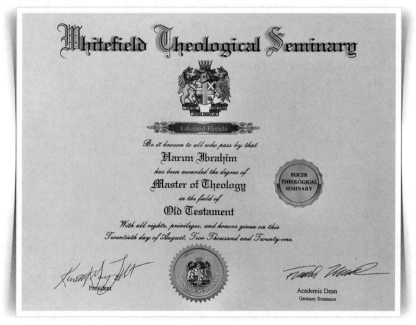

Communio Messianica has a principle that board members should have an academic theological degree. So, I continued my studies, and with the gracious help of Dr. Vogt Titus, I received my MTh degree at Whitefield/ Martin Bucer Theological Seminary in 2020. The photo shows my diploma. I am also delighted to be awarded two honorary doctorates.

19

The Global Pandemic
and a Christian Chatbot

In 2020, the globalized world faced a situation about which many futurologists had warned: a previously unknown virus caused a pandemic that spread rapidly and was remarkably more deadly than, for example, conventional influenza epidemics. The virus was SARS-CoV-2, better known as Covid-19.

When the epidemic went global in March 2020, it looked like the whole world stopped, and social media became the main communication channel. Many schools used it to instruct students at home, forcing parents to learn more about social media. Churches had to adapt and start broadcasting their Sunday meetings, praying gatherings, and Bible studies on the Web or via social media applications. Many people began to have even family get-togethers online. It was like we became inhabitants in a virtual world.

Of course, all of this also influenced the work of Al Hayat. It was a new thing for our follow-up team members to wake up and start a working day from the couch. They started getting more messages and questions because more people were at home watching TV or hanging out on social media. So, the pandemic was, actually, a very fruitful time for us, and many came to the Lord.

Al Hayat had been using social media for a long time, but because of Covid-19, we had to start producing programs virtually, too. In addition, we wanted to let our audience know that we all face the pandemic together. In early April, when the pandemic restrictions covered more than half of the global population, many of us on the Al Hayat team spent much time developing our social media ministry to meet the growing and rapidly changing needs. A few weeks later, from the 1st of May, we arranged eighteen weekly live broadcasts on social media and continued them for around two years. The program hosts were equipped with cameras, lights, and microphones, and each started to decorate a corner of their home, which became their "studio."

Those social media broadcasts mainly consisted of prayer and worship, Bible studies, and interviews with believers sharing their testimonies. We tried to comfort those who were scared because of the uncertainties caused by the pandemic.

Some of our regular TV series also became especially important in encouraging the MBB community during those strange months. One of those was *Moroccan and Christian,* made in the Moroccan Darija dialect. The hosts and viewers even celebrated Christmas together as a church virtually.

When time passed and the pandemic weakened, it was encouraging to see how well the MBB communities had survived amidst all the changes in people's daily lives. Many Muslim-background Christians were already used to communicating and gathering by way of mobile and virtual meetings, so pandemic restrictions weren't as big of a shock for their communities as they were for many traditional congregations. When many churches reported a notable decline in attendance, the reports we heard told us that a similar phenomenon did not occur in most MBB communities.

Of course, the pandemic also caused much suffering for MBBs as for everyone else. Many of our brothers and sisters died, and some have suffered from long-Covid symptoms. Movement restrictions damaged many families' income and isolated parents from their grown children.

As an Al Hayat family, we went through one of the most painful experiences in our history when we lost our beloved brother and friend Michael Heinen to complications from Covid-19 in 2021. Mike was around my age, originally from Iowa, US, and had lived overseas doing missions for many years until he became an important team member on Al Hayat. I remember when we established the channel in 2003 and were attacked by Muslims and Christians alike, we had long prayer meetings with Mike and Gary Preston. Obstacles and challenges that seemed impossible at the time were won by prayer. Mike was our longest-serving employee until he died. I can say wholeheartedly that he was a man of God.

So, even though I feel that Al Hayat was able to endure the pandemic relatively well, I will never forget that Covid-19 took the life of one of my best friends. I look forward to the day I will be reunited with Mike in heaven, and we can have long discussions about how God has used Al Hayat for the sake of His kingdom. I want to give all the glory to God for allowing me to have Mike as a brother and confidant, especially during some of the most troublesome years of my life. He and his family will be forever in the hearts of the Al Hayat staff.

MBBs Also Deserve an Annual Day of Remembrance!

One evening in May 2020, I was directing a prayer show broadcast on social media. I had several program windows open on the screen, and an advertisement appeared on one of them, catching my attention. The ad said that the present day, the 17th of May, was the International Day Against Homophobia, Transphobia, and Biphobia (IDAHOT), celebrated annually. I began to think, if there is a day for such a purpose, why don't we have a day to remember MBBs? It should be a day to educate the world about Muslim-background Christians and pray with and for them. I started to develop the idea and even got so excited that I thought of a proper name for the event: "MBB Global Prayer Day." I looked for a domain name and found that *www.mbbglobal.net* was free.

I shared the idea with the other Communio Messianica counselors and received immediate approval. So, we started planning for the first MBB Global Prayer Day. While examining the calendar for a good day later in the year, and I came up with the thought of having it on my birthday, November 18th. I thought there could never be a better birthday present for me than to have people praying with and for my Muslim-background brothers and sisters! From that point forward, November 18 has been the MBB Global Prayer Day, and we have celebrated it through live streams on various TV channels, such as Al Hayat, Mohabat TV, several YouTube channels, the www.mbbglobal.net website, and several channels belonging to GOD TV. During the 2020 commemorations, we also presented our Communio Messianica community to a large audience. Since then, these prayer days have had a significant impact by encouraging and further connecting Muslim-background Christians across the globe.

In the 2010s, a big part of TV programming moved to homes, nature, streets, and cafes. Then Covid-19 and advances in studio technology brought studio productions back into fashion. Here, we prepare for the MBB Global Prayer Day broadcast with Naser Musa and Sister Imane.

For the first MBB Global Prayer Day, I believe God gave Naser and me a clear message for all Muslim-background Christians in the form of a song. With it, we tell them, "You Are Not Alone." Naser and sister Imane from *Moroccan and Christian* sing it in the video, and it is used on prayer days and has been published on websites and social media.

The song goes like this:

> *I am rejected for my faith,*
> *For choosing to walk in Jesus' path.*
> *God promised to be with me to the end of age.*
> *Remember, sister, remember, brother,*
> *you are not alone.*
> *You are a member of our family*
> *you can call your own.*
> *Remember, you are not alone.*
> (Lyrics: Harun Ibrahim, Music: Naser Musa)

Social Media Jihad

Although there is uncertainty about the total number of MBB Christians, one thing is clear: more Muslims have come to Christ in the past decades than in the previous 1,400 years combined. I dare to say the phenomenon is primarily due to the emergence of satellite TV and, later, the internet and other new media platforms. It's been astonishing to see how Al Hayat has become the largest, most influential Christian satellite television broadcaster to reach Muslim audiences worldwide. Several informal surveys in different countries have shown that Al Hayat is the most-watched Christian channel among former Muslim Arabs.

The position and visibility of our programming are also reflected in the fact that attacks by Muslim teachers against us seem to continue non-stop. It has been interesting that Muslim teachers often openly challenge our TV hosts to debates about the arguments they present in their programs. These debates have even been attended by scholars of one of the leading

Islamic educational institutions in the world, Egyptian Al-Azhar University.

Recently, a famous young Egyptian Islamic preacher, Abdullah Rushdi, released a video criticizing the claims made by our hosts, sisters Farha and Marena, on their show. When Rushdi's video started to spread, Farha and Marena responded by releasing their own "counter-counter video," in which they questioned Rushdi's criticism and defended their original point of view.

The debate was about the Qur'anic sayings about the Jews, and as strange as it may sound in the ears of a Westerner, millions in the Arab world watch videos like this. Because of their straightforward style, I have called these debates a jihad, a holy war, through the media. This is the kind of war I love: idea against idea, interpretation against interpretation, argument against argument. As I mentioned above, if we want to end Islamic violence, we must defeat their ideology with our message—the message of the crucified and resurrected Jesus and His heavenly kingdom.

This situation forces us to be sharp in what we say. Some Muslim teachers' objections and counterarguments are pretty good, showing an intelligent mind and dedication. They force us to put effort into what we claim about Christianity, Islam, the Bible, the Qur'an, and the Hadith. If we want people to pay attention to our message, we must pay attention to it ourselves.

At the same time, we must understand that this war consists of many separate and simultaneous battles. With the changes in media use, there will no longer be a single TV show like Father Zakaria's *Questions About Faith* that shakes the whole Muslim community. Instead, the shaking must be done and the breakthroughs made with many simultaneous programs and discussions on social media, the internet, and other platforms.

Although we sometimes hear good counterarguments, most of the criticism we receive from imams, mullahs (Islamic clerics), and muftis (Islamic jurists) is not of a very high standard—not even from critics with the highest authoritative position. For example, in 2022, one of the professors of Al-Azhar University wrote a book in response to the claims of our TV host and researcher, Mohammed Lamsiah, who in 2017 published a book about the ancient manuscripts of the Qur'an. In the book *Manuscripts of the Qur'an: An Introduction to the Study of Ancient Manuscripts*, Mohammed showed how the oldest preserved manuscripts diverge so significantly that they call into question the traditional Islamic teaching of a single, unchanging Qur'an. In his counterbook, the professor tried to defend the orthodox Islamic view, but the book clearly showed that he did not really know the oldest manuscripts of his holy book and the theological problems the differences between those ancient texts raise.

It was very encouraging when Moroccan state television interviewed Mohammed and let him talk openly about his observations in studying those ancient texts. His connection to Al Hayat was not hidden, either. Despite fierce opposition from Muslim scholars, the attention secular Arab media has focused on Al Hayat has gradually become neutral or even cautiously positive.

Developing the Follow-up Ministry

Over the last two decades, the total number of salvation decisions reported to Al Hayat and its partners has risen to the hundreds of thousands. Every day, the channel and its production partners receive powerful personal testimonies of how God is moving in people's lives after they have been viewing our programs. When I read these viewer messages, it's like Christmas every day. This is hard but wonderful work!

Muslims' willingness to learn about the Christian message and the fact that there are so many converts mean that teaching the converts has become a much more significant challenge than winning new Muslims to Jesus. When I visited churches in different countries to celebrate the twentieth anniversary of Al Hayat, almost everywhere, I mentioned the challenges of the follow-up ministry as something I particularly hope people will pray for.

As mentioned above, we recorded more than 109 million viewer engagements and interactions at Al Hayat in 2023. Most of them were video views and shares on social media. However, there were also millions of comments on different platforms, and many emails and phone calls.

About ten percent of feedback given in writing or by phone includes questions or other requests for us. Viewers may ask for justification for a statement made in a program, ask for help finding a Christian congregation near their home, ask for material to research things themselves, and so on. Answering all those requests is another area in which we have tried to develop our ministry and make it as efficient as possible. For example, we have dozens of ready-made answers to the most common theological questions asked by Muslims and MBBs.

As I write this, we have about two hundred people serving in follow-up roles, either as staff or as volunteers. Some are representatives of other Christian organizations and local churches in different countries. However, more people are desperately needed. Many viewers who send us messages have to wait a long time to be contacted, but there still isn't time to respond to everyone. It is heartbreaking. We don't want anyone to feel rejected or forgotten.

Especially when we receive a question from a new believer, we want to respond carefully and with prayers. Still—as the need for advice is so urgent—we have also long examined the possibilities of using response bots as extra help, in the same way that many companies use them on their websites. The most recent project in this area has been developing Al Hayat's own AI system based on the famous Chat-GPT bot.

When the company Open AI released Chat-GPT in November 2022, they offered businesses and communities the possibility to have their own Chat-GPT bot tailored to their unique needs. So, Al Hayat's Israeli team began to examine if we could create a tailored Chat-GPT to serve our audience. Since then, the team has been programming the bot to answer our viewers' questions from the Christian point of view. Whether the user asks, "How do I know that God loves me?", "Is Muhammad the true prophet of God?", "Why was the death of Jesus necessary for the forgiveness of sins?"—or anything else about Christianity or Islam—we want the system to answer it in a theologically correct and user-friendly way.

On a visit to a Baptist congregation in Cuiabá, Brazil, where I had been invited to present the Muslim ministry. A part of our vision is to equip churches everywhere to engage with their Muslim neighbors fruitfully.

At the time of writing, the Chat-GPT bot has been installed on Al Hayat's Arabic website for trial use while the system is still under development. We are hopeful that our "Christian chatbot" can serve as a partial solution to the challenges of our follow-up ministry in the future.

If it's not going to succeed, we will not be discouraged but will develop something else.

It's in our DNA to use every means to tell the story of Jesus.

20

Together towards the Future

"Mossad agent," "traitor," "Zionist," and all the curse words one can imagine: during my thirty-five years in Christian ministry among Muslims, I have been insulted by all these expressions and many more. As a missionary, I have accepted all these vilifications as badges of honor. Of course, it's not always funny to hear such words—especially if the person saying them is standing next to you with an angry look on their face—but afterward, these comments make me smile. They reveal that our work has not been in vain and that the message has touched people and evoked emotions, even to the extent that some have gotten angry or frustrated. Fortunately, many have also changed.

When this book comes out, I am sixty-four years old. That means I am already at the age when it's time to consider retirement. At Al Hayat, we have already started preparations for it.

When I look at my life so far, it has taken a completely different turn than I thought it would.

As a young Arab boy playing in the forests of Abu Gosh with my siblings, I dreamed of becoming a delivery truck driver like my father.

As a teenager in secondary school, I studied engine mechanics and dreamed about being an aircraft mechanic.

Even in my twenties, as a kibbutz hotel accommodation manager, I could not have imagined a future like this. Despite my early doubts about Islam, I would never have guessed that I would soon become a Christian "Jesus-zealot"—still less that I would later become a missionary among Muslims. (Luckily, I have had some use for my engine mechanic skills with my cars. As a young evangelist, I could only afford cheap used cars that needed frequent repairs. Lately, it's been nice to fix up my old museum automobile, the 1967 Mercedes-Benz 250 S.)

When I look at my main character traits and how I have acted at different stages of my life, there has been greater predictability. I have always been social, passionate, tenacious, and ready to stand up for what I believe is right. I have also always been a risk-taker and an adventurer. I thank the Lord that I once dared to start a relationship with Sari and dared to move to Finland. I also thank Him for saving me from a life of nothingness so that I no longer had to risk my life by climbing home through the balcony after a bar night. Gratefully, He has also softened my fiercest tempers.

Muslims today are questioning the tenets of Islam more than ever. Yet, the need for gospel preaching among them is not diminishing: the world's Muslim population is expected to increase to 2.2 billion by 2030, thanks to the high birth rate of Muslim families.

Perhaps my character is why I have always particularly enjoyed pioneering projects. Criticizing Islam publicly in the media, setting up a denomination for former Muslims, the ideas of MBB Global Prayer Day and *The Muslim Woman* program—I've found that all these and many other projects have been such that God had almost entirely prepared them in advance and was just waiting for someone to come and take them on.

In fact, usually, when I have had an idea, I often have felt the urge to jump right into these projects. I have wanted to ensure that no one else had time to implement the same idea first. And, even if no one else has gotten the idea yet, why leave an excellent project to the next generation if you can do it now?

Later, when we have gotten a project ongoing, I have looked back and enjoyed the fruits of our hard work like an athlete after a good performance.

So, to you, young Christians—and especially to you with a Muslim background—I want to say: Take risks. Start pioneering projects. Boldly pursue the vision God has given you. If the young heroes of Islam—Khalifa Harun Al-Rashid (c. 763–809), Sultan Muhammad Al-Fatih (1432–1481), Muslim Brotherhood founder Hasan Al-Banna (1906–1949), and many others—have changed the course of history by raising armies or starting influential Islamist movements (big things from their point of view), how much more good can you do with Jesus.

So, search His will, be strong, and be brave!

From ISIS to Christ

In the previous pages, I have repeatedly referenced the values and objectives of Al Hayat and Communio Messianica.

I have talked about shining the light of Jesus Christ on Muslims and boldly unveiling Islam's deceptions.

I have talked about teaching, training, and helping new converts.

I have talked about utilizing today's technology.

In addition to all this, I have talked about doing things together. I'm glad that during all the years on IBRA Radio, Keymedia, Al

Hayat, and Communio Messianica, I've been able to develop my ideas. Still, without my colleagues and partners, all these ideas would have remained nothing but thoughts. Al Hayat and Communio Messianica are, in themselves, fruits of cooperation. There are currently sixteen media organizations from different denominational backgrounds involved in Al Hayat's program production. The mission is made possible only because of God and the love He has poured into the hearts of our friends.

This means that the events described in this book are not only the history of Al Hayat, Communio Messianica, or my family. Most events are also part of our numerous colleagues' and partner organizations' history—and the history of all individuals worldwide who have shared our dreams and prayed for us, donated to the ministry, or, for example, posted our video clips, spreading the message that way. Despite the many names in the book, many more could (and should) have been mentioned. I want to thank you all!

It's suitable to end this kind of book with a story about two Syrian men whose lives were radically changed. One of them was Youssef, a Christian-background friend of Al Hayat who distributed our material, wanting to win his neighbors to Jesus. The other was a Syrian ISIS fighter called Abou. (Names are changed for security reasons.)

Abou met his wife, Maanah, during the Syrian civil war, and she also became a fighter—a sniper—which is extremely rare in any extremist Islamic organization. They had two children, Zaid and Ayah. When the Syrian army killed Maanah in one of the battles, Abou was left alone to raise the kids. It was not easy for him, but he continued to do his "job" as a fighter.

One day in 2017, Abou received an order to kill a Christian man living in the city, Youssef. The night before the murder was supposed to be committed, Abou had a strange dream. In the dream, he saw a child telling him, "Please don't kill this man and instead help him to escape."

The following day, Abou went to do his task, but to his surprise, he saw the same child he dreamed of outside the house where the Christian man lived. Abou understood that the dream had been from God—for some reason, Allah seemed not to want him to kill the man.

Instead, Abou went to talk to Youssef and told him what kind of mission he was sent to carry out. Then he followed the advice he had received in the dream and said, "Look, I will help you and your family flee the country; here is my number. If anyone stops you, tell them to call me, and I will help you."

Luckily, no one stopped Youssef and his family, and they managed to escape to Turkey and later Europe.

From Turkey, Youssef decided to send Abou a thankyou message and linked some videos from Al Hayat's social media pages with it. At first, Abou got upset because of the Christian content in Youssef's message and blocked his number. A few months later, however, he decided to watch the videos and surprisingly became so interested in their content that asked Youssef for more links.

Through these videos, Abou accepted Christ as his Savior in 2018. Soon after that, he also fled from Syria with his children. When we heard about this testimony, we contacted and met with him. I have also been in contact with him myself. His life changed dramatically, and the whole family needs lots of prayers because they must still be in hiding and don't have any official documents. We look forward to helping them move to a safe place.

As it is written in Ecclesiastes 11:1,

Cast your bread upon the waters, For you will find it after many days.

That's the point of the Christian mission. At Al Hayat, our "bread" are the programs we produce. We cast them to our audience, and sometimes we will find a return, positive results, quickly—sometimes, like with the conversion of Abou, "after many days."

In both cases, by God's mercy, the casting of the bread has not been in vain.

Honor to whom it belongs. Here we are with our California studio's staff praying before the start of the channel's 20th anniversary live broadcast on September 1st, 2023.

Media Reactions to Al Hayat

During its history, Al Hayat has been the subject of dozens of articles in the Arabic media. Here are excerpts from some of these articles from the channel's first years, translated into English.

Words in brackets have been added afterward by the Al Hayat team to clarify the text. Some long passages of the original text have been broken into several sections to facilitate reading.

Requests to investigate Zakaria Botros

The article "Copts ask Pope Shenouda to investigate Zakaria Botros' insults against Islam" was published in a famous Egyptian newspaper, *Sout Al-Umma*, on Oct. 11, 2004. The article was written by Sahar Talaat, Fadi Habashi, and Fadi Emile, and the text is an example of the criticism Al Hayat received from the traditional Christian communities of the Middle East. Here is part of the article:

> We wonder why Pope Shenouda did not investigate Father Zakaria Botros' insults against Islam. Accountant and researcher in Coptic affairs Kamal Zakhir Moussa says that the church has to declare its official stance towards Zakaria Botros. He also asks Pope Shenouda to be more definite and transparent concerning his personal position towards Zakaria. Zakaria Botros insults everyone, ignoring the tolerance of Christianity. Jesus Christ tells his disciples to be wise as serpents and harmless as doves. It is not wise or humble to insult people's religion.

Hegumen [priest] Zakaria Botros claims that he endangers his life. Still, he says he is not afraid of being killed or assassinated, as if someone even cares about the racist rot that overflows in his weekly program.

He wants to become a hero and always speaks as if he wants to say, "Ha, I am the bravest." He claims that Christ mandates him to say what he says, but he ignores that Christ did not offend the Samaritans. He did not insult other religions or question their validity. The portrayal of priest Zakaria Botros as an evangelizing hero is an incorrect image, as evangelization doesn't mean attacking Islam or any other religion, but that we should follow what the Lord Christ taught us and not overcome evil with evil or insult with insult.

Retired Zakaria Botros lives safely in the West (not in Egypt), not caring about what might happen due to his immature views. He knows well that the fire he ignites with his shows will burn Muslims and Copts alike. [...] But the questions that Pope Shenouda must answer are: Why is he silent on the fire that Zakaria Botros is igniting? Why has Pope Shenouda not taken any action against him so far to prevent him from wearing the costume of the priesthood?

"Botros adopts an agitating style"

The article "Eight Satellite Channels Declaring War on Islam" was published in Saudi newspaper *Al-Madina* on March 23, 2007. The article was written by Dr. Turkey Bin Khalid Al-Zifeiri, Professor of Dogma and the Speaker-Imam of Abu-Bakr Alsidik's mosque in Riyadh, Saudi Arabia. In the text, Dr. Turkey made a mistake, as *Daring Question* is not a program hosted by Pastor Botros, but by brother Rachid. Here is part of the article:

Al Hayat is considered to be the most aggressive among the others because of its programs that openly and directly attack Islam. This channel has crossed all the red lines. Priest Z. Botros adopts an agitating style in his program that disregards the feelings of Muslims. He accuses Islam of being a religion that fuels lust and claims Muhammad is the real author of the Qur'an. Through the hundred episodes of his *Truth Talk* series, Z. Botros questioned everything in Islam. In his program titled *Daring Question*, which is the first live program, Z. Botros took advantage of all the impressive tools to boldly attack the Qur'an. He allocated thirty episodes out of a hundred to query and ridicule the Qur'an, fourteen episodes to question the Sunna [the traditions and practices of Muhammad], and to accuse Muhammad of being a terrorist. He extended his attack to the wives of our Messenger (prayer and peace be on him) and to our Messenger's kin. Why this silence?

"We want to know who's behind Al Hayat"

An article published in the Egyptian newspaper *Al-Osboa* on Jan. 5, 2006 called MBBs "a poisoned knife" stabbing Islam. Here is part of the text:

[The Muslim background Christians] have become a poisoned knife that stabs Islam in the back. They traded Islam for money that comes from the USA and the UK. Those people use the internet, emails, and a suspicious satellite channel, Al Hayat, which the USA finances, to raise doubts and conflicts among the Muslims and between them and the Copts in Egypt. We want to know who stands behind Al Hayat?

Christian magazine on Al Hayat's vision

Egyptian Christian newspaper *Al-Tarik* was another Christian magazine that wrote about the channel. Here is part of an article published in May 2006. The tone was much more positive than in *Sout Al-Umma*, quoted above. *Al-Tarik's* report has the wrong date for the start of Al Hayat, which was September 1, 2003. Here is part of the text:

Among the three most famous Christian channels, Al Hayat is the most controversial. Recently, many discussions have been taking place. It started on September 15, 2003. It is considered to be the most reactive channel among the others. [...] The channel's vision is that through faith, in the grace of God every day, we can reach every nation, city, and individual through the written and spoken Word of God. The channel broadcasts three programs for Pastor Zakaria, *Questions About Faith*, *Truth Talk*, and *In the Bullseye*, which provoke many questions and aggressive responses.

"A soldier became Christian through Al Hayat"

The article "Morocco's Christian Converts Irk the World of Islam" was published on the site of a Saudi-backed news channel, *Al-Arabiya*, on Dec. 13, 2006. The text was published in English and written by Sammy Ketz/AFP. Here is part of the article:

They might have Islamic names like Mohammed or Ali, but every Sunday, these Moroccan converts to Christianity go discreetly to 'church'—to the ire of Islamic militants and under the suspicious eye of the police.

"There are about a thousand of us in around 50 independent churches across the kingdom's big cities," explained Abdelhalim, who coordinates these evangelical Protestant groups in Morocco. [...]

As for Morocco's main cities, seven of these "free churches"— not linked to any international Protestant church—are in Marrakesh, six in Casablanca, five in Rabat, and even one in El Ayoun, the regional capital of Western Sahara.

"Television and the internet are very efficient methods, and in our church, a soldier became Christian through the Al Hayat channel," said 30-year-old Youssef, who also preferred to use a pseudonym.

"For many of us, Islam is perceived as a social straitjacket and not as a real faith, and Christianity as a religion of tolerance and love," said the businessman, who converted at 19 and was later followed by his family.

"Al Hayat TV is criminal, infidel, and strayed"

Saudi newspaper *Al-Madina* published an article (no. 2044, 2007) quoting General Mufti Sheikh Abdel-Aziz bin Abdallah Al-Sheikh. Here is part of the text:

> Sheikh Abdel-Aziz bin Abdallah Al-Sheikh, KSA General Mufti and Head of Senior Clerks Association, described Al Hayat TV as a criminal, infidel, and strayed channel because it airs anti-Islam programs that insult the prophet of mercy and of the right path. The mufti also said, "The channel reflects the opinion of the enemies of Islam. Allah had said to his prophet, 'We have appointed for every prophet enemies—devils among mankind and jinns.'"
>
> The mufti answered a question directed by *El Ressala* newspaper by saying, "This [Al Hayat] is a channel of infidels and deviants, and the individual Muslim who watches it should be alert and able to discern the lies and to reply. But if he lacks knowledge, then he should not watch the channel. I say this because I fear these programs might negatively affect the simple and naïve Muslims."
>
> The mufti pressed on to say that these channels are dissolute and profligate. In fact, no individual Muslim agrees or consents to such channels. It is Muslims' duty to defend their prophet's practices [the Sunna] and defeat the lies with the truth. He also said such channels should be confronted through powerful Islamic channels and programs.

Calls for an Islamic counter-channel

Egyptian newspaper *Al-Masreeyoun* wrote about the political pressure the Egyptian government was facing because of Al Hayat. The report, written by Saleh Shalaby and published on April 23, 2007, made a false claim that there are excommunicated pastors working in Al Hayat. At that time, Al Hayat was transmitted through the HotBird satellite, but later the channel became seen through Nile Sat. The *Al-Fagr* newspaper mentioned in the text is an Egyptian sensationalist publication which, for example, published part of the *Jyllands-Posten's* Muhammad cartoons in 2005. Here is part of the *Al-Masreeyoun's* article:

> The members of Religious Affairs in the Parliament have requested the government to launch a satellite channel to counter the attack launched by the Al Hayat channel against Islam, the gracious prophet (prayers and peace on him), and his companions—and to increase the time allocated for religious programming on the Egyptian TV and to re-air some of the religious programs which have been dropped, in the past, from the program-map. [...]
>
> The Parliament members expressed their resentment at the absence of an apology in a letter presented by Anes Alfiqqy, Minister of Information. [...] In his letter, he denied any connection between the Ministry of Media or Egypt Satellite Company (Nile Sat) and Al Hayat channel, saying that it has been broadcasting on the European satellite 'HotBird' since September 2003. He went on saying, "This Arabic-speaking channel airs Christianization programs by hosting church-excommunicated priests and broadcasts misleading information about the Islamic religion." He emphasized that it is almost impossible to block such channels, especially with today's high technology improvements.
>
> He, the Minister of Media, said that his Ministry, through its Radio and TV channel network, directly and indirectly explains the truth about Islam and replies to the lies aired on such channels. He also refers to the coordination between the [Egypt's] Ministry of Media and the Arab Ministers Media Council to legislate laws that govern Arab satellite broadcasts. [...]
>
> Dr. Ahmed Omer Hashim said, "If such a channel [referring to Al Hayat] aims to destroy Islam and to attack the Messenger and his companions, we should not be satisfied with less than launching an Egyptian channel or to re-air Islamic programs that were removed, such as *Spirit Talk* and the *Weekly Talk with Sheikh Sharaawi.*" [...]

Parliament member Ali Libn said launching a satellite channel would not contradict the law—as some claim that would motivate Christians to demand the state launch a Christian channel—because the second article of the Constitution gives the right to launch an Islamic channel to defend Islam. Libn stressed that the suggested channel would be a tool to convey the voice of the Islamic Research Council, which is supposed to be the higher department for the defense of Islam.

From his side, Parliament member Adel El-Bermawi questioned who stands behind Al Hayat and behind *Al-Fagr* newspaper and demanded a strict stand should be taken against them because there are plans to uproot Islam.

Some Al Hayat Programs

Since the start of the Arabic media ministry of Keymedia and later Al Hayat, the goal has been clear: to reach Muslims for Christ and to equip and disciple Muslim-background believers and Christian-background Arabic believers.

To fulfill this task, we have produced numerous TV series: evangelistic programs, day-to-day Bible teaching, Christian discipleship, worship and praise, Qur'an analyses, apologetics, personal testimonies, a special program for Muslim women, live call-in shows, etc. Here is an introduction to some of them.

The Early History of Islam

 *The Early History of Islam* explores the oldest historical sources of Islam: the manuscripts of the Qur'an and their history, the Arabic language and its roots, the disciples of Muhammad, the history of the Hadith (the traditional records of Muhammad's words and deeds), and where and how Islam ideology is developed.

The episodes are only ten minutes long. Every subject is well documented and gives the audience the sources of information so that people can go back and read it by themselves.

The producer and host of the program is a Moroccan-born Qur'an researcher and author, Mohammed Lamsiah.

Enjoying Everyday Life

Joyce Meyer's *Enjoying Everyday Life* is the longest-running show on the Al Hayat channel. The program touches especially on women's lives, as famous Bible teacher Joyce Meyer shares timeless scriptural principles to show us how to embrace God's best for us every day.

Joyce also includes her personal life in her teaching, which many who identify with her experiences have found important.

Joyce Meyer is a world-known American evangelist and *New York Times* best-selling author.

The Guide

This program aims to change Muslims' preconceived notions about Christianity and bring to light the lies and deceptions of Islam. Through the program, viewers receive researched answers to some of the most challenging questions regarding Christian and Muslim topics.

The program is hosted by a famous theologian and Bible school teacher, brother Waheed, and his wife, sister Fadwa. Both are from Sudanese Coptic backgrounds.

Brother Waheed is known for his extraordinary knowledge of the Bible and the Qur'an. He is hosting several shows on Al Hayat.

Moroccan and Christian

When Muslims accept Jesus Christ as their Savior, not only do their beliefs change, but the entire way they function in society. However, if you have lived in an Islamic culture all your life, learning a new, Christian way of life is not easy.

The series helps and guides especially new Moroccan believers in the footsteps of Christ in their everyday lives. It answers many of the ethical questions Moroccan Muslim-background people encounter when finding Jesus, such as: Is it Christian to obey the laws of Morocco and pay taxes? How should I deal with my persecutors? Should I pray for the authorities?

For the country's Muslim majority, the series explains who the MBBs are, what they believe, and how they live.

The show is produced in Darija, the Arabic dialect spoken in Morocco and neighboring countries. Sister Imane, a Moroccan believer from a Muslim background, hosts the program.

The Muslim Woman

Muslim women in the Middle East and North Africa live in dire conditions due to a combination of injustice and a lack of fundamental human rights. Based on the teachings of the Qur'an and the prophet Muhammad, these women live under the guardianship and control of their male family members. The issues of Illiteracy, child marriage, sexual harassment, limited job opportunities, domestic violence, and genital mutilation are part of numerous Muslim women's daily lives.

The Muslim Woman program was designed to speak directly and truthfully about these issues. The live weekly call-in show addresses a woman's relationship with God, her family, society, and the church.

The program is hosted by an Egyptian-born Muslim-background believer, sister Amani. Through this program, the channel has received especially many testimonies of Muslim women accepting Christ publicly.

Many male viewers have also told how this series has opened their eyes to the cruelty of Islam when they heard about the problems women face and the treatment they receive in the name of Islam.

The Qur'an Study and Analysis

This program series deals with the Qur'an and is presented in an academic way. The series' script is based on the three volumes of *The Qur'an Dilemma* book series. The program is hosted by brother Malek Meselmani and sister Farha, and it is an eye-opener to the Muslim audience and all interested in reaching Muslims. The series brings to light inaccuracies and errors in the Qur'an to shake the foundations of Islam. Through the program, many Muslim clerics have contacted Al Hayat and asked questions about Islam and Christ.

In addition to *The Qur'an Study and Analysis*, Farha and Malek host other shows for Al Hayat. One is *The Jewish Magazine* by Malek, which gives Muslim viewers a proper understanding of Judaism and opens their eyes to see that many of the Qur'anic verses and Islam's theological teachings have their roots in Judaism.

Farha's series include *What is Behind the Turban* and *Christ is the Answer*, among others.

Brother Malek is a well-known Syrian historian and researcher of Qur'anic studies who was Muslim before converting to Christianity. Sister Farha is an Egyptian MBB.

Salaam Aleikum

Salaam Aleikum is a series hosted by a Sudanese-born Christian from a Muslim background, Pastor Yassir Eric, and an American Messianic Jewish rabbi named Jason Sobel. The episodes discuss how Arabs and Jews can find reconciliation in Jesus, the Messiah.

The series was filmed in English and dubbed in Arabic.

Brothers Yassir and Jason also host the *Footsteps of Messiah* program, where they explore the biblical locations where Jesus ministered, such as the Garden Tomb, Shepherds' Field, Church of Nativity, Mount of Temptation, Mount of Beatitudes, and Via Dolorosa.

The Saudi Magazine

Christians living in Saudi Arabia are not allowed to practice their faith openly, and the conversion of a Muslim to another religion can result even in the death penalty. *The Saudi Magazine*, started in 2015, was a first-of-its-kind Christian program hosted by Saudi Christians and produced in one of the main dialects in Saudi Arabia, Khaliji. Episodes combine the Christian message with such topics as human rights, freedom to practice one's faith, and women's position in society, as well as asking provocative questions that many Saudis have relating to the society in which they live.

The series has also introduced new music to viewers: before that, no recorded Christian music in the Khaliji dialect was available. The music is composed by a famous Jordanian-born Christian musician, Naser Musa.

The program is hosted by Dr. Khaled and brother Emad. Both are Saudi Arabian Muslim-background believers.

Through the Bible

Through the Bible is a live call-in program that introduces the Bible to new believers to help them grow in God's grace and knowledge of Jesus Christ. An Egyptian Christian-background theologian, pastor, and author, Dr. Ashraf Azmy, hosts the show. Dr. Ashraf also hosts the *Al Hayat Biblical School* series.

Al Hayat Publications

The Children of Ishmael team (1999–2003) and Al Hayat's Water Life Publishing (since 2003) have published over a hundred books and booklets and dozens of shorter tracts. Below are some examples of those products.

All the books, booklets, and tracts mentioned are first written in Arabic but are also available in English unless otherwise stated.

The Ideology Behind Islamic Terrorism

This book explains why Islamic terrorism reported in the newspapers or shown on television is the last stage of a complicated and combined series of events, doctrines, and illusions. The terrorist who detonates an explosive belt or a hand grenade does not appear out of nowhere—many people are involved in the formation of that person's mind, either directly or indirectly. That's why we cannot overcome this violence without understanding the reasons behind it, especially Islam—the most critical component of the social, political, and spiritual life of the Middle East and North Africa.

The booklet documents the roots of Islamic terrorism. The author is a previous Al Hayat host, a Muslim-background believer, Rachid.

Islam Doctrine and Application

In this book, the reader will find profound knowledge about Islam expressed in simple language. Each chapter presents the reader with new and distinct information about Islam. The themes of the booklet are, for example:

- The character of Muhammad: a study on the founder of Islam
- The emergence of Islam
- The Qur'an: Is it really God's final revelation?
- Women's status in the Qur'an and Hadith
- Taqiya, the "lawful" lying: Does the Qur'an mandate it? In what cases is this principle applied?
- Jews and Christians in Islamic-ruled countries
- Jihad in Islam

The book is written by the Al Hayat team.

Manuscripts of the Qur'an: An Introduction to the Study of Ancient Manuscripts

This book is an introduction to the world of ancient Qur'anic manuscripts, which are unknown even to many Islamic intellectuals. The book identifies and classifies the most ancient preserved Qur'anic manuscripts according to their estimated age.

The author, Mohammed Lamsiah, is a Qur'an researcher, a paleographer, and one of the few people who has read all nine of the oldest preserved Qur'anic manuscripts. In this book, he employs technical, scientific tools, such as analysis of calligraphy, drawing, decoration, punctuation marks, and the material used to complete these manuscripts. He even attempts to determine the number of scribes who contributed to the codification of these texts.

The book will give the reader an understanding of the path that led to the gradual formation of the Qur'an, as Muslims know it today.

This book has been regarded as the first thorough, academic, and objective introduction to the oldest Qur'anic manuscripts. The book is available only in Arabic.

Muhammad Before Muhammad

The book presents a new interpretation of the character of the founder of Islam in his early years. The approach is objective and scholarly and is based on a careful and accurate examination of Islamic historical sources, a presentation of the most recent oriental studies on the emergence of Islam, and a reliance on extensive sources of religious and social literature in the ancient Near East.

Due to this, the book provides a broad understanding of the religious-cultural climate of Muhammad's world, and the reader's view of Muhammad and the origins of Islam will not be the same.

The author is a historian and researcher of Qur'anic studies Malek Meselmani.

The Qur'an Dilemma:
Former Muslims Analyze Islam's Holiest Book

This book is a series that comment on each chapter of the Qur'an, providing an analysis of each sura separately. At the time of this writing, the series includes three volumes and 2,010 pages of study and analysis of the Qur'an verse by verse.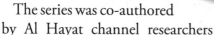

The series was co-authored by Al Hayat channel researchers Malek Meselmani and Mohammed Lamsiah, with the help of other Al Hayat team members and experts in the field.

The analysis in the book includes the following approaches:
- Critical analysis: the historical sources of the verse, its scientific and literary errors, or its literary ambiguity
- The variant readings of the verses and the semantic and doctrinal distinctions between the readings
- The traditional Islamic principle of "abrogation," which means that every new verse and command that Muhammad received from an angel always abrogated (struck down) the verses and orders on similar matters that Muhammad had received before. In the book, each abrogated verse is accompanied by a critical-historical explanation

In all of *The Qur'an Dilemma* volumes, the reader will also find a summary of resources and references, suggested readings, definitions, controversial Qur'anic texts, timelines, and maps. In addition, each volume contains various studies on the Qur'an and the Islamic faith, such as "The Compilation of the Qur'an," "The Chronological Sequence of the Qur'an," "Paradise and Hell in the Qur'an," "The God of the Qur'an," and "Islamic holidays."

The Qur'an: Its View and Treatment of Non-Muslims

This booklet details the view of the Qur'an and the Islamic faith regarding people of other religions and how it plays out in the Islamic laws imposed on non-Muslims in countries dominated by Islam.

This booklet deals with the following topics:

- How does the Qur'an view other religions?
- What is the real meaning of the Islamic expression "People of the Book"?
- What is the treatment today of non-Muslims who live in countries that apply the Qur'an's rules?
- What is the real meaning of jihad in Islam? Is it a defensive war to protect Islam or an offensive war to spread Islam's dominance worldwide?

The booklet is written by Malek Meselmani.

The Sons of Ishmael, The Daughters of Ishmael

Awlad Ismaeel (translated as *The Children of Ishmael* or *The Sons of Ishmael*) was the first book of the Children of Ishmael team and was published in 1999. The booklet includes seven testimonies of Muslim-background believers who found Christ and started to follow Him. The booklet has been translated into several languages, and more than 500,000 copies have been distributed.

Daughters of Ishmael is a similar product, including eight testimonies of women from Islamic backgrounds. The booklet was published in 2008 and has also been translated into many languages.

Both publications were compiled by Harun Ibrahim.

The Sword Verse: Qur'anic Weapon Against Peace?

The Sword verse (Sura 9.5) is one of the most extreme verses in Islam's holiest book. The verse commands the Muslims to kill non-Muslims "wherever you find them." The verse was revealed to Muhammad in the last days of his life. Because of the Islamic principle of abrogation (passages Muhammad received later in his life nullified the passages he received earlier), the command stated in the Sword verse is especially binding for all Muslims. According to Muslim scholars, the Sword verse abrogates or nullifies over a hundred pacifist verses that call for peaceful coexistence and religious tolerance with non-Muslims.

The book, written by historian and Islam researcher Malek Meselmani, extensively examines this verse. The reader will get acquainted with the following:

- What is the history and application of the Sword verse since its revelation?
- How does the Sword verse impact the politics, culture, and traditions of Muslim communities?
- How do moderate Muslims view jihad?
- When Islamic terrorist groups, such as ISIS, apply the Sword verse, are they radical or righteous Islamists?
- Is Islam really a religion of peace?
- A detailed table of 129 verses abrogated by the Sword verse, with commentary and index

The book has been translated into English, French, and Finnish. In French, the book was published under the title *Ô Allah! As-tu une arme cachée?* ("O Allah! Do you have a Secret Weapon?")

Taqīya: Deliberate Deception

One of the principles of Islam is *taqīya*. Initially, it meant that Muslims were allowed to conceal their faith under persecution or threat, but later, the term's meaning has been extended to allow a Muslim to lie to a non-Muslim if it benefits him. The principle is deeply ingrained in the Islamic world and has profoundly impacted Muslim-majority countries' politics, culture, and society.

This book will provide an answer to questions such as:
- Does the Qur'an support the principle of *taqīya*?
- Why do some leaders of Muslim nations often present contradictory statements or positions?
- How is *taqīya* used to exploit the services, education, and resources of Western nations?
- What is "civilization jihad"? Is it more dangerous than the kind of jihad advanced by terrorists?

This book is written by a Qur'an researcher, Mohammed Lamsiah.

Women in Islam – Honored or Persecuted?

The booklet is a condensed study of the status of women in the Qur'an and Islam and answers questions such as:

- What is a woman's position within the family and in society according to Islam's rule and Sharia law?
- Why do Muslim women wear the hijab?
- Why does Islam allow polygamy?
- Does the Qur'an allow wife-beating or a husband's violence?
- What is temporary marriage, known as *Mut'a* marriage?

The author is Malek Meselmani, mentioned above.

Some Examples of the Tracts

The teams of the Children of Ishmael and Al Hayat have also published several tracts, such as:

*Where Does Christ Say,
"I AM God, Worship Me"?*

The tract responds to Muslims' questions regarding Christ's divinity, particularly the often-asked question: Where did Christ say, "I AM God, Worship Me"?

Do Muslims Believe in All Prophets?
According to the tract, true belief in the biblical prophets means more than confessing their existence; it also means belief in their words and teachings.

Was Christ Crucified? Or Someone Else?
The pamphlet reveals the truth about Christ's crucifixion and responds to the Islamic claim that Christ was not crucified, but rather, someone else was made to resemble him in the eyes of the people.

God's Presence in the Qur'an and the Bible
Allah's conditional love, as portrayed in the Qur'ān, makes it difficult for a Muslim to be in a loving relationship with Allah because of human sinfulness. In sharp contrast, the Bible declares God's desire to draw close to His creation, to manifest His presence and to reveal Himself *personally*.

What Does "Christ, Word of God," Mean in the Qur'an and Holy Bible?

This brief overview looks at how the Qur'an and the Bible provide different meanings for the term "Word of God."

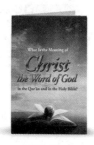

Is the Gospel One or Four?

The tract teaches that although Matthew, Mark, Luke, and John are four separate Gospels in the Bible, they are essentially one gospel of Christ and his ministry.

Does the Qur'an Acknowledge Christ's Death and Resurrection?

Muslim scholars are confused about Christ's death and resurrection. Given their numerous conflicting and confusing opinions on this serious matter, this tract questions the reader's following such scholars concerning his eternal destiny.

Where Does the Qur'an State that the Bible Is Corrupted?

Muslims charge that the Bible's text has been corrupted, an accusation that is un-substantiated in the Qur'an.

Do Christians Worship Three Gods?

In the tract, a Christian explains to a Muslim friend the Oneness of the Trinity.

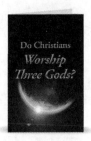

Can God Manifest Himself?

This pamphlet teaches how God has appeared to His creation in different ways to communicate His love and commitment to it. His greatest manifestation is His Son, Jesus Christ.

Does Islam Honor Christ?

The tract describes how truly loving and honoring Christ means complete belief in His divinity, teachings, crucifixion, and resurrection.

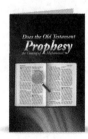

Does the Old Testament Prophesy the Coming of Muhammad?

The Old Testament prophesies herald the coming of the Messiah, who will perform miracles and preach the good news to all.

Questions from Our Audience

During the decades of ministry, we have received numerous questions from Muslim viewers and listeners.

Here are some examples of these questions. Words in brackets have been added for clarification.

- What does the term "the will of God" mean? Is His will different from His love?
- In Deuteronomy 18:18, God says: "I will raise up for them a Prophet like you from among their brethren, and will put My words in His mouth, and He shall speak to them all that I command Him." Isn't this a clear statement referring to Muhammad? Since the verse does not say from among 'yourselves' but emphasizes your own 'brethren,' doesn't this mean the promised prophet is not Jesus, Isaac's descendant, but Muhammad, who is Ishmael's?
- Did Christ's spirit depart from His body when He died on the cross?
- Could you explain to me Genesis 4:13–16? Does that mean there were other people apart from Adam, Eve, Cain, and Abel?
- Could you define Christian terms such as "Baptism" and "Confession"?
- It's written in Matthew 2:23: "And he came and dwelt in a city called Nazareth, that it might be fulfilled which was spoken by the prophets, 'He shall be called a Nazarene.'" Where can I find this prophetic word in the Old Testament?
- What happened to those already dead when the Lord died on the cross?

- What did Jesus mean when He said in Mark 14:25, "Assuredly, I say to you, I will no longer drink of the fruit of the vine until that day when I drink it new in the kingdom of God"?
- How could an uneducated man, such as Muhammad, who lived 1,400 years ago, know that plants are created male and female [if he was not a genuine prophet of God]?
- Does salvation happen at the moment we ask for it?
- Will Christ reign physically on earth?
- Although I am a Muslim, I ordered a copy of *Tell Them I Love Them*. I cannot understand how God, the King of Heaven and earth, became a man and shared our fallen nature.
- What does the Bible mean when it says that Jesus went to the lower parts of the earth?
- Would our prayers benefit our loved ones who are dead?
- What does it mean that Adam and Eve did not know they were naked until they fell into sin?
- Do the dead have any influence in the world of the living?
- I betrayed my husband because he was too busy with the computer and never paid attention to me. Later, I felt guilty, and I do not know what to do. Shall I tell him and ask for forgiveness?
- What language did the father of all humans speak? Was it Arabic, as we believe as Muslims?
- Why do you Christians not believe in the prophet Muhammad?

Al Hayat Feedback From Different Countries

Al Hayat's program producers and follow-up personnel receive millions of written comments from the audience annually. They are written on some of the channel's social media pages, sent to us via emails, text messages, or letters, or told on the phone.

Most of the comments are from Arabic countries, but because Arabic-speaking people live worldwide, we have received feedback from almost every country. During Al Hayat's early years, most reactions were negative, with insults, curses, and even death threats. Nowadays, the feedback is mostly positive.

Here is a set of viewer comments and personal stories translated into English and sorted by country. Words in brackets have been added by the Al Hayat team to clarify the text.

ALGERIA

"Even though I am a Muslim lady, I admire Al Hayat channel's excellent programs. I am honored to watch this channel that has opened my eyes to the spiritual truth I was unaware of. When alone at home, I secretly watch your beautiful programs all day. I cannot watch it in the evening when all my family is at home. Please pray for me."

Aicha

"I watch all of Al Hayat's programs with great interest and benefit greatly from the valuable information and explanations I listen to. Since childhood, I have had many questions about my previous beliefs running through my mind. Watching this channel, especially the programs discussing Islam, opened the door for me to discover the truth. Therefore, I came to know Jesus and received Him as my Savior. Because of the Al Hayat programs, I learned that God is love and has nothing to do with religiosity. I could not find God amid the massacres that swept Algeria, but I found Him in every act of love and forgiveness."

Abdelwahed

"I am an Algerian Muslim man. I watch the Al Hayat channel's good programs. The programs about Islam are my favorites among them because of the good, acceptable, and logical answers given. These answers motivate me to reconsider and study essential spiritual issues that, for a long time, I have taken for granted! Those programs portray a picture of Jesus Christ that is totally new to me."

Frias

"Many thanks for these radiant programs. I would specifically like to address the *Good News* program's presenter: Your effort to help us has been commendable. I eagerly look forward to the time allocated to your program because it gives me hope to continue living. I have been diagnosed with rheumatism for eight years now. I am nearly crippled. I often wish to die rather than tolerate the pain I go through. My family mocks me when I tell them that faith in Christ would heal me! I am ready to sacrifice everything to regain my health. Please pray for my healing."

Rachida

BAHRAIN

"On June 23, 2008, a miracle happened in my life while watching this program on the Al Hayat channel. I had many doubts about the presenter's style. I asked God that [the presenter], Pastor E. Melki, would call my name as a sign of proof! I was confused and totally exhausted. To my surprise, I heard Pastor E. Melki calling my name and age and declaring my healing from a severe fear."

Teresa

"I want to express my good feelings towards this program, which confirmed to me the Sonship of Jesus to God. The program also proved to me the carnal mind of Muhammad. May the Lord continue to use this program to deliver more Muslims from the stronghold of Islam."

A. Kulaibi

"I am a conservative Muslim, but I still ask you to pray for me. I can't really hear anything in my left ear, and I also suffer from bad headaches. Could you please send me a Bible?"

Abdel

EGYPT

"I came to know the Lord through one of the programs discussing Islam. I was a fanatical Muslim, and at the beginning, I hardened my heart and hated Christianity and Christians. I continued to watch, and the Lord visited me and gave me the understanding that salvation comes from God alone. I need some good teaching to build my faith."

E. Abdel-Gawi

"I am Mohamed, a fan of Al Hayat TV, especially the programs about Islam. Earlier on, I began to think about the issues raised by this set of programs, such as the repetition of verses in many different Qur'anic passages attacking Jews and Christians in one place and commending them in another passage. The mosque's imam answered me and said that the Qur'an had been given in different stages and situations. My question is, how would divine legislation change from one situation to another? Should not God's word remain unchangeable? How would they say that the Qur'an is the source and the measure for Arabic language's rules while the Qur'an is full of repetition, contradiction, and provokes division?"

Mohamed

"I grew up amid fanatic Muslims. I aggressively persecuted the Christians. After eleven years of studying the Bible, I concluded that even though it has not yet been contradicted, I could not believe in the incarnation. The channel's programs about Islam opened the door for me to dig deeper. Faith in Christ started to penetrate my heart, but doubt tried to take its place! I went through a cycle of divine dreams, doubt, and fear for a few months. The final dream that forever removed doubt was when the Lord appeared in shining clothes and gave me bread while I bowed my head to worship His majesty."

An MBB man

"Thank you for what you have been doing to bring us back to God. I have been a committed Muslim all my life. Not only that, but I purposely married a Christian girl and managed to convert her to Islam. Together, we have a three-year-old boy. Unexpectedly, the Lord Jesus started to visit me quite often while I was praying my Islamic prayers. Last time, while bowing down, I heard Him saying, ' You are one of My own. Follow Me with those who follow the Light.' These visions, dreams, and visitation happened after one year of my marriage. The priest in my village said he could do nothing because we live in a Muslim country but advised me to pray. Can you baptize me?"

Yasser

IRAQ

"Dear Al Hayat family, 'Lord, I stand before You empty-handed, miserable, and wretched. My life has no great performance, and it is in chaos.' This was my prayer. Right after this, and in a vision, I saw the Lord Jesus dressed in a white robe, inviting me to a great feast. He gave me a cup of water, which quenched my thirst. The only thing I did after this vision is that I confessed to Jesus with my mouth, and I believed in my heart that God raised Him from the dead. Is this enough, or must I find someone to baptize me?"

A. Hussein

This program kindled in my heart a light that will never be quenched forever. Since the first day the programs discussing Islam went on air, I never missed it to the extent that I am filled with every word you said. The credit goes to God first and to you second for shedding light in the dark and dim areas of Islam, which were kept hidden from Muslims for a long time because of ignorance and perversity. I read the Bible, pray, and fast, seeking God's face and eternal life. I want to be baptized, but there is no church here where I live. It is in my heart to form a house-church in my home and to gather those who love the Lord and teach them the Word of God."

Abdel-Salam

"I was a Muslim who practiced witchcraft. I sought advice from the spirit world, falling completely under the power of evil spirits. I couldn't get rid of them, even if I wanted to. But then I watched Al Hayat programs, accepted Jesus, and confessed my sins and addictions. I burned all my books on the spirit world. After a while, Christ appeared to me in a dream and strengthened me."

Sabri

ISRAEL

"I am a thirty-six-year-old female. As a Muslim girl, I could not see wisdom, purity, and self-control in the life of the prophet of Islam. I always doubted his claimed prophetic message. A Christian friend shared the love of Christ with me. I visited him in Egypt, and we went together to Al-Shurabia Church. There, the Lord washed away my sins and baptized me in the Holy Ghost with the evidence of speaking in tongues. That was not all. In His generosity, He revealed Himself to me in a vision. I saw smoke that came out of a fire-dripping ball, and a Shining Face started to appear until I saw the whole face of the Beloved. That was the most joyful time I have ever experienced. I am ready to testify in one of your programs."

Samia

"I am grateful to God for your programs about Islam. Many thanks for being honest and sincere in answering the viewers' questions. I wandered and staggered many times between Judaism, Christianity, and Islam. My soul suffered a lot for several years until these programs appeared to answer the questions rambling in my mind. Send a copy of *The Sons of Ishmael* booklet to my mailing address."

Menhel

"At first, I made fun of a host on Al Hayat, but then I became a big fan of his show. His words soothe my soul, strengthen my body, and fill my spirit with wisdom. I really need these programs to cope with my husband's fierce temper."

Khalida

JORDAN

"I used to be a Sheikh in Islam. I have been watching the programs discussing Islam for a long time. I recorded every word, reference, and website that was mentioned to check. I discovered that they are bitter facts that I could not overlook. Finally, I confessed that 'There are no other gods but God, and Christ is the Son of God.' I wish I could shout in every Muslim's ear that there is no other God but Jesus who died for His own, contrary to Muhammad who used his own [followers] for his earthly personal profits."

Sh. Al-Giaar

"I am a twenty-eight-year-old Jordanian man. I was born to a Muslim family. Three years ago, I came to know the God of love, peace, and joy, and I was born again through Al Hayat's commendable programs. I strived diligently to be baptized in water. A Christian friend recommended you to me to help baptize me."

Alaa

"I am an 80-year-old Jordanian lady. The Lord found and saved me through this program. Last year, I used to suffer from stones in the gallbladder, and I was scheduled to undergo surgery. When I watched one of your programs, I prayed together with the presenter. Then, when I went to the hospital, the doctors were surprised when they found out that my gallbladder is completely clean from any stone, and they canceled the operation! That was a great testimony among my relatives. I regret not sharing my testimony with the presenter and ask for forgiveness."

Khadra

"I come from a family with a Muslim father and a Christian mother. After the war in Iraq, I came on my own to Jordan. I was scared and shaky, and I could not trust anyone. I was on the verge of being deviously exploited because everyone knew I was single. One night, I dreamed I was in a pit, and an older man stretched out his hand to pull me out of the hole. I did not see his face, and he disappeared. Then I entered a small room in the neighborhood, and behold, a dove was present in the room. I could not see it, but I heard the sound of its wings. I stretched out my hands for inspection to take it out, and when I grabbed it, it was a fish, not a dove, a golden color that started to change to silver. I asked aloud, 'Who are you?' A voice answered me, 'I am the life.' Shortly after, I was flipping through the TV channels and was attracted to a religious program. I continued to watch until I noticed the logo of Al Hayat, and it was as if someone told me that it was the fish I had seen."

A Jordanian woman

KUWAIT

"Dear Al Hayat, I have watched your program for a while. I feel comforted, encouraged, and joyful every time I watch you. I am a Kuwaiti man whom the Lord visited eleven years ago. Five years later, He visited my wife, then my children, and finally my sister-in-law. The Holy Spirit, today, is wooing the hearts of my brother Mohamed and Dalia, my sister, through dreams and visions similar to what I experienced before. Please pray for me and my loved ones to live our faith openly."

Saher

"Thank you, Al Hayat, for proving that God can do the impossible anytime. I am a 24-year-old married woman living with my husband in the Arabian Peninsula. I am Christian in my spirit, soul, and being, but no one knows about it, and I can't let others know lest I be killed. My husband and my whole family are Muslims. I used to be, but now I am not because of the truth revealed to me. I was a veiled Muslim while in university before I was married. One day, one of my Christian colleagues asked me to attend her sister's wedding at church. I apologized to her that I couldn't enter a church, but then I had an idea to go, watch, and make fun of their unworthy speech. I did, and the minute I stepped in, a strange feeling enveloped me, and I couldn't make a single laugh! Suddenly, I found my feet taking me to stand in front of a picture of the crucified Christ. I don't know why tears streamed down my cheeks. Quickly, I moved into an isolated corner, sat down, and wiped away my tears. Suddenly and unexpectedly, I heard a voice saying: 'Welcome, I have been waiting for you all these years; you are in the right place; don't leave.' I tried to see who was talking to me, but I couldn't see anyone, and my heart began beating louder and faster. During the wedding ceremony, the pastor talked about the love of Christ and that He's our only way out of sin. I found a copy of the Bible on the church's bench, and I should admit that I stole it to read when alone. I did, and I liked it very much, and it's still with me. Since that night, I believed in Christ secretly. I continued watching and listening to Al Hayat's programs while alone at home. Months passed, and I was forced to marry a rich Muslim man. I want to tell him the truth, but I know I will be killed. I want to shout out that I am a Christian. Please pray the Lord will open a way for me to live for Christ who met me and whom I love."

Hala

LEBANON

"I was born into a Muslim family. Since the age of nine, the mark of the cross has occupied my thoughts. I used to gaze at crosses on top of churches. When I turned twelve, a friend of mine, upon my request, gave me the symbol of the cross as a gift. My mother learned about that cross, and since then, she has waged war against me. When I turned seventeen, Christ appeared to me in a dream and gave me bread to eat. Later, I found the answers to my questions on a Christian website. I left my family, was baptized, and am determined to follow Christ all the way to the end."

Rachel

"I would like to say Hallelujah to our Lord Jesus Christ for opening many new doors to help the lost get back to Him. I wanted to know if Joyce Meyer has planned to visit Lebanon to preach the Word. I belong to the Rock of Ages Church. I used to be a Muslim. I lived in darkness, but now I am in the light. Could you send me some of Joyce's booklets translated into Arabic to share with people from my background?"

Ali Khalil

"Al Hayat TV, my ID shows that I am Muslim and Islam is my inherited religion, but I believe in Jesus Christ and His Word. All through my life, I never felt that I belonged to Islam. I lived with a confused mind and a distracted spirit. My wife was a fanatic Muslim. While she was reading the Qur'an, I would read the Gospel, which led to many disharmonies in our marriage. One day, I openly expressed my admiration for the Gospel because of its many spiritual teachings. That was the end; my wife sued me. The judge considered me an apostate and divorced us. The board of the school I used to teach at fired me because the same judge who divorced us was the head of the board of that school. It was a very costly price, but it was worth my freedom from the intellectual chains and the blackness of the darkness of Islam. Today, the Lord Jesus is present in my heart. I am ready to appear on Al Hayat to help others see the light."

Ahmed

LIBYA

"I am a twenty-seven-year-old Libyan man. I was born and raised in a Muslim family. As I was flipping over the channels, I came across Al Hayat TV, and I stopped there because I heard a man exposing mistakes in Islam. That really pierced my ear. Every time the name of Jesus was mentioned, my heartbeats sped up. I wanted to know more about Jesus, but I fell asleep. I had an amazing dream: Muslims were trying to force me to pray in the mosque by beating me up. I resisted them and escaped but fell into a dark pit. My persecutors could not find me. In the pit, I saw a light that was approaching me. I was terrified. A man with a shining face said to me, 'Come.' As I moved towards Him, He sprinkled water on me, and when I sat down, He poured all the water over me. I was overwhelmed with joy. I heard Him saying, 'Your sins are rolled away; you are free.' Could you explain this dream to me?"

Ali

"I was born as a Muslim. I like your programs and am convinced of the basis of the Christian faith, but I do not know how to become a Christian. It is a high risk to declare my new belief. Could you help me to take a further step forward?"

M. Al-Subaai

"I lived as a Muslim for twenty-four years. After watching Al Hayat TV and especially the *Enjoying Everyday Life* program, the Lord showed mercy on me and opened my eyes to see Jesus. One night before I went to bed, I drew a small symbol of the cross so nobody would notice it. To my surprise, the Lord visited me at five o'clock in the morning and showed me a big shining cross. Thank you, Joyce."

Nabil

MAURITANIA

"I am a Mauritanian man found by the Lord eight years ago. Since then, He taught me many things. Now, I am serving Him by planting house churches. By His grace, we formed seven of these churches. Each is formed of twelve members. Our biggest problem is getting Bibles and literature because of the difficult transport conditions. Could you help, please?"

Aldah

MOROCCO

"I grew up as a committed Muslim. I always thought in my heart that Isa [Jesus] is by far greater than Muhammad. Later, in a dream, I saw myself standing by the beach, and suddenly, an earthquake hit. I lifted my eyes to heaven and saw a star bigger than the moon. In the middle of that glorious star, I saw the face of Jesus and heard Him saying to me: 'Do not fear, for I am with you.' This dream settled the issue forever."

Al-Mernissi

"Since I was sixteen years old, many questions had been rambling in my mind. Whenever I asked them to the Muslim leaders, I would get the same answer: 'Do not question!' Just recently, as I was flipping over the channels, I accidentally came across Al Hayat and its program about Islam. I found answers to some of my questions, and since then, I have become a committed viewer of this channel. I am determined to find the truth for myself."

Fatima

"Al Hayat led me to my Savior. While still a Muslim, I knew nothing about God's love or salvation. The Qur'an only taught me words such as hell, fire, punishment, and that I am good for nothing. I feared death and the torture waiting for me in the grave by my torturer. Therefore, I lived my life in horror. I thank God for putting Al Hayat across my path, opening my eyes to the reality of Islam, its Messenger, and his lifestyle. I wept, knelt, and asked God to show me the right way and what to do. That same night, the Lord appeared to me in a dream, holding a cross of light in His hand, and said, 'I am the Way; rid yourself of all the Qur'anic books and the Qur'anic verses hanging there and replace them with the cross.' It has been a year since I received Jesus, during which time I have known His love, mercy, and compassion, which redeemed all the days of horror and bitterness I lived. I never experienced happiness until Christ came into my heart."

Loulouaa

"I used to be a Muslim. A series of curses dominated my life until I lost all sense of existence and died spiritually. I tried to regain what I lost by reciting more of the Qur'an, praying, calling upon the name of the Messenger of Islam, and visiting so-called holy places and Sufi sheiks. All my efforts went with the wind, and Satan continued to reign over my life. I thought one day, why has Satan not been defeated by all this effort? I stopped praying and started asking the Creator to lead me to the right path. One day, I was flipping over the channels and thought, why not try the Christian channels? I was surprised and suspicious as I watched and heard all the miracles going on. But when I noticed that people were healed, delivered, and wept genuinely, I wondered, is it possible that all these people are fooled, cheating, and pretending? I decided to try Christianity since I wouldn't lose anything more than what I lost as a Muslim. So, despite all my doubts and confusion, I believed in Jesus and noticed great changes for the better in different places in my life. On the other hand, Satan hasn't given up on me yet. Therefore, I count on your prayers to help me be completely delivered. Please send me a copy of the Bible so I can live a victorious life."

Moloud

"I am a middle-aged Moroccan man. I admit I am a sinner. As a Muslim, I pray and fast but live in fear. I cheat on my wife, practice homosexuality, lie, and steal. Your programs on Islamic doctrine exposed to me the fallacy of Islam. If I believed in Jesus Christ, would He forgive my sinful past? What if I fell into sin again?"

Hashim

OMAN

"Even though I am a Muslim, I watch the Al Hayat channel's meaningful programs, especially *Questions About Faith*. I would like to know if there are verses in the Bible that could be used to help those possessed by evil spirits. I would like you to send me more information about the basis of the Christian faith and a copy of the Bible."

Zina

"I have been watching this channel for a while and became a committed viewer of your smart, commendable, and informative programs several months ago. These programs portrayed a new and completely different picture of Jesus in my mind. I want to know more about the basis of the Christian faith."

Amina

"Even though I was born to a Muslim family, Christ Jesus sealed my heart with His love since childhood, even years before I knew to read and write. I just want to know: Do I have the right to consider myself a Christian? I have not read the Bible yet!"

Hamed

QATAR

"I have been watching your programs about Islam, especially the special episode allocated to comment on what was said in the *Cairo Today* program. I was really shocked by the rude and rough way that Mr. O. Adeeb handled your programs' spiritual questions. Therefore, I beg you to accept my apology on behalf of the Muslims and invite me to answer the questions you raise."

M. Al-Qet

"Many thanks for *More Than Dreams'* excellent drama that helps rescue people from hell. I am a thirty-two-year-old

Muslim man. I have been watching the different episodes of this excellent drama, and I found myself drawn to Christ Jesus and completely convinced of His love. I started to read the Bible secretly until the truth of Christ was fully revealed to me."

Emad

"After watching Al Hayat's programs and reading the New Testament for the last seven months, the Lord Jesus conquered and reigned in my heart. I have been a Muslim for more than twenty-five years. To be honest, I should tell you that I am afraid of the threats of my friends. Could you help me through?"

Taha

SAUDI ARABIA

"I am from a Muslim background, but I lived all my life as a wanderer and a lost soul because I could not find in Islam anything that backs up the idea of a Holy God. Therefore, I wandered away from God and became an atheist. The more I watched the behavior of the Muslims, the more I hated Islam. Three years ago, I discovered your Al Hayat TV and started to watch your program to make fun of your religion. Little by little, a sense of security overwhelmed me, and I discovered that salvation is only in Christ. I want to let you know that many well-educated Saudi figures are watching Al Hayat's programs with great interest but in secret lest the authorities would torture them."

Saad

"I found answers to my questions through this highly respected channel. I became a Christian, and my love for the Lord Jesus fuels my faith. Before I tuned in to Al Hayat's programs, my information about the Christian faith was very shallow. We were taught that Christianity is the religion of killing and worshipping the symbol of the cross and is perverted. I grew up hating this belief. But God showed me the truth and the light in Christ Jesus."

A. Aziz

"May 11, 2007, was a turning point in my life when Christ appeared to me in a dream, although I was still Muslim. I did not recognize Him; His head was covered, and no light came from Him. He told me, 'I am the Christ,' and showed me the scars of wounds on the cross. Gently and lovingly, He seated me, laid hands on my head, and prayed over me. He said to me: 'Fahed, you are mine; what you see now is just a pale shadow of the reality of My substance and truth, and what I just showed you is merely to attract you to Me,' and then He disappeared. Today, I believe in Him, but I need to know more."

Fahed

"I am a 22-year-old Saudi girl. This program has caught my attention and directed my thoughts toward Isa [Jesus]. I am determined to invite Him to enter my heart and forgive my sins. My Arabic-speaking Ethiopian maid encouraged me to tune in to Al Hayat's meaningful programs. Please send me Christian literature to help me become more acquainted with the Lord."

Elham

"I have watched your programs, and I think they spread lies about Islam. It's dismaying to see churches with homosexuals in them. Is this Christianity? If not, why don't you legislate to ban such churches?"

Anwar

SUDAN

"Four years ago, I came out of the darkness of Islam to the light of Christ, and I was baptized. Now I am facing many disappointments and pressures. Please pray for me."

Dalia

"Even though I am a Muslim, I believe Jesus is the light to all nations and speaks to our souls. God is alive, and He cares and shows love to His people. I think the Bible has the secrets to this life. Therefore, please send me a copy of the Bible."

Hussein

"I am a 28-year-old married woman. One year after I was baptized in water, I married a converted man so we could uphold each other. A year later, my husband returned to Islam and threatened to tell my family about my faith in Christ, which would be a huge family catastrophe in our culture, and I am not yet strong enough in the faith to stand this trial. My husband went and told my family, and they began to torture and humiliate me in different ways until, under heavy pressure and just hoping to escape the torture, I told them that I had returned to Islam. Still, the love of Christ is engraved in my heart, and He is my life. It was in the face of intimidation that I denied Him. Now I live a dual life, as a Muslim in front of others, but Christ is enthroned in my heart."

Gamila

SYRIA

"I am a 66-year-old MBB male. I could not move my right hand for almost a year due to an unknown sickness. I stretched my left hand towards the screen and prayed with the host of one of Al Hayat's commendable programs. To my surprise, I discovered my hand was completely healed the next day. Pray for a complete recovery of my 27-year-old daughter, Fatima, who had surgery a couple of years ago and is not yet fully recovered."

Ghazy

"I come from a Muslim family. A year ago, I was invited to watch the Jesus movie. I thought I would watch a story similar to that of the founder of my family's religion. To my surprise, I saw a totally different story. I was impressed by the love, compassion, and forgiveness that Jesus offered to humankind. Even though I have many questions running in my mind about some passages in the Bible, I am totally convinced of the basis of the Christian faith."

An MBB man

"For the last five years, I suffered from dizziness, high blood pressure, and deafness in my right ear. The doctor told me he had been treating me with the best medicine he could and added that my right ear was completely dead, but he had been treating the left one to keep it functioning properly. The next day, I turned my TV on the Al Hayat channel and heard the host say, 'There is a lady whose right ear is deaf. The Lord will heal her if she prays with me now.' I did, and my ear opened, and I could hear again. I shouted joyfully, 'He has healed me!'"

Samia

TUNISIA

"I am a Tunisian well-educated man. I am a holder of a Ph.D. in chemistry. Since childhood, I strived diligently to study and figure out some of the mysteries in this world. I am pleased with Al Hayat channel's programs, especially the programs about Islam, because they discuss, analyze, and compare some important spiritual issues—a thing that I really miss in the other Jewish, Christian, and Muslim spiritual channels I watch. In the latter group of channels, I do not find studies showing similarities and differences between the religions. Please send me a copy of the Bible in Arabic and French."

Khalid

"Even though I am a Muslim and have a Ph.D. in Islamic studies, I find your channel to be of great help for me to find out about the basis of the Christian faith. I received a copy of the Bible and started to read it, but I could not understand some biblical terminologies, which sounded difficult and strange for the Muslim reader. Could you send me books to help solve this problem?"

Houssine

"Dear Al Hayat, Thank you for your Islam programs, which shed light on dark areas and deliver people. I believe the Muslim leaders should clarify their viewpoint about the *ayat as-sayf* [the Sword Verse, Sura 9.5], which urges Muslims to kill non-Muslims. Is it valid or abrogated? Why do Muslim leaders intentionally ignore Muhammad's invasions? In my opinion, dipping the amputated parts of the body in boiled oil is considered a kind of terrorism. I do not believe that God, the Creator of this beautiful universe, would torture His creatures as Islam does."

Ibrahim

"I started to watch Al Hayat's programs a year ago. Five months later, I gave my life to our beloved Savior. A month later, my mother also gave her life to Jesus after watching your programs discussing Islam. It did not stop there, but the love of the Savior looked very contagious as it quickly consumed the hearts of my three sisters, my brother, my brother-in-law, my cousin, his wife, my aunt's husband, and a friend of mine."

Murad

UNITED ARAB EMIRATES

"First, I apologize for my audacity, but I want to be honest. I am from the UAE, where I was born and grew up as a Muslim female. Challenging religious issues was tough for me, but thanks to God, who helped me. Initially, I couldn't tolerate listening to a lady who teaches or seeing her. One day, I heard her preaching on life's cares and problems, and I did not know why I was drawn to listen to her. Right after her speech that day, I received the Lord Jesus as my personal Savior, and Joyce became my favorite preacher. Thank you for conveying the Word of God."

An MBB woman

"Resentment, anger, hatred, and commotion were my feelings when I first watched this program. 'How would this infidel dare to tell all these lies about Islam?' The only way for me to expose his lies was to study the references. It shocked me to discover that the host was telling the truth! I tried to seek help from the Muslim leaders, but I got a second shock when they gave me a blind answer by saying, 'Just take it by faith, do not question.' I could not take this as an answer to big questions like, How could a man in his sixties get married to a six-year-old girl? How could he marry his daughter-in-law? How could the same man approve of adult breastfeeding? I praise God for this program, which opened my spiritual eyes."

A. Atif

"I have been watching this program regularly, and I came to a point where I am totally convinced that I need to check my inherited beliefs. Please send me whatever material you have. I am eager to find out the truth very quickly. I have the energy to read, analyze, and understand 50 pages/day. I can dedicate 10 hours/day to watching and listening to debates. I am thirsty for the Truth."

Mutwally

"At the age of eighteen, I discovered that I am not free to choose my beliefs. I cried and suffered secretly because I could not find a trustworthy person to confide in to help me come out of this dark life. I met for a few hours a person who was visiting my country. I felt he was very kind, loving, and compassionate. Lately, he admitted that he is a Christian, and I loved him more because of the spirit he mirrors. Tears gush down my cheeks every time I read the testimonies of the MBBs on the Al Hayat website because I am one of them now. Even the dreams the MBBs saw while asleep are the same as mine. For instance, a cross fixed on the moon and a white dove."

Hanae

YEMEN

"I was born and raised in a Muslim conservative society. My family and relatives persecute me because I chose to put my faith in the Lord Jesus Christ. I am determined that nothing can separate me from my Savior and the joy that He gives while walking through persecution and trials. I would like Al Hayat TV to air programs that address and encourage the persecuted Christians worldwide, especially in Yemen."

Ali M. Saleh

"I came to know the Christ, the Lord, through a friend. The Word of our Savior melted the accumulated ice on my heart, brought me warmth, and motivated me to seek harder. I am part of a group of national converts. We meet together, read, discuss, and spread the Word of God. Because of Joyce's testimony, she has become our example of serving the Lord faithfully, sacrificially, and wholeheartedly. Kindly send us some of Joyce's printed material."

Emad

"I became a Christian in 1992 while listening to Christian media. I still need to learn much about the basis of the Christian faith, especially as I live in a country that forbids and deprives converts from making decisions for their own lives. I formed a group of MBBs to spread the Word, but we stopped it as such a group is considered illegal. I feel paralyzed because I want to teach the Word but lack a good Christian education. I want to study in a Bible school. Could you help me?"

Hussien Alhindi

"I was born into a Muslim family. When I was five, the Lord introduced Himself to me in a dream and stamped my heart with an awesome impression of Himself. I did not know then who was that Supreme Being. When I turned ten, He revisited me in a dream and took me to heaven. There, He showed me more, opened His arms wide, and told me that I am His daughter and He has chosen me. A friend gave me a copy of the New Testament. I struggled a lot between Islam and these dreams. Finally, at the age of seventeen and at the climax of the confusion that I lived in, the Lord settled the issue in a third dream by saying, 'I AM the Truth.' I woke up, and my spirit was completely saturated in peace and joy that I have never experienced before."

Ebtisam

NON-ARABIC COUNTRIES

"Thank you for your programs on the teachings of Islam! I always try to watch every episode because they are very informative, and the issues are presented in a friendly way. I don't quite agree with all the interpretations, but these programs are a good example of how to deal with sensitive spiritual issues."

A Muslim man, the British Isles

"My daughter experienced a healing after watching one of your programs. She had been suffering from heel pain so bad for a long time that she could no longer walk. I encouraged her to pray with the host of your program, and she did. Then she felt the warmth in her heel and started walking, jumping, and shouting for joy!"

Zakko, the Netherlands

"I went through a tough time. I lost my joy in life and stayed at home. I found the Al Hayat channel and started watching it for the first time. The teachings I heard led me to Jesus. The Lord strengthened me and my faith in Him. I lost my job, but I found the Lord Jesus."

Abdel-Aziz, the Netherlands

"I am a Muslim, but I love Christ and hold Him up as my example. I have not yet experienced salvation in Him, but I believe He will not leave me. I watch Al Hayat to get answers to my many questions. All your programs are very good and a great help to the searching soul. I am very sure that Christ will not leave those who love Him. Would you pray that I may experience salvation?"

Male, the Netherlands

"I was a drug addict and drug dealer. One day, as I was watching one of Al Hayat's programs, the host said: 'Stand up now, lay your hand on the TV, and pray with me.' I had a significant problem that day and thought of killing someone. My life was completely upside down. I prayed, thinking that no power could deliver me from the bondage of drugs, sex, etc.… I looked in the mirror, wept, filled with unbelief, and slept. The next day, I discovered that the problem was solved, and until today, I have never wanted to retake drugs. I thank God for this miracle, which, for me, is by far more significant than curing cancer. Please continue to pray for me to know the Lord more intimately."

Naji, Belgium

"Thank you for illuminating my darkness, restoring my spirit, which was about to be strained by Islam's ignorant and carnal rules. The cutting of heads, as is going on in Iraq and Algeria, and the raping of young girls, as is happening in the Gulf, is the real Islam. I left my country to escape such crimes."

Goueiria, France

"I was born and raised in an Algerian Muslim family. Being forced to, I used to practice all the requested rituals, such as worshipping, fasting, and praying. Every time I practiced the rituals, I felt like my heart had been squeezed. I moved to France and watched Al Hayat TV, and my life has changed after faith in Christ entered my heart and the love of Jesus saturated me. I began to explore what I was ignorant of—because of Islam's chain of fear—about Christ, the fountain of love. Today, I love God, pray, and worship God out of love and not fear."

Bushara, France

"Leave Islam alone. Instead of trying to evangelize the Muslim world, try to study Islam. It is spreading worldwide, and many monks and priests are converting to Muslims. You cannot stop it. I say this in the name of the only God who has no son born of woman."

Mohamed, France

"I am an Algerian mother of two children and have lived in Italy for twelve years. I have been a Muslim all my life. I started watching Al Hayat programs, which not only changed my understanding of Islam but also helped me to receive Christ as my Savior. I pray that your programs will open the eyes of Muslims to the truth."

Ghania, Italy

"I am still in shock after realizing I have been following the wrong religion all my life. I desperately need more teaching, and I watch your programs and read the material you sent me. I am thirsty for living water."

Saida, Italy

"Thank you for bringing the message of Christ to my heart and directing me to a local church in Athens where I was born again. I feel at home there, and the Word of God nourishes me. Thank you for introducing me to both Christ and His church body."

M. Kamara, Greece

"We tried for four years to have a child. I underwent several painful treatments, but finally, the doctors gave up and stopped the treatments. I watched one of your programs where the host said: 'You've been patiently hoping for a child, now it's your turn.' I took these words personally. I went to the hospital again for an ultrasound scan. The doctor chuckled loudly: 'There's a baby in the womb! I've been doing this job for twenty years, and I've never seen such a miracle.'"

A. S., Denmark

"Through the TV screen, your words have been like the healing plaster I so badly needed on the wounds of my heart since Saddam Hussein killed our twenty-four-year-old son. My husband fell ill after hearing of our son's death. We are thankful to God that He has anointed you to speak His Word. If it were not for God, we would not be alive today. We pray for you daily."

Iraqi mother, Denmark

"Thank you very much, Al Hayat; you are a great source of blessing to many. I grew up in a conservative Catholic family. I always felt that I was missing something. Religiousness did not quench my thirst for the living God. I watched your programs, and some of them I opposed very aggressively. One time, the Lord opened my eyes. The program host said, 'Your name is Leyla, and you are forty-seven. The Lord has healed you of gynecological disease. You were already scheduled for surgery, but you don't need surgery.' I was saved and healed at the same time. I would like to know more about the baptism of the Holy Spirit."

Leyla from Iraq, Finland

"Al Hayat, you are doing a good job. I wish I could start translating your programs into Chinese for those viewers who really need what you have to say. Please pray for China and me."

Adel, China

"I studied Islam in Algeria. I watched Al Hayat, and although I didn't understand everything linguistically, the Lord's presence touched me. I started to follow the programs regularly and was born again. I returned home and told my family that I found— or rather—that Jesus found me."

Mohamed, Cameroon

"Glory to God! I am an ex-Muslim woman from Pakistan. I became a Christian through your TV programs. Jesus Christ is my Lord and Savior."

Amany, Pakistan

"I have moved from Syria to the US. I found the Al Hayat website by chance a while ago, and I am very grateful for it. Every day, I spend three to four hours on your courageous website. Thank you, and may the Lord guide you always!"

Jamil, USA

Photo Captions List